The Search for a European Identity

This book examines the link between political identity and legitimacy in the European Union (EU). Stimulated by the crisis of legitimacy and identity suffered by the EU after the referenda on the Constitutional Treaty, the editors have developed a theoretical framework to examine the interplay between these two items in the problematic development of the EU into a fully-fledged political actor.

The contributors to the volume seek to:

- Redefine the key notions in the rigorous way of political philosophy, thus avoiding the generic or imprecise language usage found in a large part of the literature on identity.
- Test these concepts in the analysis of EU policies that may reveal the world views and the principles upon which EU legislation is based, and whose degree of acceptance on the side of the citizens is an indicator of how far a shared political identity has developed.

Featuring case studies on foreign and environmental policy, biosafety policy, biotechnology regulation, civil society, human rights promotion, as well as studies on the role of memory, space and external views on the process of European identity-building, this book will be of interest to students and researchers of political science, political philosophy, European politics and European studies.

Furio Cerutti is Professor of Political Philosophy at the Department of Philosophy, University of Florence, Italy.

Sonia Lucarelli is a Senior Researcher and Lecturer at the Department of Politics, Institutions, History, University of Bologna, Italy.

Routledge/GARNET series: Europe in the World
Edited by Mary Farrell and Karoline Postel-Vinay
Centre for International Studies and Research (CERI), France

Editorial Board: Dr Mary Farrell, Sciences Po, Paris; Dr Karoline Postel-Vinay, CERI, France; Professor Richard Higgott, University of Warwick, UK; Dr Christian Lequesne, CERI, France; and Professor Thomas Risse, Free University Berlin, Germany.

International Advisory Committee: Dr Salma Bava, Jawaharlal Nehru University, New Delhi, India; Dr Knud Erik Jørgensen, University of Aarhus, Denmark; Professor Sunil Khilnani, SAIS, John Hopkins University, USA; Dr Anne-Marie Legloannec, CERI, France; Dr Xiaobo Lu, SIPA, Columbia University; Professor James Mittelman, University of Washington, USA; Dr Karen Smith, London School of Economics, UK; Professor Elzbieta Stadtmuller, University of Wroclaw, Poland.

The Routledge GARNET series, Europe in the World, provides a forum for innovative research and current debates emanating from the research community within the GARNET Network of Excellence. GARNET is a Europe-wide network of 43 research institutions and scholars working collectively on questions around the theme of 'Global Governance, Regionalisation and Regulation: The Role of the EU', and funded by the European Commission under the 6th Framework Programme for Research.

1. EU Foreign Policy in a Globalized World
Normative power and social preferences
Edited by Zaki Laïdi

2. The Search for a European Identity
Values, policies and legitimacy of the European Union
Edited by Furio Cerutti and Sonia Lucarelli

The Search for a European Identity

Values, policies and legitimacy of the European Union

Edited by Furio Cerutti and Sonia Lucarelli

LONDON AND NEW YORK

First published 2008
by Routledge
2 Park Square, Milton Park, Abingdon, Oxfordshire OX14 4RN

Simultaneously published in the USA and Canada
by Routledge
270 Madison Avenue, New York, NY 10016

Routledge is an imprint of the Taylor & Francis Group, an informa business.

First issued in paperback 2010

© 2008 Furio Cerutti and Sonia Lucarelli selection and editorial matter; individual contributors, their contributions

Typeset in Times New Roman

All rights reserved. No part of this book may be reprinted or reproduced or utilised in any form or by any electronic, mechanical, or other means, now known or hereafter invented, including photocopying and recording, or in any information storage or retrieval system, without permission in writing from the publishers.

British Library Cataloguing in Publication Data
A catalogue record for this book is available from the British Library

Library of Congress Cataloging in Publication Data
    The search for a European identity: values, policies and legitimacy of the European Union / edited by Furio Cerutti and Sonia Lucarelli.
        p. cm. – (Routledge/GARNET series – Europe in the world; 2)
    Includes bibliographical references and index.
    ISBN 978-0-415-44687-7 (hardback: alk. paper)
    ISBN 978-0-203-92677-2 (e-book: alk. paper)
        1. European Union. 2. European Union countries – Foreign relations.
3. European Union countries – Social policy. 4. European Union countries – Politics and government. 5. Environmental policy – European Union countries. 6. Human rights – European Union countries. I. Cerutti, Furio. II. Lucarelli, Sonia.
    JN30.S43 2008
    341.242?2 – dc22

2007048593

ISBN13: 978-0-415-44687-7 (hbk)
ISBN13: 978-0-415-66407-3 (pbk)
ISBN13: 978-0-203-92677-2 (ebk)

Contents

List of tables	vii
List of contributors	viii
Acknowledgments	xi
Acronyms and abbreviations	xii

PART I
Theorizing the link between identity and legitimacy — 1

1 Why political identity and legitimacy matter in the European Union — 3
  FURIO CERUTTI

2 European political identity, foreign policy and the Others' image: An underexplored relationship — 23
  SONIA LUCARELLI

PART II
Memory and space — 43

3 Europe, war and remembrance — 45
  CHIARA BOTTICI

4 Identity and capital cities: European nations and the European Union — 59
  GÖRAN THERBORN

PART III
Politics and ethics: the regulation of technology — 75

5 Global warming and European political identity — 77
  DIMITRI D'ANDREA

6	EU food safety policy and public debate ELENA ACUTI	93
7	EU red biotechnology regulation and European values RENATA BADII	108

PART IV
Social and civil Europe 123

8	The European social model(s) and the self image of Europe VAÏA DEMERTZIS	125
9	The double face of civil society DEBORA SPINI	142

PART V
Outside the EU: policies and images 157

10	Human rights promotion ROSA BALFOUR	159
11	Judicial policies and European enlargement: Building the image of a rule of law promoter DANIELA PIANA	176
12	How do the Others see us? European political identity and the external image of the EU LORENZO FIORAMONTI AND SONIA LUCARELLI	193
13	Conclusion FURIO CERUTTI AND SONIA LUCARELLI	211
	Index	219

Tables

11.1 Assessment on Europeanization by legal experts in EU
     epistemic communities   184
11.2 Trust of citizens in the judicial system in Central and Eastern
     European countries   185
12.1 Main external images of the EU   195
12.2 World powers today (and in 2020)   199
12.3 Europe vs. USA influence in world   202

Contributors

Elena Acuti is a PhD student at the Department of Philosophy, University of Florence. Her current areas of research are political realism, ethical and political issues in the EU's biotechnology policy.

Renata Badii is a post-doctoral Fellow at the Department of Philosophy, University of Florence. She has worked on political thinkers such as Norberto Bobbio and Carl Schmitt. She has written several entries for A. Cantini, P. Meucci and D. Spini (eds) *Le parole per dirlo: breve dizionario della globalizzazione*, ETS: Pisa (2008).

Rosa Balfour is a Senior Policy Analyst at the European Policy Centre in Brussels and a Research Fellow at CeSPI (Centre for Studies in International Politics) in Rome. Her area of research is European foreign policy. Recent publications include: (with Antonio Missiroli) 'Reassessing the European Neighbourhood Policy', *EPC Issue Paper* no. 54, June 2007; (ed.) *L'Europa allargata: come cambia la politica estera europea?*, Soveria Mannelli: Rubbettino 2005.

Chiara Bottici is a post-doctoral Fellow at the Department of Philosophy, University of Florence. She has contributed to various international journals such as the *Journal of Political Philosophy*, the *European Journal of Social Theory*, *Epoché: A Journal for the History of Philosophy*, *Iride* and *Quaderni Forum*. She is the author of *A Philosophy of Political Myth*, Cambridge: Cambridge University Press 2007 (Italian translation forthcoming at Bollati Boringhieri) and *Uomini e stati. Percorsi di un'analogia*, Pisa: ETS 2004 (English translation forthcoming at Palgrave).

Furio Cerutti is Professor of Political Philosophy at the Department of Philosophy, University of Florence and a recurrent Visiting Scholar at the Center of European Studies, Harvard University. He has recently published *Global Challenges for Leviathan. A Political Philosophy of Nuclear Weapons and Global Warming*, Lanham, MD: Rowman & Littlefield 2007. He has also co-edited *Political Identities and Conflicts*, Basingstoke: Palgrave 2001 and *A Soul for Europe*, two vols, Leuven: Peeters 2001 (translated into Italian and Farsi).

Dimitri D'Andrea is Senior Researcher and Lecturer in Political Philosophy at the Department of Philosophy, University of Florence. His publications include: *L'incubo degli ultimi uomini. Etica e politica in Max Weber*, Rome: Carocci 2005; (co-editor with E. Pulcini) *Filosofie della globalizzazione*, Pisa: ETS 2001; *Prometeo e Ulisse. Natura umana e ordine politico in Thomas Hobbes*, Rome: Nuova Italia Scientifica 1997.

Vaïa Demertzis is a PhD student in Political Science at the Institute for European Studies, Université Libre de Bruxelles. She is currently working on the issue of the construction of a supranational social solidarity in the EU.

Lorenzo Fioramonti is a Research Fellow at the University of Bologna and Pretoria (South Africa). He holds a PhD in comparative politics and has published widely on the European Union's external relations, civil society and development aid in international journals such as *Development in Practice*, *European Foreign Affairs Review* and *Third World Quarterly*. He is the editor of the *CIVICUS Global Survey of the State of Civil Society*, Bloomfield (USA): Kumarian Press, 2007.

Sonia Lucarelli is Senior Researcher and Lecturer of International Relations at the University of Bologna. She has written on International Relations theory, EU foreign policy and the external image of the EU. Among her publications: (ed.) *Beyond Self Perception: The Others' View of the European Union*, special issue of *European Foreign Affairs Review*, 3/2007; (co-editor with Ian Manners) *Values and Principles in EU Foreign Policy*, London: Routledge 2006; (co-editor with Claudio Radaelli) *Mobilising Politics and Society? The EU Convention's Impact on Southern Europe*, London: Routledge 2005; *Europe and the Breakup of Yugoslavia. A Political Failure in Search of a Scholarly Explanation*, The Hague: Kluwer 2000.

Daniela Piana is a Senior Researcher and Lecturer at the Department of Sociology and Political Science, University of Florence. She is the author of several articles on constitutionalism, judicial policies in post-Communist countries and rule of law. She has recently published two books: *Le istituzioni nella mente*, Soneria Mannelli: Rubbettino 2005, and *Costruire la democrazia. Ai confini dello spazio pubblico europeo*, Padua: Liviana 2006 (Romanian translation forthcoming).

Debora Spini is Adjunct Professor of Philosophy of Social Sciences at the University of Florence and a faculty member at Syracuse University in Florence. She has published on post-national democracy and legitimacy in the age of globalization. Among her publications: *La società civile postnazionale*, Rome: Meltemi 2007.

Göran Therborn is currently Professor and Chair of Sociology in the Social and Political Sciences Faculty at Cambridge University. Previously he was co-director of the Swedish Collegium for Advanced Study in Uppsala, and Professor of Sociology at Uppsala University. He has published numerous books and articles on many different topics. His recent publications include: *European Modernity and Beyond. The Trajectory of European Societies 1945–2000*, London: Sage 1995, 2000 (updated French edition Paris: Fayard 2008); (co-editor and co-author) *Asia and Europe in Globalization: Continents, Regions, Nations*, Leiden: Brill 2006; (author and guest editor) 'Eastern Drama. Capital Cities of Eastern Europe, 1830s-2006', Special Issue of *International Review of Sociology*, 16 (2), 2006; (editor and co-author) *Inequalities of the World*, London: Verso 2006; *Between Sex and Power. Family in the World 1900–2000*, London: Routledge 2004.

Acknowledgments

This book is the main output of a research project pursued in 2006–7 under the heading *Normative Issues of Regional and Global Governance* (coordinated by Furio Cerutti, executive coordinator, Andrew Gamble and Mario Telò) in the framework of the GARNET Network of Excellence on *Global Governance, Regionalisation and Regulation: the Role of the EU* (EU Sixth Framework Programme 2005–10; call identifier: FP6–2002-Citizens-3).

Most chapters have been intensively discussed in a series of seminars held at the Department of Philosophy, University of Florence, with the participation of the research team (led by Sonia Lucarelli) of the Forum on the Problems of Peace and War, also based in Florence. Moreover, in a preliminary form some chapters have been presented at the ECPR Joint Session of Workshops in Nicosia (April 2006), at the conference 'The Europeans' organized at Florence in the framework of the research project mentioned above (May 2007), at the ECPR General Conference in Pisa (September 2007) and at the GARNET Annual Conference 'Pathways to Legitimacy?' (Warwick, September 2007).

The editors wish to thank the participants in the various workshops and conferences for comments and insights, and are particularly grateful to the anonymous reviewers of the book project and to those who accepted to review specific chapters: Dario Castiglione, Marco Duranti, Wynn Grant, Gerdien Jonker, Sandra Kröger, Javier Lezaun, Liborio Mattina, Luigi Pellizzoni, Bo Stråth, Karin Tilmans, Monica Toraldo di Francia, Camil Ungureanu, Ian Welsch and Jay Winter.

Finally, the editors are grateful to Renata Badii and Lisa Tormena for their invaluable research assistantship.

Acronyms and abbreviations

ACGF	American Corn Growers Foundation
BEPG	Broad Economic Policy Guidelines
BSE	bovine spongiform encephalitis
CAHBI	Council of Europe committee of experts on the progress of biomedical science
CC	climate change
CCJE	Consultative Council of European Judges
CCPE	Consultative Council of European Prosecutors
CEECs	Central and Eastern European countries
CEPEJ	Commission for the Efficiency of Justice
CFSP	Common Foreign and Security Policy
CSCE	Conference on Security and Cooperation in Europe
CSOs	civil society organisations
DG	directorate-general
EC	European Community
ECCP	European Climate Change Programme
ECHR	European Convention for Human Rights
ECJ	European Court of Justice
ECSC	European Coal and Steel Community
EEA	European Environment Agency
EEC	European Economic Community
EES	European Employment Strategy
EESC	European Economic and Social Committee
EFSA	European Food Safety Authority
EGE	European Group on Ethics in Science and New Technologies
ENP	European Neighbourhood Policy
EP	European Parliament
EPPOSI	European Platform for Patients' Organisations, Science and Industry
ESM	European social model
ETS	European Emissions Trading Scheme
EU	European Union
EuropaBio	European Association of Biotechnology Industries

Eurordis	Rare Diseases Europe – European association of patients affected by rare diseases
Eurostat	European statistics
GM	genetically modified
GMO	genetically modified organism
GSP	generalized system of preferences
GW	global warming
ICT	information, communication, technology
IPCC	Intergovernmental Panel on Climate Change
ITRE	Industry, Transport, Research and Energy Commission
MEP	Member of European Parliament
MS	member state
NAPs	national allocation plans
NATO	North Atlantic Treaty Organisation
NGO	non-governmental organisation
OECD	Organisation for Economic Cooperation and Development
OMC	Open Method of Coordination
QMV	qualified majority voting
SEA	Single European Act
SIT	social identity theory
TEU	Treaty on European Union
TRIPs	trade-related intellectual property rights
UN	United Nations
UNESCO	United Nations Educational, Scientific and Cultural Organisation
WHO	World Health Organization
WSF	World Social Forum
WSSD	World Summit on Sustainable Development
WTO	World Trade Organization

Part I
Theorizing the link between identity and legitimacy

1 Why political identity and legitimacy matter in the European Union

Furio Cerutti

In this introductory chapter I first take note of the various and confusing meanings of 'identity' that can be found in academic and political discourse andpropose a phenomenological rather than normative approach to it, based on a reflexive notion of identity (what the citizens and the elites perceive as shared values and principles: a process of self-identification). Given the ineliminable double nature of the European Union (EU) (half a regulated singlemarket with high integration, half a would-be polity), in the section on 'Political identity' I argue that it is only possible for it to possess, if any, a thin, strictly political identity, which does not tend to cancel the national identities, or to replace Europe's cultural diversity. As for legitimacy, I stick to a broad understanding of it based on its conformity with models of good governance, supported but not able to be replaced by its economic performances, and 'wrapped' in shared memories and symbols (see the section on 'Legitimacy'). Why in a union of states identity is still an essential condition for institutions and policies to be legitimized, and what makes the development oa European identity so difficult, is explained in 'What has identity to do with legitimacy?'. In the conclusion I argue that only the correction and relativization of old notions about democracy can clear the way for a non-populistic understanding of it in the would-be polity that is the EU.

Definitions

Political identity (and legitimacy) in the EU can be broached in so many ways that the question can only be raised if all the authors mean the same thing. A credible answer is no. There is hardly so confused and polysemic a topic in European affairs as identity. What follows is a catalogue of this not-so-productive diversity:

1 identity as a set of things (say, European security and defence Identity) or
2 as a set of laws (constitutional first of all) and court rulings or public policies generated by the EU;
3 European identity as a substantive definition, derived from normative ethics, of what the EU ought to be (a deliberative democracy in the

Habermasian sense as in Eriksen (2005), a superpower, a caretaker for the rest of humanity) or
4 European identity as a substantive definition, based on historical and philosophical considerations, of what Europe could and should be [a civilian power, see Telò (2006); a regional state, see Schmidt (2006); an offspring of Renaissance Humanism and Enlightenment, see Rudolph (2001)];
5 political identity as a reflexive feature: how the Europeans, common citizens and elites, perceive the Union, how far they perceive themselves as European, what potential for identity formation and for legitimating EU policies and institutions is or is not contained in their mindset. A further question, beyond the phenomenology of European identity, regards how far those potentialities may correlate with the evolution of world politics, in which Europe's future is embedded.

I call 1 and 2 analytical approaches based on a reified notion of identity, 3 and 4 respectively a hypernormative and a moderately normative approach, and 5 a phenomenological approach. My first preference is for 5 and only at a distance for 4, but in the following I will at least sketch the reasons for rejecting 1–3. This starts with a political and meta-scientific consideration based on my assessment of the present predicament of the EU as a deep crisis that could develop into an existential crisis if the present discrepancies between the member states increase and no new strategy is devised in order to address the post-enlargement and post-referenda paralysis.[1] Things being as they are,[2] I cannot help sensing some intellectual futility, largely out of touch with the political process, in approaches such as those regarding the legislation passed in Brussels or even the EU declaratory policies (Manners 2006) as sufficient proof of the existence of our identity as Europeans; or those inferring from an interpretation of Rawls' *Theory of Justice* (it could as well be Plato's *Republic*, for that matter) the prescription for making the EU a superpower (Morgan 2005), a theorem that is light years away from what the Europeans wish for and what they can effectively bring about. For all scholars, but particularly those who are citizens of the Union and do not need to evoke a promising if a little fictional EU as a land of salvation to be gazed at from the shores of Bush's America [cf. again Morgan (2005) and Rifkin (2004)], the prevailing interest seems to me to lie elsewhere: we are interested in deploying our best analytical and critical tools rather than in developing prescriptive wishful thinking, in order to find out if a *political* enterprise as tortuous and open-ended as the European process still has a chance of becoming consolidated; that it will go on and thrive is not certain, and an eye should be also kept on the possibly disrupting consequences of this enterprise running indefinitely out of steam. Furthermore, to look with curiosity at the multifarious appearances of a European consciousness as can be read from what citizens and elites think and imagine, wish or reject, to conjecture where these attitudes may lead, and what could lead them in one direction rather than another is a more exciting intellectual task than inventing and touting the perfect formula capable of making

Europe a state or a community. To understand identity formation in the odd EU beast[3] the phenomenological sociology of Schütz, Berger and Luckmann is a better source of inspiration than an approach from a historicist (finding Europe's identity in its past) or engineering (let us make a blueprint of it and then wait for the people to implement it) angle; even good old Hegel, who in the *Phenomenology of Mind* studied the process through which self-consciousness evolved from personal and collective experience, can inspire us to develop a phenomenology of the European consciousness that integrates empirical and theoretical tools in order to interpret in an evolutionary context what people think and where they are heading. In the end, it is as ever less the academic debate and rather the attitude of the people (leaders, elites, citizens, in varying configurations) that determines if and which 'idea of Europe' or normative project will play a role (and how much of it) in shaping the final design of tomorrow's Union. This is why it is the method of studying the identity–legitimacy complex rather than the debate on its possible contents that is at the centre of this chapter.

Having sketched in this first round the contours of my position in the research on identity, I will now define it in a more systematic manner.

Political identity

If 'political identity' is to be used as a conceptual tool connected to 'legitimacy', we have to agree on a well-defined language, which excludes *four* fairly common usages.

First, political identity is not whatever feature (a governance mechanism, a set of policies or declarations) may be attributed to the EU or produced by it as an institution, but only what is clearly or confusedly perceived and talked about by Europeans (common citizens and elites) as a communal issue. Just to mention an extreme example, the notion of a 'European defence identity' made of military units, common procurement and joint command is a conceptually abhorrent reification of the identity concept. Policies and institutions are not 'identity' in themselves, but only as far as they are perceived by the individual actors as something which is meaningful to their self-description as Europeans as well as relevant to the image of themselves they want to project onto external actors. Political theory is different from objectivistic *Soziographie*.

Second, when talking about political identity we are not necessarily assuming an inescapable *path dependence* that is a dominance of the past over what we would like to be in the present and the future. The cultural heritage, the 'idea of Europe' celebrated in so many philosophical and historical books from Husserl to and Gasset, from Croce to de Rougemont and Gadamer does matter, but what is more important for the understanding of political reality is the re-elaboration we make of it in our projects for the future. Here we should not overlook that in the age of globalization the cultural heritage itself is changing more rapidly than ever and producing 'glocal' life forms, which admittedly are often inspired by American rather than European models.

Third, identity is not based primarily on *exclusion*, and Huntington's view that 'we know who we are when we know whom we are against' is an oversimplification, and a distorting one at that. It means taking a pathological development, e.g. the ethno-nationalist identity, for the very nature of identity. Suggestions aimed at shaping European identity as what is opposed to American culture and politics or, on another count, to Islam are not very far from this approach. Yet it is true that even the identity of a liberal and tolerant group, made predominantly of the sense of having certain shared values and goals, needs to be accompanied by the distinction between 'us' and 'the others'; otherwise identity vanishes into diffusiveness and does not accomplish its task of defining political groups, giving them internal cohesion and making their coexistence and interaction possible ('good fences make good neighbours'). Group identity[4] always contains two moments: the *mirror*, in which the group reflects and redefines its features, in a conversation among members of a group (development of a common political culture, constitutional debates), and the *wall*, by which the group (nation, political party, social community) gives itself a self-contained image which also defines its relations to other groups in a more open or exclusive or aggressive way.[5] New and post-national it may be, but European identity cannot be *cosmopolitical* in the sense that Europeans should see themselves as citizens of the world who just happen to live on the European continent, but refuse to identify themselves as citizens of a particular polity with certain geopolitical problems and interests (cf. Fuchs 2000); or should take responsibility as representatives for the rest of humankind, as suggested by Bauman (2004). The universalistic values on which the Union is based should rather be reconciled with the inevitable particularistic features of the European polity by keeping the configuration of the EU open to those values, but this constitutive philosophical and legal problem cannot be addressed here,[6] although it remains relevant to its legitimacy, if this is meant in the sense outlined in the following section on 'Legitimacy'.

Fourth, the identity that plays a pivotal role for legitimacy is *political*, not social or cultural.[7] Epistemologically and ontologically, society and polity are two different things, the second is not simply a by-product of the first, as some Marxists and most sociologists would have it, and has specific features: the ability to make ultimate decisions acting as one sovereign actor[8] (in this sense it is premature to call the EU a polity, as it is at best a would-be polity) and the normative framework (usually a constitution plus ordinary legislation, but also the ethics of patriotism or civic obligations) in which the preferences and projects of social groups are put in hierarchical order and reconciled with each other.

In its *core definition*, political identity is the overarching and inclusive project that is shared by the members of the polity, or in other words the set of political and social values and principles in which they recognize themselves

Why political identity and legitimacy matter in the European Union 7

as a 'we'. More important than this set (identity) is the process (self-identification through self-recognition)⁹ by which the people recognize themselves as belonging together because they come to share, but also modify and reinterpret those values and principles which are the framework within which they pursue their interests and goals.¹⁰ To do so, a degree of homogeneity in the *political* culture (say, an orientation favouring liberal democracy) is needed as a pre-condition, while a convergence of the entire cultural world (language, religion, morality, images of the world and forms of everyday life, cf. Joas and Wiegandt (2005)) is not. This is why to speak in the same sentence of the 'European cultural and political identity' is flawed, and leads inevitably to denying the Europeans any chance of achieving a political self-awareness of themselves as an actor, since a unified European culture exists and will exist to as small an extent as a European society – perhaps with the exception of football. On the other hand, a thick cultural and political identity could foster the dangerous image of a Fortress Europe, or result from the ethnocentric projection of mistaking one's own national or ideological identity for the European identity as a whole (Mummendey and Waldzus 2004). With regard to the history of modern nation-states, developing a purely political identity that is not backed by a unitary culture is admittedly an unprecedented *challenge*, one it is not yet clear if the Europeans are up to. Recent signs do not go in this direction: the debate on the failed Constitution, particularly its rhetorical preamble, was burdened by the temptation to establish a European cultural identity, with or without 'Christian roots', by means of an international treaty, while the cancellation of all common symbols (the flag, the anthem) from the next envisaged treaty, as provided for by the European Council of June 2007, reveals a frantic, if unrealistic fear of loss of identity on the part of certain national leaderships or public opinions.

On the one hand, the problem is whether in Europe a political design can take hold that out of the persisting diversity of culture and society and beyond the functional ties dictated by the single market, but also building on them, can achieve the consensus and stabilize the institutions that are necessary to take the Union to full actorness within and without. So far this design has failed to score a decisive step forward twice (in 1954 and 2005), and could even be reversed, by the effect of stagnation (cf. Alesina and Giavazzi 2006) and outside pressure rather than by anti-European forces. The Constitution project and the elites supporting it were not equal to the complex requirements raised by that design. Whatever may happen now, the emergence of a European self-identification process depends on future political developments much more than on cultural pre-givens. More precisely, we are speaking of a twofold dependence. First, it depends on the type of Union: a predominantly *intergovernmental* entity (of British flavour) aimed at best regulating the single market does not need much of a political *idem sentire* on the part of its citizens.¹¹ Vice versa the predominantly intergovernmental nature of the Union and its failure to act jointly on major issues is the first, though by no means the only, reason why identity among the citizens is very slow in developing. As a counterfactual example, think of how far the sense of being European would have been enhanced had the European governments spoken with one voice against or in favour of America's intervention in Iraq. It is indeed the effect of shared decisions in *high political issues* such as war and peace or reshaping versus dismantling the social protection network that could generate political identity, along with communicative conditions that will be mentioned later; it is not mere institution building or constitutional debates or identity-promoting policies such as establishing more public symbols of unity or launching awareness campaigns, although all of these would hold some sway.

On the other hand, there is no reason why a mature political identity of the Europeans should not form along the same contours as in European multilevel governance, which rules out a European identity overriding and replacing national identities; it rather prefigures a composite identity structure, for example in the sense of the typology (nested, cross-cutting, marble cake identities) sketched by Risse in the concluding chapter to Herrmann *et al.* (2004), and typical of a 'flexi-polity' (Lord and Beetham 2001) in which the degree of unity and self-identification varies from policy area to policy area and varies over time because the still open territorial borders also intersect with evolving functional borders.[12] This seems to fit the postmodern, more agile political culture of post-national (or rather, not-only-national) Western democracies, in which the unicity of allegiance to either the region or the nation-state or the union or federation or superstate is overcome; nor is the EU a superstate, except in the fantasies of Europhobes. This is the point missed in the *Bundesverfassungsgericht* ruling of 1993[13] with its request to have at the European level a *demos* with exactly the same traits as the culturally homogeneous *etnos–demos* in which elder EU citizens including this writer were born. The alternative to this obsolete perspective is however less the idea of a new political identity generated by means of constitutional patriotism, lastly because we have now learnt that the Europeans are not going to have a Constitution with its evocative force; rather it is or could be the idea that out of partly converging interests and ideas we Europeans can achieve a much stronger commonality or even unicity of action in some policy areas, including the build-up of more legitimate institutions as well as the sharing of the political principles that support them. It is not even said that these institutions have to be less and less intergovernmental and more communitarian to allow for the development of a stronger sense of being one party under many (but not all) profiles; if by a fortunate set of circumstances the European Council were over a long period able to set high political issues of EU and world politics on its agenda and to make enforceable decisions on them, the identity-building effect would be nearly the same.

Having sketched the lexicon of identity discussed preliminarily with the authors of this volume, it remains to me to raise and briefly respond to two questions of delimitation: '*Whose identity?*' and 'What is the stuff from which self-identification is distilled?'

To the first question, in a nation-state the answer would be: the citizens'. But this is different in a post-national, compound quasi-polity such as the EU, in which the citizens are only partly direct members of the polity, while indirect membership through the national governments remains prevailing in weight. In a mix whose proportions can only be defined from case to case, European identity has to be studied by looking at elites, opinion leaders and bureaucracies as well as at common citizens, whose choices only hold full direct sway in the case of referenda. Here lies one of the reasons why in several chapters of this book the press, being a medium of conversation of the elites among themselves, has been used as a main source for the study of European self-identification processes.

Second, the stuff from which self-identification is distilled does not exactly coincide with the experience of the EU as such. The cognitive ability and the will to distinguish between the Union institutions and the member states cannot be credited to be very developed among the now half a billion Europeans; it should be cautiously tested when interviewing people, inside and outside the Union. Where this ability has not been established, it seems safe to assume that in a majority of cases what the people, particularly outside the elites, have in mind while assessing the legitimacy and performance of the emerging polity is 'Europe' (the composite effect of what the EU and the member states have done) rather than the EU as a distinctive body.[14] Its *popular image* on the continent is said to be that of a big market for all, characterized by freedom of movement, and also a bloc competing with others on the world stage (Díez Medrano 2003). This minimalist picture should, however, be complemented by the more political traits that can be read in the Europeans' ascertained openness towards having a common foreign and, even more, security and defence policy (respectively 68 per cent and 76 per cent according to Eurobarometer 2006).

Lastly, a few words on *how to study political identity in empirical terms*, also with regard to this volume, even if this cannot be seen as full implementation of the ideal methodology I am going to sketch; this would have required much greater funding, more time for setting up and testing the single tools, and more contributions in other issue areas, with the likelihood of exceeding the limits of a single volume. First, qualitative analysis should prevail over quantitative. The results of elections and referenda are too rough and momentary a tool to reveal the citizens' 'soul'; opinion surveys are fundamental, but can be distorted by ill-formulated questions or by the omission of essential questions. Quantitative data can prevail only in the first approach to the issue, or *faute de mieux*, as long as a more refined and penetrating analysis is not available.

In particular, I would like to stress the importance of the *content analysis*:

10 *Furio Cerutti*

- of what the media directly or indirectly tell the public about Europe (this is carried out in most chapters with regard to the press only, TV being far beyond our funding);
- of constitutional and parliamentary (in the European Parliament as well as national chambers) debates, which is done only occasionally in the chapters; but also
- of the motivations with which national and EU policies are introduced and the debates accompanying them, which would require a more thorough examination of the available archives and in-depth interviews with the policy-makers involved. I again want to stress that analysing a policy (say, foreign or security or human rights policy) adopted by the Union and attributing it by default the meaning of representing European identity is not the correct way to go about investigations. However, policy analysis (cf. Cedermann 2000; *contra* Herrmann and Brewer 2004) does become relevant to our research the moment in which, as we have tried to do here, the focus is shifted to the motivation and meaning of a policy in Europe's political cultures and public opinions on the one hand and the reception given to it by the media and the citizens interviewed on the other.

Legitimacy

The legitimacy of the EU (of the Union itself as an institution, then of its policies and lastly of its leaders) is an only slightly less polysemic notion to identity; for example, legitimacy is easily mistaken to be *consensus*, which is a phenomenon not unambiguously related to it, while the *legal* legitimacy based upon the treaties is just a background element of political legitimacy; but it remains subject to the theoretical disagreements which I am now going to discuss.[15] Its link to identity is hardly addressed in most of the literature written under this heading, while it is highlighted in only a segment of the literature on legitimacy (very clearly in Scharpf 1999; cf. also Schmidt 2006).

My own approach rests on the following theses:

1 legitimacy cannot be reduced to output legitimacy, nor input legitimacy easily replaced with the latter;
2 properly said, legitimacy does not comprise two equal and exchangeable components, because output legitimacy is the set of conditions for legitimacy to be able to work rather than a second type of legitimacy;
3 there is a deeper, Weberian layer in the notion of legitimacy which goes beyond input legitimacy itself as based on 'what the people will'.

On thesis 1. Output legitimacy, based on the performance of the EU as a caterer of wellbeing to the citizens (Scharpf 1999), is just one component of the whole; to see it as all-encompassing and capable of legitimizing the Union altogether is not just (normatively) a technocratic reduction of the European process; it is (analytically) out of touch with the real history of European integration, as this process is known to have gone for better or for worse beyond the stage of a single market that makes economic actors, acting on their predefined self-interest, cooperate.[16] Cooperation complemented by integration among the member states has got them involved in high political questions such as the reshaping of the welfare state, also as a consequence of the Maastricht stability criteria, the attitude towards other peoples (the Doha Round; the scrapping or preserving of the Common Agricultural Policy, which also involves questions of international justice and impacts on the EU's image)[17] and last but not least in security crises such as in Lebanon 2006 or Iran – although the EU remains an incomplete security community, being embedded as a junior partner in the larger community of NATO and being incapable to speak with one voice on all occasions. In other words, legitimacy in and of the EU is neither the nation-state legitimacy model written large nor the legitimacy of an entity that can choose to act one day as a market regulator and the next as a fledgling polity. As it has developed in the last 20 years, this *double nature of the beast* is at work at all times and does not allow for the political aspects and deficits of the process to be silenced by a better economic performance.

In other words, the integration process has gone beyond the point in which the legitimacy of the EC/EU may have been totally based on what it did for our economic wellbeing. It has thus acquired or claimed to possess a political substance whose nature and extent remain so far unclear, and far from giving birth to a fully-fledged polity; but it has in any case unleashed 'democratic' expectations, even if the meaning and procedure of democracy at a post-national, but non-federal, level have not been redefined. The scholars' task under these circumstances is to clear the way from the relics of an obsolete set of notions and to help forge redefined concepts.

On thesis 2. To prevent confusion and unduly mistaking terms, the expression 'output legitimacy' should be dismissed and replaced with 'substantive conditions of legitimacy' (cf. Cerutti 1996): whatever their fundaments, as we are going to see, the legitimacy claims (related to 'input legitimacy') of a polity or regime allow for its effective legitimization only if it also proves able to provide the basic common goods (security, minimal wellbeing, legality); performances that are fragmented between the Union and member states rather than shared. Being a condition of something is not the same as being the thing itself.

On thesis 3. (Input) legitimacy is mostly defined as what results from the 'will of the people' (where government *by* the people prevails) being the basis of government, thus making the even costly decisions of some on behalf of others acceptable to the latter, when (Bartolini 2005: Ch. 3) in collective decisions neither unanimity nor exit are available to the ruled.[18-] But this regards only the procedural rule that makes legitimacy possible, that is, its being generated from a presumably ultimate authority (the will of the people). Most real people, however, are not fully satisfied with this procedural foundation of legitimacy and look to substantive elements beyond and underneath it: to grant legitimacy to a polity they want to have grounds to perceive its *conformity to a model* of just and good governance, which citizens have in mind and refer to in an emotional and/or discursive way, as it embodies the deep-seated values, principles and overall goals they believe in as members of a polity. In other words this property can be attributed to political power only if this is able to justify its existence and its actions by claiming to be somehow related to fundamentals or sources of collective life that are not of an everyday nature (Weber: *ausseralltäglich*). This is what I call Weberian legitimacy, the ground layer of any other version of 'legitimacy': for the EU it means its claimable conformity to, say, a democratic, social and federative polity model which guarantees peace and some protection from the side-effects of globalization.[19] Without the people feeling like this, the mere input of the 'will of the people' (for example, in an election whose issues do not relate to those models) is not sufficient to establish the legitimacy of power, nor do economic performances or benefits by themselves enhance the loyalty of the people (there is little Europeanism among the French farmers, who benefit most from the Common Agricultural Policy).

Finally and most importantly, it is not even the sum of the conformity to a model upheld by shared beliefs plus the credibility achieved by a well-performing regime that can ensure that the EU or one of its policies will be recognized in their legitimacy claims. The good economic and social reasons (satisfaction with former EU policy results and further expectations of gains) and the acceptance of (existing pieces of) EU government because it is 'democratic' or even 'social' have to be linked to each other and embedded in the shared belief that the EU institutions are 'our' government for certain, though not all matters of governance. But this cannot be done and communicated if they are not at the same time perceived as somehow embodying a shared *memory* of our controversial history (cf. Chapter 3 by Chiara Bottici) and speaking to us through accepted and understandable *symbols,* including the shaping of the politically relevant space of capital cities, as Göran Therborn shows in his chapter. The Union is not a new nation or supernation, but political discourse on it must take place inside the countries as well as transnationally if its polity moment is to survive and to develop with legitimacy.

An example: the downfall of the Constitutional Treaty at the hand of the Dutch and French voters came not only from the lethal blend of an overdose of Weberian legitimacy (the normative overweight of the Constitution itself) and diminished performance (the presumed inability of the Union to protect underprivileged layers from the effects of globalization), but also from a large lack of an emotional and symbolical grasp on the citizens' souls by the political elites, which were almost unanimously in favour of ratification. The European integration process is much more complicated a business than politicians, technocrats and social scientists obsessed with economic models of politics have been able to understand, and the disaster in France and the Netherlands has given everybody bitter food for thought.[20]

Recapitulating this section, to denote the case in which (Weberian) legitimacy is successfully claimed thanks to motivating decisions in high politics, and the claim is made more credible by good performances and also comes 'wrapped' in shared memories, narratives and symbols, I propose to speak of *substantial legitimacy*. Substantial legitimacy[21] is not an empirical quantity that can be easily measured by quantitative tools such as polls on the approval rating of a public policy. In its core, legitimacy resides in the reservoir of meanings, arguments and symbols to which political power can reasonably resort in order to justify its existence and behaviour. It is the job of the political leadership to decide what meanings and symbols to activate at a given stage of the political and social conflicts that the polity has to deal with, thus actualizing legitimacy, translating it into consensus and stabilizing it around institutions; actualizing legitimacy is the process we habitually call *legitimization*, in which the conditions now known as 'output legitimacy' first play a role.[22] The several fathers and mothers of the Maastricht Treaty succeeded in this enterprise, appealing at the right moment to the Europeans' search for a new role after the end of the Cold War and to the economic and symbolic promise of the single currency to come. In contrast, in order to push forward political integration, the luckless fathers and mothers of the constitutional project chose the wrong instrument, a legal text evoking the image of a bureaucratic superstate, submitted it to popular vote, as if the EU were a single democracy with a traditional *demos*, and also chose the wrong timing (the sluggish economic recovery and lingering unemployment favoured the populist search for a scapegoat, which was found in 'Brussels').

What has identity to do with legitimacy?

The link between legitimacy and political identity in the EU can be best understood as a problem: why should there be *one* actor (or, more philosophically, one subject), the EU, seeking legitimacy for its actions? Only when people come to find that staying united is at the same time convenient for their well-being and relevant to their image of collective life can a new polity reach the critical point of acceptance. In other words, they would then find that decisions concerning ultimate issues such as peace or war, openness or closure towards the rest of the world, social solidarity or deregulated competition should not be left to the veto power of national governments, or the dynamics of globalization, but rather made within the new polity, whatever (federal, semi-federal, multilevel, etc.) method of government this may have chosen.

Substantial legitimacy thus contains as a core condition the political identity or rather *self-identification* of the people involved. Only institution building or policy-making perceived as legitimate by a public that feels it is *one* actor can *create meaning* for the recognition of the new polity, meaning being the scarcest resource in the post-modern globalized world as well as a powerful basis of allegiance and participation.[23] It is only by grasping the complex legitimacy–identity link, particularly in front of such a strange beast as the EU, that we acquire the conceptual tools and the sensitivity that are necessary to keep our eye on *political change*, which always includes legitimacy crises or even the disruption of the polity – against which the EU is also not safeguarded.

Now, in the case of the EU the legitimacy problems surrounding institution building and policies are complicated by the circumstance that, beyond all questions regarding the social, economic or legal substance of the issues, a question of political *entitlement* remains open: in a Union only those acting as members of the whole ('the Europeans' as a sole constituency) called to justify or delegitimate new institutions and policies are entitled to decide for the whole. The French and Dutch majorities against the Constitutional Treaty were instead allowed to decide for the rest of Europe because they were called to the polls on that particular French or Dutch election day, rather than on the same day for all Europeans; this *built-in democratic deficit* was the result of a choice made by a European Council, unaware of how political identity and legitimacy play into each other, and should be focused on well before all worries about the much talked-about 'democratic deficit' of the Commission. Referenda should have not been held, as I argue below in the 'Conclusion', and the main reason for that is the lack of a political discourse among Europeans rather than the lack of a common election day, which was however to be observed if the referenda were to be legitimate.

Finally, it is obvious but perhaps not pointless to remember that neither identities nor legitimization processes are *monolithic*. On the one hand, national identities still play a prevailing role in European countries; however, not without fractures along regional and local or class and generational lines. On the other hand, on the acceptance of the EU itself Europeans have been for a long time and indeed remain divided into roughly two halves for and against the Union, according to the recurrent results of the Eurobarometer.[24] From this point of view, the question of the legitimacy of the European institutions remains open and controversial, a matter of a *political and cultural struggle* between nations, parties, ideologies and interest groups, in a constellation that is bound to change depending on economic developments, social movements and the communicative strategies of future leaderships, but still bound by the double nature that does not allow for the market regulator to ignore politics nor for the would-be polity to expand into a classical state.

At the moment, however, the growth of a political identity among European citizens and elites and its impact on the Union being felt as a trustworthy and efficient institution is made difficult or even smothered by several structural factors.

First comes what I have dubbed the double nature of the beast, the constraints that each of the two natures, market regulator and quasi-polity, put on each other. This ambivalence is made even more visible by its two sides being distributed among countries with contrasting attitudes, the UK and Denmark on the market-only side, France, Germany and Italy on the polity side. The two terms of the ambivalent nature are, however, unlikely to remain unchanged, even if the functionalist spillover from functions of economic regulation and integration into politics does not work as it did in previous decades: if ever, the European polity will only become fully-fledged as the result of political decisions.

Second, there is a difficulty that is previous to granting or refusing legitimacy to the Union: its scarce visibility, the difficulty for the public to focus on and become familiar with Delors' *objet politique non identifié*, which is an absolute and odd cognitive novelty (the federative, but non-federal polity; the multilevel system of governance, in which even experts can get lost) for generations that have still been socialized with the pyramidal and homogeneous modern state model in mind; a model in which government of, by, for and with the people (Schmidt 2006) tends to coincide, while these sides are now being disconnected and distributed, part on the member states, part on the Union.[25]

Third, this is aggravated by two structural circumstances: EU legislation is executed not directly by Union institutions, but by the national ones, which retain the gratitude expressed by those favoured by the legislation, while in case of protest they can still resort to 'EU-bashing'. Also, while fundamental economic policies (think of the Stability Pact, or the EU stance in WTO (World Trade Organization) negotiations) are determined at EU level, the cake baked under those policies is then distributed among social groups, lobbies and generations at the national executive and legislative level, which thus seems to be the true venue of decision-making and attracts a lot of attention – also because national debates are immediately 'readable' by the public.

The last reason resides in the communication structures through which the EU is perceived or 'framed'. They are still overwhelmingly national, with the EU being a preoccupation or a scapegoat for politicians and journalists (whose political culture remains widely national) rather than a free-standing entity. Suffice it to remember that of the whole volume of European information flows only 7.5 per cent regards the EU, while 62 per cent of the information citizens possess on the Union comes from the TV, which with its event-related news is hardly instrumental to the understanding of the complex EU institutional framework.[26] The communicative deficit regarding Europe is the so far failed Europeanization of national public opinions (cf. Schmidt 2006) rather than the lack of a Europe-wide public sphere based on its own media. Or, in the case of Euronews, the lack of serious efforts to advertise this multilingual TV channel across Europe and its aseptic style, with some policies, but no politics coming into its reporting and debates.

Conclusion

The first use of the notions of legitimacy and political identity that I have tried to redefine is to help us better examine the question of how far the EU can be regarded as a polity and has attained political actorness. In a further step, they are essential in order to understand how far a *post-national polity* can arise, based on patterns of political identity and legitimacy that are different from those of the nation-state as well as of the neo-medieval empire conceptualized by Jan Zielonka (2006). This is perhaps the paramount question: if voters, journalists, intellectuals and politicians in the member states remain conceptually stuck to national patterns, if they believe that the same 'national' type of glue or cement must be put to work in the EU in order to make some European identity keep the citizens together and to legitimize in their eyes the authority of the Union, this belief is doomed to unleash competition with the nation-states, in whose eyes 'Brussels' will remain a den of techno-bureaucrats, despite all pretensions of being home to all Europeans. A chance for European identity to put down roots is given only if we conceive it as a purely political identity, not competing with national identities on the same level, being *thin* rather than thick, as large as is needed to make the polity moments of the Union legitimate (with no extension to matters outside EU competence), and capable of asserting its present *finalité politique* (the governance of globalization) in a measure compatible with its double nature. That the EU must come to terms with (in comparison with the nation-state) slimmed-down legitimacy does not mean that it can give up its constitutive elements and be happy with an *Ersatz* legitimacy such as 'output legitimacy'.

Let us lastly mention another framework condition, which has already emerged in this text and needs to be more clearly formulated: I mean clarification of the usage of 'democracy', not just in scholarly discussions but in political discourse as well. Its articulation into government of, by, for and with the people, as most recently developed by Vivien Schmidt (2006), is an important step in this direction. Another one would be to clarify that democracy does not have its supreme model in direct democracy, which is almost a mockery (like in the 'constitutional' referenda, see Cerutti 2005) when explicitly or unconsciously applied to a Union of (27) states and only secondarily of citizens, with a degree of complexity in government never heard of in previous polities and – as we have just seen – little or no communication among the people and the peoples. What representative democracy may mean in this context, and how much *countermajoritarian democracy* is needed to prevent democracy from degenerating remain open questions which must be discussed if the notion of legitimacy is to make sense in the EU framework. Last but not least, a crucial question is how far democracy in its most widespread sense as an electoral and parliamentarian check on government can go in a Union of states based on multilevel governance. The problem is whether the interests and ideals of the peoples of

Europe are better served by continuous checks of that kind, which do indeed misuse the fascination of 'democracy' and help paralyse the process, or by the continuation and acceleration of an integration that, beneficial to all as it has proved to be, cannot but be elite driven; all the more given the ultra-complex and for the common citizens difficult-to-comprehend nature of the odd EU beast. This was so even in less complex times: had the myriads of German and Italian medium-sized or small states held referenda on each step of the *Reichsgründung* and *Risorgimento* respectively, Germany and Italy as states would possibly never have come into existence. It is true that Europe, if at all will become one polity by the *word* and not the *sword*, but this is exactly why words such as democracy should be carefully tested before being used in the EU debate. Otherwise this word remains surrounded by the polysemies and misrepresentations that characterize much of the debate in the member states on EU legitimacy, with delegitimizing effects not just on the Union but on the member states as well, because they seem to have just lost portions of their sovereignty.

Refocusing our attention on a more problematic understanding of legitimacy and identity as is attempted in this book goes hand in hand with a suggestion regarding our *research programme*. It is a suggestion to shift our main attention from policy analysis and the study of formal institutions to what in German classical philosophy was called the subjective or active side of history, 'agency' being a pale successor to that notion. I mean the degree of meaningfulness of the EU in the minds of citizens and national or European elites, the motivations they feel while acting in one way or the other in EU policy-making, and the resulting degree of participation in European politics,[27] seen in its interplay with national politics.

On this volume

While the contents of the chapters shall be discussed in Chapter 13, it may be useful here to outline the structure of the volume. Its main thrust lies, as mentioned above, in exploring the relevance that ethically significant EU policies as well as certain aspects of its foreign policy may have for the fostering of a political identity among Europeans and the legitimization of the Union. We regard the inquiry into the contents of a common attitude that may arise around policy issues (first among the policy-makers and then the public, the two levels researched by most of our authors) more productive than those methodologies that just look at how far a (presumably) holistic national identity remains untouched or spills over into a European one. Identities are not things that can be moved around like blocks of wood, so the question 'how much do you feel European, or just French, or European and French, or French and European' is only a very rough and initial tool.[28]

Policies on biosafety and medical technology are by definition ethically relevant because they touch upon notions of life and nature that are constitutive of our stance in the world; policies on climate change may raise questions in the near future regarding our effective solidarity with future generations. We assume that ethically relevant policies such as those mentioned (see the Chapters 5, 6 and 7) will assume an enhanced role in the decades ahead, because they challenge the modern model of adversary politics and rather require a joint effort of humankind in saving global commons such as the atmosphere.[29] As the former ethical neutrality of technology and of its public regulation is fading away, we also assume that these policies, that is, the way they are formulated and how they are received by the public, play and will play a role in shaping the developing Europeans' identity.

That foreign policy plays a major role in this shaping is not in need of any demonstration, even less in the case of the EU human rights policy examined in Rosa Balfour's (Chapter 10) contribution; besides, human rights issues share ethical relevance with technology-related ones. However, in this volume a further, rarely investigated dimension of that role is examined, that is, the effect that the external image of the Union[30] might have on the identity formation process among the Union's citizens (see Chapter 12 by Fioramonti and Lucarelli as well as the theoretical introduction to this research area developed by Sonia Lucarelli in the next chapter).

Two more policy areas are investigated with regard to their effects on identity-building and to what they may contribute to the Union's legitimacy. Vaïa Demertzis looks at the 'European social model', which is an identity-promoting signal or codeword rather than a policy, while Daniela Piana goes through the attempted Europeanization of the judiciary in the enlargement countries with an eye to those effects. Another significant codeword for European identity formation is 'civil society', which Debora Spini examines both in its conceptual definition(s) and empirical evidence.

A book whose theoretical frame of reference stresses the importance of the symbolic elements for the substantial legitimacy of the EU could not fail to explore this level of identity formation as well. This is done, again in both the conceptual and the empirical dimension, in Chapter 3 by Chiara Bottici on the memory of the Second World War and the Holocaust in present-day Europe, while Göran Therborn looks from the viewpoint of historical sociology at the role of politically defined space, specifically the typology of European capital cities, including Brussels, in the shaping of each polity's identity.

Since the authors are political philosophers and political scientists, with the participation of a sociologist, the book has a strong multidisciplinary and to an extent interdisciplinary character, which we believe to be particularly suited to a matter as intricate and elusive as the identity and legitimacy of a new powerful, but still undefined and incomplete, polity.

Notes

1 At the time of writing, autumn 2007, it is unclear or even unlikely that the current Intergovernmental Conference and the following Council meetings can

generate such a strategy, which would require a strong leadership that does not exist in Europe at this time.
2 That Europe was politically short of steam and that it was approaching the 2004 enlargement without a cohesive and determined leadership was already clear at Nice 2000, well before the debacle of 2005.
3 Cf. Mayer and Palmowski (2004).
4 I follow Berger and Luckmann (1966: 174) in using this expression instead of the currently widespread 'collective identity', since this retains for me an aftertaste of totalitarian ideology, which makes group identity a hypostasis and places this collective entity over the individuals.
5 More in Cerutti (2001). Unlike my own views, boundary formation is put at the centre of identity formation by Eisenstadt and Giesen (1995); for its role in the EU see Cederman (2000). I am grateful to the members of the Political Philosophy Group in my university's department of Philosophy for the help received in preparing this chapter, particularly in discussing the existing literature.
6 See however Beck and Grande (2004).
7 This notion of a European identity being political and not cultural is not far from the notion of civic identity used by authors such as Bartolini (2005) and Herrmann et al. (2004), but I cannot discuss similarities and differences here.
8 Herrmann and Brewer (2004) also sees the relevance of this element for the differentiation of social and political identity. It is impossible to address their complex relationship here, and for argumentative purposes in this text I stress the distinctiveness of political identity.
9 This is perhaps what Vivien Schmidt (2006: 17–20) alludes to when she writes that identity is more an issue of doing than of being.
10 The most recent snapshot of some of the fundamental values heeded by the Europeans is in Arts and Halman (2004). In the multilevel European polity things are made more complicated by the fact that sharing for example views on social solidarity and protection by the state so far has not translated into the citizens' wish to transfer competence in this field from national governments to the EU. Holding identical views in matters of social policy does not yet mean requesting and legitimizing an EU social policy. For a view on how values and principles along with their interpretation shape European identity see Lucarelli (2006).
11 See Moravcsik (2002). Eder (2001) rightly points out that a greater complexity of society (a higher degree of EU integration, in our case) requires more 'collective identity'.
12 Examples of these variations are the transfer of issue areas from pillar to pillar and the extensions of qualified majority voting on the one hand, and the successive enlargements on the other.
13 Its rightfulness has been upheld among others by Scharpf (1999: 10) which limits the acceptability, but not the usefulness of a book that remains the most penetrating discussion of the relationship between identity and legitimacy.
14 EC\EU history is correctly intertwined with the history of the member states in Judt (2005).
15 On the plurality of legitimacy claims in the case of the EU cf. Lord and Magnette (2004).
16 The reduction of legitimacy to output legitimacy is also criticized in various ways by Olsen (2004) and Bartolini (2005).
17 As for the still little researched problem of how far the external perception of Europe (by which I mean the EU + member states) feeds back into identity formation within the Union see Fioramonti and Lucarelli (Chapter 12) as well as Lucarelli (Chapter 2) in this volume.
18 At a first sight EU decision-making in foreign policy has little need to find full political legitimacy, as exit is formally available and has been also practised in

high controversial situations like the Iraq war, as the EU simply ceased to exist as an international actor (technically it was a suspension of partnership rather than the exit of opting-out partners).
19 This is just an example of what many, though not all Europeans may expect from the EU when thinking about its legitimacy.
20 More in Cerutti (2005).
21 It is perhaps worth remembering that 'substantial' regards the very core of something, whereas 'substantive', as opposed to 'procedural', looks at the specific contents of a process or institution.
22 The link between legitimacy and legitimization cannot be further discussed here, and is best explained using single concrete examples. The complex structure of legitimacy is differentiated by Fuchs and Schlenker (2006) into legitimacy/trust and subjective/objective legitimacy.
23 How these two elements develop (or rather struggle to develop) in the EU and play into each other cannot be further developed here (see Cerutti 2003 and more in-depth Schmidt 2006).
24 This also holds true in the case of the Constitutional Treaty: the referenda killed it politically, but let us not forget that it was ratified by a large number of parliaments and a majority of Spanish and Luxembourgian voters. Also, according to Eurobarometer (2007) 66 per cent of EU citizens still support the idea of a Constitution, although this finding cannot be easily translated into a probable majority of voters in every country (this Eurobarometer having been made available a few days before this volume went to the publisher, its data could be taken note of only in this introduction). As for the rate of acceptance, in the sense of having a positive view of the EU, it was 46 per cent in 2006 and it is 52 per cent in Eurobarometer (2007)
25 This difficulty has been enhanced by the legal–bureaucratic Eurospeak of the Brussels institutions, which seem determined to make the EU impermeable to the understanding of the citizens. A paradigmatic example seems to be the case of the utterly confusing coexistence of the 'Council of Europe' and 'European Council', which a name change of the latter would easily have avoided.
26 See Garcia and Le Torrec (2003). Cf. also Seidendorf (2007).
27 This is said without ignoring the problem signalled in Vivien Schmidt's formula of 'policy-making without politics in the EU, politics without policy in the member states', Schmidt (2006: 5 and *passim*).
28 Books and articles based exclusively on the corresponding findings of the Eurobarometer or similar surveys seem to have no awareness of this.
29 A theory of global challenges can be found in Cerutti (2007).
30 Cf. Lucarelli (2007).

References

Alesina, A. and Giavazzi, F. (2006) *The Future of Europe*, Cambridge, MA: MIT Press.
Arts, W. and Halman, L. (2004) (eds) *European Values at the Turn of the Millennium*, Leiden: Brill Academic.
Bartolini, S. (2005) *Restructuring Europe*, Oxford: Oxford University Press.
Bauman, Z. (2004) *Europe: an unfinished adventure*, Cambridge: Polity.
Beck, U. and Grande, E. (2004) (eds) *Das kosmopolitische Europa: Gesellschaft und Politik in der Zweiten Moderne*, Frankfurt: Suhrkamp.
Berger, P. L. and Luckmann, T. (1966) *The Social Construction of Reality: a treatise in the sociology of knowledge*, Garden City, NY: Doubleday.

Cedermann, L.-E. (2000) (ed.) *Constructing Europe's Identity: the external dimension*, Boulder, CO: Lynne Rienner.

Cerutti, F. (1996) 'Identità e politica', in F. Cerutti (ed.) *Identità e politica*, Rome: Laterza.

——(2001) 'Towards the political identity of the Europeans. An introduction', in F. Cerutti and E. Rudolph (eds) *A Soul for Europe: on the political and cultural identity of the Europeans*, Vol. 1, *A Reader*, Leuven: Peeters.

——(2003) 'A political identity of the Europeans?', *Thesis Eleven*, 72 (1): 26–45.

——(2005) 'Europe's deep crisis', *European Review*, 13 (4): 525–40.

——(2007) *Global Challenges for Leviathan*, Lanham, MD: Rowman & Littlefield.

Díez Medrano, J. (2003) *Framing Europe*, Princeton, NJ: Princeton University Press.

Eder, K. (2001) 'Integration through culture?' in K. Eder and B. Giesen (eds) *European Citizenship between National Legacies and Postnational Projects*, Oxford: Oxford University Press.

Eisenstadt, S. and Giesen, B. (1995) 'The construction of collective identity', *Archives Européennes de Sociologie*, 36: 72–102.

Eriksen, E. O. (2005) (ed.) *Making the European Polity*, London: Routledge.

Eurobarometer (2006) *Public Opinion in the European Union. Standard Eurobarometer 66. First Results*, European Commission, Public opinion Analysis, Brussels. Online. Available HTTP: < http://ec.europa.eu/public_opinion/archives/eb/eb66/eb66_highlights_en.pdf > (accessed 19 November 2007).

——(2007) *Public Opinion in the European Union. Standard Eurobarometer 67. First Results*, European Commission, Public opinion Analysis, Brussels. Online. Available HTTP: < http://ec.europa.eu/public_opinion/archives/eb/eb67/eb_67_first_en.pdf > (accessed 19 November 2007).

Fuchs, D. (2000) 'Demos und Nation in der Europaeischen Union', in H.-D. Klingemann und F. Neidhardt (eds) *Zur Zukunft der Demokratie. Herausforderungen im Zeitalter der Globalisierung*, WZB-Jahrbuch 2000, Berlin: Edition Sigma 2000.

Fuchs, D. and Schlenker, A. (2006) 'European identity and the legitimacy of the EU', Background paper Team 12, EU-Consent: Work package V, presented at the II Work package V Conference, Lodz, March 30-April 1, 2006. Online. Available HTTP: < http://www.eu-consent.net/library/brx061012/Klingemann_Lodz0603.pdf > (accessed 19 November 2007).

Garcia, G. and Le Torrec, V. (2003) 'Le cadrage médiatique de l'UE: exploration comparée des mécanismes du frame-setting et du frame-sharing', in G. Garcia and V. Le Torrec (eds) *L'Union européenne et les médias*, Paris: L'Harmattan.

Herrmann, R. K. and Brewer, M. B. (2004) 'Identities and institutions: introduction', in R. K. Herrmann, T. Risse and M. B. Brewer (eds) *Transnational Identities: becoming European in the EU*, Lanham, MD: Rowman & Littlefield.

Herrmann, R., Risse, T. and Brewer, M. B. (2004) (eds) *Transnational Identities: becoming European in the EU*, Lanham, MD: Rowman & Littlefield.

Joas, H. and Wiegandt, K. (2005) (eds.) *Die kulturellen Werte Europas*, Frankfurt am Main: Fischer.

Judt, T. (2005) *Postwar: a history of Europe since 1945*, New York, NY: The Penguin Press.

Lord, C. and Beetham, D. (2001) 'Legitimizing the EU', *Journal of Common Market Studies*, 39 (2): 443–62.

Lord, C. and Magnette, P. (2004) '*E pluribus unum*? Creative disagreement about legitimacy in the EU', *Journal of Common Market Studies*, 42 (1): 183–202.

Lucarelli, S. (2006) 'Introduction', in S. Lucarelli and I. Manners (eds) *Values and Principles in European Foreign Policy*, London: Routledge.
——(2007) (ed.) *Beyond Self Perception: the Others' view of the European Union*, special issue of *European Foreign Affairs Review*, 12(3).
Manners, I. (2006) 'The constitutive nature of values, images and principles in the European Union', in S. Lucarelli and I. Manners (eds) *Values and Principles in European Union Foreign Policy*, London: Routledge.
Mayer, F. and Palmowski, J. (2004) 'European identities and the EU', *Journal of Common Market Studies*, 42 (3): 573–98.
Moravcsik, A. (2002) 'In defence of the "Democratic deficit": reassessing legitimacy in the European Union', *Journal of Common Market Studies*, 40 (4): 603–24.
Morgan, G. (2005) *The Idea of a European Superstate*, Princeton: Princeton University Press.
Mummendey, A. and Waldzus, S. (2004) 'National differences and European plurality: discrimination or tolerance between European countries', in R. K. Herrmann, T. Risse and M. B. Brewer (eds) *Transnational Identities: becoming European in the EU*, Lanham, MD: Rowman & Littlefield.
Olsen, P. J. (2004) 'Survey article: unity, diversity and democratic institutions: lesson from the European Union', *Journal of Political Philosophy*, 12 (4):461–95.
Rifkin, J. (2004) *The European Dream*, Cambridge: Polity Press.
Rudolph, E. (2001) 'Historical manifestations of European identity and its failures', in F. Cerutti and E. Rudolph (eds) *A Soul for Europe: on the political and cultural identity of the Europeans*, Vol. 1, *A Reader*, Leuven: Peeters.
Scharpf, F. (1999) *Governing in Europe*, Oxford: Oxford University Press.
Schmidt, V. (2006) *Democracy in Europe: the EU and national polities*, Oxford: Oxford University Press.
Seidendorf, S. (2007) *Europäisierung nationaler Identitätsdiskurse?* Baden-Baden: Nomos.
Telò, M. (2006) *Europe: a civilian power? European Union, global governance, world order*, Basingstoke: Palgrave Macmillan.
Zielonka, J. (2006) *Europe as Empire*, Oxford: Oxford University Press.

2 European political identity, foreign policy and the Others' image
An underexplored relationship
Sonia Lucarelli

The literature on European identity is large and ever growing and approaches to the topic variegated,[1] but none of them focuses on the impact that foreign policy[2] has on the process of identity-building. Such an absence of focus on foreign policy is striking, particularly if we consider that, according to the Eurobarometer surveys, not only do Europeans have their own image of the role of the European Union (EU[3]) in the world, but they tend to find the EU's international stance legitimate, positive and worth pursuing (Eurobarometer 2007; Transatlantic Trends 2006).

Given this interest shown by citizens in foreign policy, it is striking that, thus far, so little attention has been paid to the role of the EU's foreign policy in the processes of self-identification of the Europeans as a political group. Equally noteworthy is the fact that the literature dealing with the EU's distinctive role in world politics – frequently described as the 'EU's international identity' – does not pay any attention to the 'domestic' repercussions of the EU's international stance on the European polity-building process at large, and on the processes of identity and legitimacy construction among EU citizens in particular. All this reflects theoretical developments in the field of International Relations (IR), where, in spite of a general rediscovery of identity as a fundamental component of politics, there is a widespread tendency to treat identity as if it were an attribute of an institution, being it a state (Wendt 1992) or the EU (Whitman 1998; Manners and Whitman 1998), rather than as a defining element of a group of *people*.

This analysis aims to bridge the gap between these branches of literature and to propose a framework for the analysis of the EU's foreign policy which draws both on social identity theory (SIT) and IR and underlines the relevance of foreign policy for processes of identity construction in the EU.

The chapter first deals with the literature on the EU's international role and on political identity in the EU in order to highlight the theoretical and empirical gaps between the two. It then proposes a theoretical framework, which builds on SIT and IR literature and combines it with specific attention to the role of external perceptions in the processes of self-identification, and finally it offers some general conclusions.

The EU's foreign policy and the political identity of the Europeans: a missing link

During the first five decades of its life, most discussions on the EU's relations with the rest of the world focused on politics, policies and practicalities: the study of the EU's external relations was primarily concerned with 'what are the policies?' rather than 'what do the policies tell us about the EU?' More recently, discussions of the EU's relations with the rest of the world have changed, with emphasis increasingly placed on how the EU participates in world politics and how this participation reshapes the EU. This has been the case particularly since the end of the Cold War, with the launch of the Common Foreign and Security Policy (CFSP) in the Maastricht Treaty and the subsequent efforts of the EU to combine widening (enlargement), deepening (treaty reform), as well as broadening the international tasks (from peacekeeping to conflict management) of the Union. Building a more efficient foreign policy and making sense of the EU's international role have become essential components of the overall integration process. Recently, EU documents have underlined that the EU has a specific international stance in world politics, it is guided by values 'which have inspired its own creation' (Treaty establishing a Constitution for Europe, Part III, Title V, Art. III-292) and is inspired by an ethics of responsibility (Lucarelli 2006b). At the same time, scholarly literature has rediscovered more than a mere interest in the concept of a civilian power Europe (Whitman 1998; Telò 2006).

As a matter of fact, building on François Duchêne's idea of a 'civilian power Europe' from the early 1970s (1972, 1973), a large stream of scholars has since emerged following in his footsteps (e.g. Whitman 1998; Telò 2006). Terms such as *civilian power*, *normative power* (Manners 2002), *structural foreign policy* (Keukeleire 2000, 2004; Telò 2001: 264), *normative area* (Therborn 2001: 85), *gentle power* (Padoa-Schioppa 2001) and *norm-maker* (Björkdahl 2005; cf. Checkel 1999) have been coined to capture the idea of the EU as an international actor with specific qualities which make it different from 'traditional powers'. Whether it is to enrich the concept (Telò 2006) or to revise it (Manners 2002), these authors share Duchêne's views that the EU is internationally different because its initial *telos* (peace through integration), its historical developments and its current institutional and normative framework make it better suited to spreading universal values.

This literature frequently refers to the EU's international distinctiveness in terms of 'identity', based on the idea that the EU possesses a distinctive 'international identity' (Manners and Whitman 1998; Manners 2002), characterized by its history and values. For Ian Manners, for instance, it is the EU's 'constitutional norms that represent crucial constitutive factors determining its international identity' (Manners 2002: 241).

This 'distinctiveness thesis' has attracted a lot of attention but also raised criticisms. Some scholars have questioned whether it is appropriate to claim that the EU exports 'universal norms' and that its approach to norm diffusion is different from that of the USA. Indeed, the claim of spreading universal values is very common within the USA too (cf. Nau 2002; Stephanson 1995). Precisely the US experience, however, has already demonstrated that the failure to define the relationship between universality and particularity is bound to generate criticism and distrust in the 'recipients' of normative politics who might easily regard reference to universalism as purely instrumental to the pursuit of particular political objectives. In the case of the EU, failing to understand this relationship could easily have internal repercussions on the fragile European political identity, given the still weak state of identification with, and legitimization of, the EU among the Europeans.

A second criticism concerns the lack of empirical support provided by the *distinctiveness* literature. This has given rise to a branch of literature with the aim of testing the idea of 'EU distinctiveness' empirically (Bicchi 2006; Smith 2006; Panebianco 2006; Scheipers and Sicurelli 2007; Elgström and Smith 2006) or evaluating its logical-deductive coherence (Diez 2005; Hyde-Price 2006). These studies are precious in showing the pitfalls of the EU's foreign policy, but they limit their attention to the characteristics of the EU's external relations and its impact on the target environment.

What is completely missing in all this literature is an investigation into the extent to which this alleged distinctiveness is associated with a specific European political identity *of the Europeans*. In other words, what can we learn about the Europeans' self-awareness (as a group) by looking at the EU's foreign policy? One might say that they are two completely separate matters since identity is something that the individuals and groups develop on the basis of their own historical and cultural experiences. Moreover, one might argue that the EU's foreign policy is shaped by the interlinking of bureaucratic constraints and political negotiations among the member states, rather than by political identity. I believe, on the contrary, that there is a close link between policy (including foreign policy) and the self-identification of the Europeans as a political group. As we will see, not only is foreign policy one of the contexts in which the political values of the group are brought into existence through political implementation (regardless of how compromised and mediated this can be), but it is also one of the mirrors in which the Europeans can view themselves as a political group. This first type of mirroring exercise (as we will see there is another mirroring exercise activated by foreign policy) is fundamental for the process of identity formation (see Cerutti in this volume; see also Taylor 1994; Turner *et al.* 1987). A fully-fledged research project on the EU's distinctiveness should also emphasize the link between the EU's distinctive international role and the European political identity, avoiding treating 'identity' as if it were a given attribute of the polity in its 'objective' existence.

Interestingly, such a lack of attention to the relationship between foreign policy and identity also characterizes the branch of literature explicitly devoted to the analysis of European political identity. This literature fails to study if and how the EU's foreign policy is relevant to the construction of a European political self-consciousness. The focus is rather on fundamental elements such as the relationship between national and European identities (Maier and Risse 2003), comparisons between elites and mass self-identification processes (e.g. InTune – http://www.intune.it), the role of institutions in the construction of identity (Herrmann *et al.* 2004), the role of history and memory (Eder 2005), and the existence and characteristics of a European public sphere (see note 1). Very little or nothing is said about how the EU's international role feeds back into European political identity. For instance, in the 137 pages of the final report of the IDNET research project – a useful investigation into European identity – the word 'foreign policy' is mentioned only once, in quick recognition of the fact that a comparison between EU and US foreign policy would also be useful for an analysis of European identity (Maier and Risse 2003: A39).

The reason might be that foreign policy is – erroneously – scarcely seen as capable of igniting public debate and mass mobilization even at the national level. It might be that, as a public sphere has developed more in the areas in which the EU has more competences – i.e. on monetary issues, internal markets, etc. (Meyer 2007; cf. Van de Steeg and Risse 2007) – scholars have attributed to EU foreign policy a much less relevant (or nonexistent) role in the process of self-identification. It might also be that most of the literature deals more with 'identity' as a given quality rather than with self-identification as a *process*.

Whatever the reason for the lack of attention to foreign policy in analysing identity and legitimacy, recent events have made it even more compelling to fill this gap. Before 2003 never had the intellectual and political elites been engaged in such a vibrant debate on European specificities and differences from the USA (e.g. Kagan 2003; Rifkin 2004; Habermas and Derrida 2003). The European Security Strategy can be read as a response to this debate (Lucarelli and Menotti 2006) as well as the large support of the Europeans for a common EU voice in crisis management (83 per cent) – independent from the USA (82 per cent) – and their conviction that the EU has a more positive international role than the USA in a wide range of areas (Eurobarometer 2005). Since 2003, the European public debate on *who we Europeans are and what we stand for* has been very much characterized by reflections on what the EU's foreign policy is and should be.

The following section deals with the relationship between identity, legitimacy, foreign policy and the role of external Others, so as to clarify how a focus on self-identification and foreign policy can be merged into a conceptualization also apt for use in analysing the case of the EU.

Identity, legitimacy, foreign policy and external image

When taking political decisions, individuals are influenced by their normative and cognitive framework of reference. Identity produces the cognitive lenses through which they conceive themselves, the world and the others. At the same time, identities are associated to socially binding norms according to which individuals evaluate the 'appropriateness' of an action (March and Olsen 1998). If we translate it into foreign policy, political identity matters since it provides the structural context of meaning and norms within which state representatives and decision-makers shape 'their appreciation of the world, of international politics, and of the place of their states within the international system', to use the fitting words of Jutta Weldes (1999: 9).

But *which* identity are we talking about? How does it influence foreign policy? Can we also analyse the possible feedback of a policy into self-awareness? And, finally, are there conditions in which the political identity of a group is more vulnerable to such feedback? I will touch on each of these questions in order.

Which identity?

Here I focus attention on *political* identity as the type of identity which is most relevant to political action. The term happens to be all too frequently confused with other forms of social identity. This is particularly the case of *cultural* identity, which a large amount of literature considers to be indispensable for political identity and the main form of identity behind the role definition of a state.

Antony Smith (1992), for instance, treats political identity as the 'essence' of a nation which is pre-given with little possibility of being affected by politics, including foreign policy. A variant of this position is represented by those who regard political identity as a phenomenon which is 'constructed' (instead of pre-given) but predominantly through sharing cultural experiences rather than through political history (Rudolph 2001). Samuel Huntington takes a similar approach on American identity, when he claims that the core of this identity is the Anglo-Protestant culture of the initial settlers: even the set of political principles that is usually regarded as constitutive of American identity as a *civic* identity (namely liberty, egalitarianism, individualism, populism, laissez faire), affirms Huntington, is but 'Protestantism without God' (2004: 69). An extreme version of this essentialist position is represented by Huntington's reduction of identity to belonging to a larger civilization (Huntington 1996).[4] Others are more articulated in describing the relationship between political and cultural identity and tend to attach an ambiguous role to culture. For instance, Jepperson *et al.* affirm that 'cultural or institutional elements of states' global or domestic environments […] shape identity', and then define culture as 'collective models of nation-state, authority and identity, represented in customs or laws' (Jepperson *et al.* 1996: 52, 56), i.e. culture is a collective model of identity and at the same time influences identity. This reasoning is likely to generate a vicious circle and does not contribute to understanding the precise role of culture in the definition of identity.

With Furio Cerutti, I regard political identity as a construction that is not and cannot be derived *directly* from a common culture, as 'the set of social and political values and principles that we recognize as ours, or in the sharing of which we feel like 'us', like a political group or entity' (Cerutti 2003: 27; see also Cerutti 2001, Ch. 1 of this volume; Lucarelli 2006a). Such values and principles do not shape the identity of the citizens by themselves: they need to be *interpreted*.

Culture, history, policies and institutions are the frameworks in which values interpretation takes place and thereby play a paramount role in shaping political identity, but do not coincide with it. Policy is also an explicit framework in which values interpretations are observable, as we shall see. The importance of values *interpretation* for self-identification is recognized by some parts of socio-psychological literature. For instance, Fox (1996) maintains that what characterizes pan-Hispanic identity in the USA is the shared interpretation of a set of core values (populist democracy, personal liberty, etc.). In the case of the EU's foreign policy, a close investigation reveals that the EU's peculiarity in world politics derives precisely from a European interpretation of some widely shared values and principles (Lucarelli 2006b; Lucarelli and Manners 2006). The EU interpretation of very general values and principles frequently diverges from that provided in other political contexts in that we see (i) the translation of a value into different guiding principles, or (ii) the peculiar interpretation of a value in the light of another (here, clearly, what counts is the hierarchical order among values in different political communities) (Lucarelli 2006b). An example of the first process (the translation of a value into specific principles) is provided by the rejection in the EU of the death penalty, which in the Charter of Fundamental Rights derives directly from the value of dignity (Ch. 1, Art. 2.1). Here the 'right to life' (expression of the value of dignity) is read together with an interpretation of the value of justice, where justice does not translate into directly proportional punishment for the offence. The different stance of the EU and the USA on this aspect is well known, and has created problems relating to the release of prisoners from Europe to the USA as a form of cooperation in the fight against terrorism.

As for the second process (specific interpretations of a certain value in the light of other values or principles), embedded liberalism – an economic liberalism that should support domestic economic stability and social security – is a telling case. The peculiar interpretation given in Europe to liberalism as a value and a pillar of order has made it possible for European societies to develop the strongest welfare state systems in the world, despite the liberalization of markets. This was made possible by two other values and a principle of the European tradition: solidarity, justice and the principle of the rule of law. The result has been a peculiar understanding of liberalism, which sees the logic of free trade strictly tied to the need to also safeguard the other two values. As this has been applied since the beginning within the EC/U and its member states, it has also begun to influence the EU's foreign policy. The Treaty on European Union (TEU) affirmed that international cooperation, as an aim of the Common Foreign and Security Policy (CFSP), should help developing countries to smoothly and gradually integrate into the world economy, while at the same time calling for their sustainable social and political development (Art. 130u). Furthermore, some positions undertaken by the EU at the WTO negotiations can hardly be explained by looking at the material benefits, but more as ways to support underdeveloped countries. Some observers point to the Commission's position on the TRIPs agreement (Trade Related Intellectual Property Rights) as a case in point (Van den Hoven 2006).[5]

Where do such interpretations come from? 'Our' specific interpretation of a value/principle is the result of our culture, history (or, better, of the shared meaning attributed to this history), constitutional and legal practices, and coherence with respect to other shared values.

Michael Walzer (1992) argues that it is history that provides the crucial difference between the way in which group identity unfolds in the USA and in Europe. Leonie Huddy (2001: 142) mentions studies of the early 1990s that show how German students experience a historical sense of guilt which makes them reluctant to endorse a patriotic identity even when their German identity is underlined in the interview question.

Another fundamental framework of interpretation, the one we focus most attention on in this book, is *policy*. Policy-making is a sort of communicative act which turns values into action, thereby interpreting them. This communication is immediately visible to the informed public that is constantly engaged in a *process* of self-identification (Bloom 1990). Therefore, policy is not only an intervening variable in the process of identity-building, but also a framework in which identities are observable.

The fact that political identities are debated, shaped and interpreted in a (set of) public sphere(s) should not convey the idea that political identities are completely unstable elements.[6] Rather they tend to be *stable around a core set of political values* which give a meaning to the political community. This set of values represents the core of the *reductio ad unum*. Should that set of core values with a specific interpretation become subject to contention in the group's public space, then the very identity of that group would undergo a severe transformation or could be at a risk of breaking. This, clearly, does not refer to the ordinary political dialectic among exponents of different political groups in a democratic system, as they diverge on many things but not on core political values. The Haider case in Europe might serve as a case in point, as it revealed a European consensus on safeguarding certain fundamental European values. A EU/ropean political identity, more than self-awareness in highly homogenous linguistic/cultural groups, cannot but emerge from the Europeans and their institutions' recognition of a core set of political values.

As we have seen, policy is both a context in which interpreted values can be observed at work, and an intervening variable in the process of identity formation. Foreign policy has the specific characteristic of producing – more than other branches of politics – external images of the *polity* that can then feed back into the domestic self-identification process, as we shall see below.

Identity and foreign policy

Current research on foreign policy and international relations makes frequent reference to the concept of identity. Yet, although with rare exceptions (Hopf 2002), it shows similar shortcomings to those that we have seen affect research on the EU's international distinctive role. Alexander Wendt (1992) had the merit of drawing the attention of mainstream IR to the issue of identity by using the concept to challenge Realism's epistemological foundations (though sharing part of its ontological basis, contrary to the earlier constructivist contributions of Nicholas Onuf or Friedrich Kratochwil).

In Wendt's view, identity is the 'property of international actors that generates motivational and behavioural dispositions' (1999: 224). According to Wendt (1999: 21), it represents a relatively stable intersubjective structure within which *a state* defines its interests, role and expectations about its Self, in interaction with relevant Others. Such a perception of the Self, in turn, shapes its interests – therefore interests are defined by identity. However, according to Wendt, the state, which exists prior to interaction, has some interests which are independent from the social context – physical security, autonomy, economic well-being and collective self-esteem (1999: 235ff.). In Wendt's view, a state has a 'corporate identity' – 'the intrinsic, self-organizing qualities that constitute actor individuality [...] For organizations it means their constituent individuals, physical resources, shared beliefs and institutions in virtue of which individuals function as "we"' (Wendt 1994: 385) – and three other types of 'social identities': type, role and collective identities (1999: 224ff.), which exist only in relation to others (taking the others' perspective).

Precisely because of his state-centric approach, though recalling that identities are constituted in interaction, Wendt ends up treating both states and their identities as given. His anthropomorphic concept of state, the absence of normativity, the exclusion of domestic processes of articulation of a state's identity, his failure to deal with concrete articulations of identity are among the most serious criticisms of Wendt's constructivist approach (Zehfuss 2002; Hopf 2002: 281–94). I believe that the greatest pitfall of Wendt's approach lies in its absence of reference to the *peoples'* political identity. An anthropomorphic treatment of states as actors with an identity is by no means Wendt's prerogative, rather it has long been a somewhat popular practice in IR, but it is striking that it has also been maintained in a social constructivist framework. The practice is misleading and generates confusion with respect to the original concept of identity as pertaining to individuals and groups.[7]

I will refer to what is frequently called 'state identity' as state 'role' (cf. Holsti 1970; Walker 1987; Aggestam 1999). Roles refer to patterns of expected or appropriate behaviour and are determined by both an actor's own conceptions about appropriate behaviour and by the expectations of other actors (Elgström and Smith 2006; Wendt 1999: 227–28). Ultimately, role conceptions can be regarded as behaviourally related elements of identity (Elgström and Smith 2006). However, as the 'actor' in question is a political system in itself (a state, a polity like the EU), its identity cannot be seen as a hypostasis but should always be considered as an attribute of the citizens. This means that the interaction through which a role is defined also involves the 'domestic' social level. What is the link between political decision-makers and the (political) identity of the group?

As political self-identification is reproduced through a series of habits (Hopf 2002: 10–11), experiences of 'everyday life' (Berger and Luckmann 1966: 23), norms and roles, it is deeply rooted in society, shaped through a social interaction process in which policy-makers also take part. Not only are decision-makers part of the social game of the production and reproduction of social identities, but, like each member of the group, they are influenced by the meanings that such identities provide. As a matter of fact, by definition identities have a paramount function in providing meaning, by creating a grid of orientation in a sea of complexity, also in the specific context of international politics (Hopf 2002: 4–5).

Moreover, identities imply interests: this means that interests are not endogenously given – as assumed by most traditional IR literature – but are identity contingent. Hopf's example is illuminating:

> The United States has an obvious economic interest in low crude oil prices – or does it? [...] The United States has an obvious economic interest in the most efficient transportation of gas from the Caspian Sea to western markets – or does it? The answers to these questions are well, no, sort of; it depends; and what do you mean? The complexity stems not from the idea that the United States has no unified interest but from the fact that there is no such a thing as an allowed economic interest. Every single question demands an understanding of the identity politics underlying US relations with the Middle East [...] and Russia.
> (Hopf 2002: 16–17)

Though it might appear the contrary, the 'identity politics underlying US relations with the Middle East' mentioned by Hopf is a form of enlivened, enacted group identity and not an attribute of a stereotyped item called the USA. Decision-makers take political decisions on the basis of a social cognitive structure developed in the context of socially shaped identities. Their decisions are all at once telling of the political identity of their group and likely to give rise to debate within the same group and outside it. This brings us to the next question.

Can we conceptualize the feedback from policy to identity?

As we have seen, politics is one of the main frameworks in which political values are interpreted. The observation of political performance is equally the observation of 'values at work'. At the same time, policy is the framework within which the legitimacy of the political entity that took the decision for the group is put to the test, for the procedures adopted (legal legitimacy), its efficacy (output legitimacy) and its conformity with the core values of the group. It should be underlined, however, that political decisions have different prospects of entering the public debate, and possibly constituting part of the self-identification process, depending on their *salience*. This salience might depend on the type of identity (e.g. decisions regarding imported meat in a Muslim country) or/and on specific external circumstances (e.g. decisions regarding global warming in the last few years). As not all issues are equally salient, not all political decisions have the same relevance in the public debate, or in processes of identity construction (cf. D'Andrea's chapter, Chapter 5).

Alongside this direct feedback from politics to the political identity of the citizens, there is indirect feedback which passes through the relationship between the latter as a political group and outside groups – the so-called 'Others'. In IR, Others are usually associated with other states or group of states. However, Others may also refer to other categories of referents, such as our own past. Ole Wæver (1998) underlines how, in the case of the EU, the internal coherence of the process rests on the positive affirmation of a set of values to avoid reverting to Europe's precedent history – the real Europe's Other. The re-elaboration of a group's memory, for instance, is a key component of a self-identification process (cf. Bottici, Chapter 3). Of interest in this respect are the analyses of Neumann (1996a) and Hopf (2002) on Russia's identity, also developed in relation to a physical (Europe – according to Neumann) as well as a cognitive Other (its own past and current role; Hopf 2002).

The relevance of 'Others' (particularly of physical Others – other individuals, other states) is appreciated in both socio-psychological (Taylor 1994; Turner *et al.* 1987) and IR literature (cf. Rumelili 2004; Neumann 1996b). Upon reviewing the available literature, Others are seen to be treated as relevant to the self-identification process in three broad respects:

Recognition. The main theorists of recognition (Charles Taylor, Alessandro Pizzorno, Axel Honneth and Nancy Fraser) have underlined the relevance of this process in identity formation. In his illuminating work on rationality and recognition, Pizzorno (2007) reads recognition as 'the reciprocal attribution of identity, [...] constitutive of any form of sociality [...] simply reflects the arrival on the scene of new actors' (2007: 190). A macroscopic example of the formation of a system of reciprocal recognition, continues Pizzorno, was the formation of the European state system after the peace of Westphalia, which involved a double form of recognition: the vertical recognition by local authorities of states' sovereignty, and the horizontal reciprocal recognition of a system of states each with its own area of jurisdiction (2007: 190).

The relevance of recognition in identity formation is also underlined by a popular author on the topic Charles Taylor. Taylor's treatment of recognition entails a normative theory of multiculturalism, however his description of recognition is also useful for our purposes. He asserts that 'our identity is partly shaped by recognition [...], often by the *mis*-recognition of others'. Eventually, he continues, 'a person or group of people can suffer real damage, real distortion, if the people or society around them mirror back to them a confining or demeaning or contemptible picture of themselves' (Taylor 1994: 25). Shifting it to the relationship among groups, we can affirm that Others are relevant in the first place as active actors engaged in a process of (mis)recognition, and (mis) representation of a group to which group members are sensitive. In other words, the Others produce a second mirror for us, the first being provided by the direct observation of our political action. In order for this feedback from external recognition and representation to self-categorization to take place, group members need to acknowledge the Others' images of them. This gives rise to complex dynamics of mutual (though frequently asymmetrical) influence.[8]

Distinctiveness and Otherness. Others, however, are not only relevant to processes of identity formation for what they actively *do* (recognizing or not-recognizing the group) but also as inactive objects of our comparisons. Self-categorization theory finds a key psychological motivation for an individual's endorsement of group affiliation in his/her need 'to differentiate [his/her] own groups positively from others to achieve a positive social identity' (Turner *et al.* 1987: 42). This is what Furio Cerutti calls 'wall identity' (1996; Introduction to this volume). Such differentiation is not necessarily oppositional but entails assuming the positive distinctiveness of one's group with respect to comparable Others. A similar understanding of the role of Others in shaping identity is contained in Iver Neumann's analysis of the role of Russia's main Other – Europe – in the shaping of Russia's identity (Neumann 1996a). As for European self-awareness, who are Europe's Others? Do Europe's Others differ from those of the EU? Relevant Others are not simply those that are not me, but those who I consider to be relevant with respect to me. With respect to whom are the Europeans and EU institutions underlining their *distinctiveness?* It is rather easy to claim today that alongside the traditional differentiation with respect to non-Western countries, in the past few years the USA has also emerged as a relevant external Other with respect to whom Europe/EU's positive distinctiveness has been affirmed. This emerges clearly both from the opinion polls[9] and from an analysis of the press debates (see Fioramonti and Lucarelli, Chapter 12, as far as the debate on global warming is concerned).

Though not necessarily being oppositional, differentiation is frequently regarded as being related to conflict. Part of sociological and IR literature underlines how antagonism creates or reinforces group cohesiveness. Suffice it to recall here the importance of conflict and boundaries in Simmel's understanding of groups' cohesion (cf. Cederman and Daase 2003: 16–17) or the famous idea that war contributes to a stronger sense of national cohesion according to foreign policy analysis (Mueller 1973). In IR, critical constructivists contend that identity always forms in contrast to Others, and that there is a relationship between identities and counter-identities (Campbell 1992).

As far as the EU is concerned, some scholars have pointed to a modern mode of differentiation based on a net juxtaposition with respect to external Others (Neumann 1998, 1999), while others have pointed to a post-modern mode of differentiation, grounded in the fear of disunity rather than fear of the Others (Wæver 1998; Schimmelfennig 2001). Bahar Rumelili argues that in reality the EU uses both modes of differentiation according to the specific Other it is dealing with: '[the] EU's interactions with Morocco, Turkey, and states in Central and Eastern Europe are situated differently on the dimensions of difference, social distance, response of other, and hence exemplify different kinds of self/other relationships' (Rumelili 2004: 29–30). Though very penetrating, Rumelili's analysis suffers from the same shortcomings as IR studies of the 'EU's international identity': a treatment of identity as an attribute of 'the EU'. What we can gain from her analysis is the idea that Self–Others relations do not always entail *Othering practices* (practices of conflictual differentiation).

External labelling, boundaries and meaning. The likelihood of a group member internalizing group identity depends both on 'less permeable group boundaries and higher incidence of external labelling' (Huddy 2001: 140). Others' labelling is an important element in that it creates cognitive boundaries between members of a group and outsiders. Labelling is more or less difficult depending on the main criteria adopted, which can be more or less subject to ascription (e.g. labelling based on the colour of skin is easier than labelling based on the political orientation). In this regard, external observers find it easier to label a 'European identity' rather than an EU/ropean one (Lucarelli 2007).

The role of boundaries in identity formation is debated in several branches of literature from the socio-psychological literature mentioned above, to sociology (e.g. George Simmel, Shmuel Eisenstadt, Bernhard Giesen), from political science (e.g. Albert Hirschmann), to anthropology (Frederik

Barth) (for an overview, see Cederman 2001). In an SIT perspective, boundaries are both created by the members of a group as a by-product of self-categorization processes, and imagined by outside Others. Moreover, they can be seen as identifying the contour of a group of people either sharing some similarities (e.g. having a European passport) or having internalized the *meaning* of group membership (e.g. the difference between having European citizenship and having a European identity). Boundaries as meanings are what count more for identity formation processes. The Others can influence internal debate on meaning, perhaps even expressing a different view of what meaning is attached to belonging to the 'in-group'. This can generate significant interaction between the Others' views and internal processes of identity construction. Suffice to think of the internal EU/ropean debate generated by Ronald Rumsfeld's declarations on a division between New and Old Europe, with diverging views and attitudes towards world politics and global threats. This was *de facto* an attempt at influencing international attribution of meaning to collective belonging.

Politological literature has underlined the role of 'blaming' in influencing future behaviour, and socio-psychological literature has demonstrated that it can induce a redefinition of a group's identity (here the case mentioned above of the sense of self-recognition of the Germans, influenced by historical blaming for nationalistic political identity, is telling).

To conclude, foreign policy is relevant to the process of the political self-identification of the individual in a group, not only because it is one of the important frameworks within which core values and principles of a political group are interpreted (assume a specific meaning around which political identity can be articulated and legitimization processes can take place), but also because it is the main context in which the group interacts with external Others. Others are both passive and active actors in the self-categorization process. *Malgré eux* they are a term of comparison to state *distinctiveness* (in more or less oppositional terms); as active players, they reproduce an image of ourselves with which we can compare our self-representation, particularly if those Others are relevant sources of our self-esteem from whom we demand *recognition*.

Are there conditions in which the political identity of a group is more vulnerable to such feedback?

Each process of self-identification is subject to sensitivity to the acknowledgement of performance by the group and to its relationship with relevant Others, but the degree of such sensitivity is contingent upon: (a) the salience of the issue area in which the performance takes place; and (b) the degree of consolidation of the group's self-awareness.

Salience refers to the fact that decisions in some areas might put core values of the political group under strain and therefore cause the group to re-evaluate a fundamental element of its group identity and the legitimacy attributed to the institutions of reference. This, for instance, was the case behind the EU's response to Haider's electoral victory in Austria in 1999. Salience becomes particularly high in cases of 'ideational shocks', i.e. severe challenges to a group's core beliefs in a certain area, likely to undermine beliefs in other sectors and, ultimately, impose an internal debate on the basic elements of a group's identity (cf. Marcussen 2000; Flockhart 2005). Examples abound in recent European history, from the mad cow disease (see Acuti, Chapter 6), to the aforementioned recent transatlantic divide in the case of the Iraqi war and the intellectual and political debate that followed. The extent to which a situation is perceived as an ideational shock depends on the identity of the group, both in terms of 'content' (core values) and 'cohesion' (the extent to which a threat to such values challenges the cohesion of the group).

Cohesion or maturity of the group's identity, therefore, is a key element of its sensitivity to external challenges (Lucarelli 2006c). This is an important element in the analysis of identity transformation, something which is usually neglected in literature. In the case of a political identity in the making like the EU, the self-identification construction process is particularly sensitive to the image that the political group gives of itself through its politics and policy, also including foreign policy, as it should in principle be sensitive to its relationship with external Others.

Conclusion

Analyses of the Europeans' political identity have rarely dealt with the relationship between this sense of belonging and the EU's foreign policy (in the wider sense of the word – see note 3). At the same time, analyses of the EU's distinctive role in the world do not deal with the political self-identification of the Europeans, but at best with a stereotypical 'EU international identity'. Drawing from socio-psychological and IR literature, I have attempted to sketch a relationship between the political identity of the group, foreign policy and external images. Moreover, I have underlined how foreign policy is relevant in several ways. In the first place, foreign policy is relevant to identity directly, as a context in which values are interpreted and acknowledged by the group. In other words, foreign policy provides a first type of mirror in which the group can view itself and its values. However, foreign policy is also relevant to self-identification indirectly, insofar as it has an impact on external Others who function as a second mirror in which the Europeans see themselves reflected. Others are also relevant to self-identification as active providers of recognition, an indispensable component of self-identification processes. I have also underlined that such a relationship between foreign policy and self-awareness is particularly important in cases of less consolidated political identities, such as the one developing among Europeans.

In the forthcoming chapters in this book, we will see several examples of policy areas with different degrees of salience and, thereby, of impact on the processes of self-identification. As far as foreign policy is concerned, we will analyse the relationship between EU policy in the area of human rights and Europeans' political identity (Balfour in this volume). We will also explore the impact of two different forms of *Otherness*: Europe's past (with particular reference to Second World War memories, see Bottici, Chapter 3), and the image of the EU within a group of non-European countries (Fioramonti and Lucarelli, Chapter 12).

Acknowledgements

I am grateful to my fellow editor to this volume for illuminating discussions on the topic and his sharp comments on the first draft of this chapter. Also particularly useful were comments by Chiara Bottici, Lorenzo Fioramonti and Arlo Poletti; as well as bibliographical suggestions by Elena Pulcini, Dimitri D'Andrea and Laura Lanzillo. Thanks also go to the participants in the fourth Pisa ECPR General Conference (September 2007) at which a version of this chapter was presented, particularly to Knud Erik Jørgensen for his comments and Ole Elgström for his encouragement.

Notes

1 Several European projects have been devoted to the analysis of the role of the media in the emergence of a European public sphere or more specifically of European identity. Among them: EMEDIATE – http://www.iue.it/RSCAS/Research/EMEDIATE; EURONAT – http://www.iue.it/RCSAS/Research/EURONAT; EUROPUB – http://europub.wz-berlin.de; IDNET – http://www.iue.it/RSCAS/Research/Tools/IDNET; ConstEPS – http://www.monnet-centre.uni-bremen.de/pdf/flyer_2.pdf; EU-CONSENT – http://www.eu-consent.net. Other projects mainly deal with opinion surveys (cf. Fuchs and Schlenker (2006); EURONAT – http://www.iue.it/RCSAS/Research/EURONAT –; In Tune – http://www.intune.it). For a review of the literature see Cerutti's Introduction to this volume.
2 Here I consider foreign policy in the broad sense of 'the sum of official external relations conducted by an independent actor ... in international relations' (Hill 2003: 3). In the EU's case, this includes both Pillar I and III external relations and the more 'traditional' foreign policy developed in Pillar II.
3 From here onwards I will use the EU to refer to both the EU and the European Community (EC).
4 For the homologation of the concepts of culture and civilization, see Benhabib (2002; in particular pages 20–21 of the Italian edition 2005).
5 Clearly, this does not tell the full story of the EU's positions at the WTO negotiations, where interests matter as much as values (if we grant that for analytical reasons they can be kept separate).
6 Turner assumes that social identities are highly labile, while other scholars consider them more stable (Huddy 2001: 147–49).
7 On the relationship between ontological and social identity, between man and the social world, see Berger and Luckmann (1966: 50, 61). SIT deals with individual and social identity as two poles of a continuum (Huddy 2001).
8 In chapter 12 of this volume, Lorenzo Fioramonti and I have attempted to verify the degree of information that the Europeans receive on the Others' image of the

EU in a set of specific circumstances. A wider research project would include an interactive dimension.

9 According to Eurobarometer (2005), EU citizens believe that the EU has a more positive role in comparison with the USA in peacemaking (63 per cent versus 25 per cent), environmental protection (62 per cent versus 18 per cent), the fight against terrorism (60 per cent versus 43 per cent), global economic growth (50 per cent versus 38 per cent), and the fight against world poverty (49 per cent versus 20 per cent).

References

Aggestam, L. (1999) *Role Conceptions and the Politics of Identity in Foreign Policy*, Oslo: Arena Working Paper 99/8.

Benhabib, S. (2002) *The Claims of Culture: equality and diversity in the global era*, Princeton: Princeton University Press (Italian edition: *La rivendicazione dell'identità culturale*, Bologna: Il Mulino 2005).

Berger, P. and Luckmann, P. (1966) *The Social Construction of Reality: a treatise in the sociology of knowledge*, Garden City, NY: Doubleday.

Bicchi, F. (2006) 'Our size fits all: normative power Europe and the Mediterranean', *Journal of European Public Policy*, 13 (2): 286–303.

Björkdahl, A. (2005) 'Norm-maker and norm-taker: exploring the normative influence of the EU in Macedonia', *European Foreign Affairs Review*, 10 (2): 257–78.

Bloom, W. (1990) *Personal Identity, National Identity and International Relations*. Cambridge: Cambridge University Press.

Calhoun, C. (2002) 'Imagining solidarity: cosmopolitanism, constitutional patriotism, and the public sphere', *Public Culture*, 14 (1): 147–71.

Campbell, D. (1992) *Writing Security: United States foreign policy and the politics of identity*, Minneapolis, MN: University of Minnesota Press.

Cederman, L.-E. (2001) 'Political boundaries and identity trade-offs', in L.-E. Cederman (ed.) *Constructing Europe's Identity: the external dimension*, Boulder, CO: Lynne Rienner.

Cederman, L.-E. and Daase, C. (2003) 'Endogenizing corporate identities: the next step in constructivist IR theory', *European Journal of International Relations*, 9 (1): 5–36.

Cerutti, F. (1996) (ed.) *Identità e politica*, Roma-Bari: Laterza.

——(2001) 'Towards the political identity of the Europeans. An introduction', in F. Cerutti and E. Rudolph (eds) *A Soul for Europe: on the political and cultural identity of the Europeans*, Vol. I, *A Reader*, Leuven: Peeters.

——(2003) 'A political identity of the Europeans?', *Thesis Eleven*, 72 (1): 26–45.

Checkel, J. T. (1999) 'Norms, institutions and national identity in contemporary Europe', *International Studies Quarterly*, 43 (1): 83–114.

Diez, T. (2005) 'Constructing the self and changing Others: reconsidering "Normative Power Europe"', *Millennium*, 33 (3): 613–36.

Duchêne, F. (1972) 'Europe's role in world peace', in R. Mayne (ed.) *Europe Tomorrow: sixteen Europeans look ahead*, London: Fontana.

——(1973) 'The European Community and the uncertainties of interdependence', in M. Kohnstamm and W. Hager (eds) *A Nation Writ Large? Foreign policy problems before the European Community*, Basingstoke: Macmillan.

Eder, K. (2005) 'Remembering national memories together: the formation of a transnational identity in Europe', in K. Eder and W. Spohn (eds) *Collective Memory and European Identity: the effects of integration and enlargement*, Aldershot: Ashgate.

Elgström, O. and Smith, M. (2006) 'Introduction', in O. Elgström and M. Smith (eds) *The European Union's Roles in International Politics: concepts and analysis*, London: Routledge.

Eurobarometer (2005) *Public Opinion in the European Union. Standard Eurobarometer 63*, European Commission, Public opinion analysis, Brussels. Online. Available HTTP: < http://ec.europa.eu/public_opinion/archives/eb/eb63/eb63_en.pdf > (accessed 19 July 2007).

——(2007) *Public Opinion in the European Union. Standard Eurobarometer 67. First Results*, European Commission, Public opinion analysis, Brussels. Online. Available HTTP: < http://ec.europa.eu/public_opinion/archives/eb/eb67/eb_67_first_en.pdf > (accessed 19 July 2007).

Flockhart, T. (2005) 'Complex socialization and the transfer of democratic norms', in T. Flockhart (ed.) *Socializing Democratic Norms: the role of international organizations for the construction of Europe*, Basingstoke: Palgrave.

Fox, G. (1996) *Hispanic Nation: culture, politics and the construction of identity*, Tucson, AZ: University of Arizona Press.

Fuchs, D. and Schlenker, A. (2006) 'European identity and the legitimacy of the EU', Background paper Team 12, EU-Consent: Work package V, presented at the II Work package V Conference, Lodz, March 30-April 1, 2006. Online. Available HTTP: < http://www.eu-consent.net/library/brx061012/Klingemann_ Lodz0603.pdf > (accessed 19 July 2007).

Habermas, J. and Derrida, J. (2003) 'Nach dem Krieg: die Widergeburt Europas', *Allgemeine Zeitung*, 31 May, p. 33 (the same article appeared also in *Libération*, under the title 'Europe: plaidoyer pour une politique extérieure commune').

Herrmann, R. K., Risse, T. and Brewer, M. B. (2004) (eds) *Transnational Identities: becoming European in the EU*, Lanham, MD: Rowman and Littlefield.

Hill, C. (2003) *The Changing Politics of Foreign Policy*, Basingstoke: Palgrave.

Holsti, K. J. (1970) 'National role conceptions in the study of foreign policy', *International Studies Quarterly*, 14 (1): 233–309.

Hopf, T. (2002) *Social Construction of International Politics: identities and foreign policies*, 3rd edn, Ithaca, NY: Cornell University Press.

Huddy, L. (2001) 'From social to political identity: a critical examination of social identity theory', *Political Psychology*, 22: 127–56.

Huntington, S. (1996) *The Clash of Civilizations and the Remaking of World Order*, New York: Simon & Schuster.

——(2004) *Who are We? The challenges to America's national identity*, New York: Simon & Schuster.

Hyde-Price, A. (2006) '"Normative" power Europe: a realist critique', *Journal of European Public Policy*, 13 (2): 217–34.

Jepperson, R., Wendt, A. and Katzenstein, P. (1996) 'Norms, identity, and culture in national security', in P. Katzenstein (ed.) *The Culture of National Security*, New York: Columbia University Press.

Kagan, R. (2003) *Paradise & Power: America and Europe in the new world order*, London: Atlantic Book.

Keukeleire, S. (2000) *The European Union as a Diplomatic Actor*, Discussion Paper no. 71, Centre for the Study of Diplomacy, University of Leicester.

—— (2004) 'EU structural foreign policy and structural conflict prevention', in V. Kronenberger and J. Wouters (eds) *The European Union and Conflict Prevention. Legal and policy aspects*, The Hague: Asser Press/Cambridge University Press.

Lucarelli, S. (2006a) 'Introduction: values, principles, identity and European Union foreign policy', in S. Lucarelli and I. Manners (eds) *Values and Principles in European Foreign Policy*, London: Routledge.

—— (2006b) 'Interpreted values: a normative reading of EU role articulation and performance', in O. Elgström and M. Smith (eds) *The European Union's Roles in International Politics: concepts and analysis*, London: Routledge.

—— (2006c) 'Values, identity and ideational shocks in the transatlantic rift', *Journal of International Relations and Development*, 9 (3): 304–34.

—— (2007) (ed.) *Beyond Self Perception: the Others' view of the European Union*, special issue of *European Foreign Affairs Review*, 12 (3).

Lucarelli, S. and Manners, I. (2006) (eds) *Values and Principles in European Union Foreign Policy*, London: Routledge.

Lucarelli, S. and Menotti, R. (2006) 'The use of force as coercive intervention', in S. Lucarelli and I. Manners (eds) *Values and Principles in European Union Foreign Policy*, London: Routledge.

Maier, M. L. and Risse, T. (2003) (eds) *Europeanization, Collective Identities and Public Discourses. Final report*. Online. Available HTTP: < http://www.atasp.de/downloads/030625_risse_idnet.pdf > (accessed 19 July 2007)

Manners, I. (2002) 'Normative power Europe: a contradiction in terms?', *Journal of Common Market Studies*, 40 (2): 253–74.

Manners, I. and Whitman, R. G. (1998) 'Towards identifying the international identity of the European Union: a framework for analysis of the EU's Network of Relationships', *Journal of European Integration*, 21 (1): 231–49.

March, J. and Olsen, J. (1998) 'The institutional dynamics of international political orders', *International Organization*, 52 (4): 943–69.

Marcussen, M. (2000) *Ideas and Elites: the social construction of economic and monetary union*, Aalborg: Aalborg University Press.

Meyer, M. F. (2007) 'Discussing Europe: the emergence of a European public sphere in the foreign policy domain?', paper presented at the International Conference *The Europeans. The European Union in search of political identity and legitimacy*, GARNET – JERP 5.2.1, Florence, 25–26 May 2007.

Mueller, J. (1973) *War, Presidents and Public Opinion*, New York: John Wiley & Sons.

Nau, H. R. (2002) *At Home Abroad. Identity and power in American foreign policy*, Ithaca, NY: Cornell University Press.

Neumann, I. B. (1996a) *Russia and the Idea of Europe. A study in identity and international relations*, London: Routledge.

—— (1996b) 'Self and other in international relation', *European Journal of International Relations*, 2 (2): 139–74.

—— (1998) 'European identity, EU expansion, and the integration/exclusion nexus', *Alternatives*, 23: 397–416.

—— (1999) *Uses of the Other: the East in European identity formation*, Minneapolis, MN: University of Minnesota Press.

Padoa-Schioppa, T. (2001) *Europa, forza gentile*, Bologna: Il Mulino.

Panebianco, S. (2006) 'Promoting human rights and democracy in European Union relations with Russia and China', in S. Lucarelli and I. Manners (eds), *Values and Principles in European Union Foreign Policy*, London: Routledge.

Pizzorno, A. (2007) *Il velo della diversità. Studi su razionalità e riconoscimento*, Milan: Feltrinelli.
Rifkin, J. (2004) *The European Dream*, New York: Polity Press.
Rudolph, E. (2001) 'Historical manifestations of European identity and its failures', in F. Cerutti and E. Rudolph (eds) *A Soul for Europe: on the political and cultural identity of the Europeans*, Vol. I, *A Reader*, Leuven: Peeters.
Rumelili, B. (2004) 'Constructing identity in relating to difference: understanding the EU's mode of differentiation', *Review of International Studies*, 30 (1): 27–47.
Scheipers, S. and Sicurelli, D. (2007) 'Normative power Europe: a credible utopia?', *Journal of Common Market Studies* (2007), 45 (2): 435–57;
Schimmelfennig, F. (2001) 'Liberal identity and postnationalist inclusion: the Eastern enlargement of the European Union', in L.-E. Cederman (ed.) *Constructing Europe's Identity: the external dimension*, Boulder, CO: Lynne Rienner.
Sjursen, S. (2006) 'What kind of power? European foreign policy in perspective', *Journal of European Public Policy*, 13 (2): 169–81.
Smith, A. (1992) 'National identity and the idea of European unity', *International Affairs*, 68 (1): 55–76.
Smith, K. E. (2006) 'The limits of proactive cosmopolitanism: the EU and Burma, Cuba and Zimbabwe', in O. Elgström and M. Smith (eds) *The European Union's Roles in International Politics: concepts and analysis*, London: Routledge.
Stephanson, A. (1995) *Manifest Destiny. American expansion and the Empire of Right*, New York: Farrar, Straus and Giroux.
Taylor, C. (1994) 'The politics of recognition', in A. Gutmann (ed.) *Multiculturalism: examining the politics of recognition*, New Jersey: Princeton University Press.
Telò, M. (2001) 'Reconsiderations: three scenarios', in M. Telò (ed.) *European Union and New Regionalism: regional actors and global governance*, London: Ashgate.
——(2006) *Europe: a civilian power? European Union, global governance, world order*, Houndmills, Basingstoke: Palgrave MacMillan.
Therborn, G. (2001) 'Europe's break with itself. The European economy and the history, modernity and world future of Europe', in F. Cerutti and E. Rudolph, *A Soul for Europe. On the cultural and political identity of the Europeans*, Vol. II, *An Essay Collection*, Leuven: Peeters.
Transatlantic Trends (2006) *Key Findings 2006*. A project of the German Marshall Fund of the United States and the Compagnia di San Paolo, with additional support from the Fundação Luso-American, Fundación BBVA, and the Tipping Point Foundation. Online. Available HTTP: < http://www.transatlantictrends.org/trends/doc/2006_TT_Key%20Findings%20FINAL.pdf > (accessed 19 July 2007).
Turner, J. C., Hogg, M. A., Oakes, P. J., Reicher, S. D. and Wetherell, M. (1987) *Rediscovering the Social Group: a self-categorization theory*, Oxford: Blackwell.
Van de Steeg, M. and Risse, T. (2007) 'The emergence of a European Community of communication: insights from empirical research on the Europeanization of public spheres', unpublished paper, Center for Transnational Relations, Foreign and Security Policy, Freie Universität Berlin. Online. Available HTTP: < http://www.atasp.de/downloads/eps_vandesteeg_risse_070513.pdf > (accessed 19 July 2007).
Van Den Hoven, A. (2006) 'European Union regulatory capitalism and multilateral trade negotiations', in S. Lucarelli and I. Manners (eds) *Values and Principles in European Union Foreign Policy*, London: Routledge.

Wæver, O. (1998) 'Insecurity, security, and asecurity in the West European non-war community', in E. Adler and M. Barnett (eds), *Security Communities*, Cambridge: Cambridge University Press.

Walker, S. G. (1987) (ed.) *Role Theory and Foreign Policy Analysis*, Durham: Duke University Press.

Walzer, M. (1992) *What it Means to be an American*, New York: Marsilio.

Weldes, J. (1999) *Constructing National Interest: the United States and the Cuban missile crisis*, Minneapolis: University of Minnesota Press.

Wendt, A. (1992) 'Anarchy is what states make of it', *International Organization*, 46 (2): 391–426.

——(1994) 'Collective identity formation and the international state', *American Political Science Review*, 88: 384–96.

——(1999) *Social Theory of International Politics*, New York: Cambridge University Press.

Whitman, R. (1998) *From Civilian Power to Superpower? The international identity of the European Union*, London: MacMillan.

Zehfuss, M. (2002) *Constructivism in International Relations: the politics of reality*, Cambridge: Cambridge University Press.

Part II
Memory and space

3 Europe, war and remembrance
Chiara Bottici

The aim of this chapter is to explore the role that memories from the Second World War play in the construction of the European identity. To this end I propose to substitute the concept of collective memory with that of collective remembrance as a theoretical tool better equipped to capture the ongoing process of elaboration of a traumatic past such as the European one. The analysis of the practices of remembrance that takes place at three levels (institutional, public and pedagogical) will show that a struggle for the definition of the past in the light of the construction of a political identity is taking place.

War and remembrance

Many authors have criticised the very idea of a collective memory as a spurious notion. Most notoriously the historian Reinhart Koselleck observed that only individual human beings can have memories so that every use of the term *memory* beyond the limits of the individual mind should be rejected as a misleading metaphor and replaced by more appropriate terms such as tradition or historical consciousness (Koselleck 2000: 19–20). The concept of collective memory is suspected of a primordialist connotation, as if it would presuppose a sort of collective soul, or spirit of a nation (Klain 2000: 127–50, 135).

On the other side, we have the sustainers of the concept of collective memory. As he introduced this notion in the thirties, Maurice Halbwachs did not mean a mere metaphor or the reified memory of the collective – be it the nation or the race. He wanted to point to something that happens when we remember, i.e. to the fact that when we remember we always recall the viewpoint of a given social group through whose eyes we see the event, because individual memories are always socially framed (Halbwachs 1980: 34).[1]

The critics of the concept of collective memory are right in reminding us that it is ultimately individual human beings who remember. At the same time their criticism seems to be misplaced from a twofold point of view. From an empirical perspective, it risks overlooking two fundamental facts.

First and foremost, there is the performative impact of the act of remembering. When someone remembers something and expresses it through language s/he has an impact on her/his audience that can in turn be the subject of other acts of remembering. This can be a person who shares the same experience of the past, or simply agrees on its relevance, and is therefore willing to frame it in the same way. This is a sufficient condition, formally speaking, to talk about a collective memory. In this sense, the term *collective* does not presuppose any sort of collectivist or nationalist connotation, but simply indicates a collection of individuals.

Second, there is also more generally speaking a philosophical problem with the critics of collective memory. They overlook an important distinction between two possible sides of the process of remembering. Ricoeur talked about the distinction between an active and a passive act of remembering; that is, what Greeks used to call *anamnesis* and *mneme* respectively. To remember something can be a completely passive act, as when we say that 'something came to my mind', but it can also be the result of an active act of research. To remember can be to have memories or to look for memories (Ricoeur 2000: 6). And, as we will see, it is in particular this active side of memory that is relevant for us.

As a way to avoid the misunderstandings generated by the concept of collective memory and to insist on this active side, we will use the concept of collective remembrance. Whereas memory may be understood as denoting an object, remembrance always designates a process. For instance Jay Winter and Emmanuel Sivan used this concept in order to examine the collective remembrance of war by emphasising agency, the product of individuals and groups who come together not necessarily at the behest of the state or any of its subsidiary organizations, but because they have to speak out (Winter and Sivan 1999: 9). From the point of view of an analysis of the different modes of collective remembrance of war, the advantage of such an approach is clear. The men and women whose activity they explore in their book lived through war as trauma and their decision to act in public – by creating associations, by writing memoirs, by speaking out in a host of ways – responds in the first place to the need of collectively elaborating such a trauma.[2]

For our purposes, the concept has also the further advantage of not assuming as given any relationship between the acts of collective remembrance and the dominant forces of a given polity. Whereas the term collective memory can come to suggest the idea of an entity that is already given, be it the ideological covering of political institutions or the mental furniture of a given population (what the French would call *mentalités*), the term remembrance always denotes a process rather than an object. The question remains therefore open as to what role these acts of remembrance play within a given social and political context. And this is the question that I want to address by analysing what I will call 'the politics of remembrance'.

Europe, war and remembrance 47

With respect to a traumatic past, as certainly is the Second World War, there can either be a need to remove it or to speak up about it. It is in particular with the passage of time, when trauma is decoupled from its actual psychological roots, that the events of a traumatic past can become an issue in the public agenda. This is the reason why according to many it is in subsequent generations (starting from that of grandchildren) that a traumatic past has more chances to be elaborated. This holds not only for the victims' community, but also for its complement, the community of former-generations perpetrators (Giesen and Junge 2003: 335).[3] There certainly is an ethical side in engaging in acts of remembrance of the victims of war. This is what Avishai Margalit (2002) tried to convey with his idea of an ethics of memory. However, what I want to emphasise in this work is the political role that these acts of remembrance play in the context of European integration, and, in particular, the role they play within the process of identity-building.

Remembering together?

Formally speaking, it is enough to have two people remembering together in order to speak about collective remembrance (Eder 2005). However, if we want to emphasise the collective dimension in the practices of remembrance we need to look at the different levels of social life. Here, I will distinguish between three levels: institutional, public and pedagogical.

The *institutional* remembrance stems directly from the activity of institutions. Sites for collective remembrance can therefore be law texts, policies, official declarations, public rituals, institutional places with particular historical significance – what Pierre Nora (1996–98) called *lieux de mémoire*. Even if European institutions have only a limited power in terms of cultural policies, acts of collective remembrance of the Second World War abound at the level of institutional memory, both below and above the level of the member states. The first important reference to the role that the Second World War played in triggering the process of European integration is inscribed in the first of its treaties. In the Preamble of the Treaty constituting the European Coal and Steel Community (ECSC), signed on 18 April 1951 in Paris, we read that the six pioneering countries

> [...] resolved to substitute for *historic rivalries* a fusion of their essential interests; to establish, by creating an economic community, the foundation of a broad and independent community among peoples long divided by *bloody conflicts*; and to lay the bases of institutions capable of giving directions to their future destiny; have decided to create a European Coal and Steel Community (emphasis mine).
> (Treaty constituting the European Coal and Steel Community, Preamble)

48 *Chiara Bottici*

Legal texts are important carriers of institutional memory given their codified and normative nature. They last in time, and therefore have a crucial stabilising effect. But moreover, they are normative sources that directly link a given vision of the past with the will to construct something in the present and in the future. An analogous reference to the Second World War indeed recurs in subsequent documents. As it has been shown through an analysis of all the successive treatises and the proceedings of the European Convention, the same narrative 'Europe out of the war' recurs in them all. In this sense, we can speak of an *acquis historique communautaire* (Larat 2005: 288). In contrast to the complete body of EU legislation accumulated so far, which is referred to as the *acquis communautaire*, the guiding lines of the *acquis historique* have no juridical value of their own, but are inscribed in crucial components of institutional remembrance, where they exercise their legitimating impact. Like the *acquis communautaire*, this narrative has a crucial normative impact, as it is shown by the fact that it must be recognised by applicant countries when joining the EU (Larat 2005: 288).

Another way to show the stabilising effect of institutional remembrance is to look at its ritual side. An explicit reference to the Second World War as the founding event of the European construction was for instance present in the famous Schuman Declaration of 9 May 1950. This declaration, which is always presented as the act of birth of the European project, explicitly referred to the desire to make war 'not only unthinkable, but materially impossible'. The Schuman declaration is remembered every year on 9 May, Europe Day.[4] Even though Europe Day is not strongly felt by European citizens, ritual commemoration is an important part of the collective remembrance among the elites: through rituals the memory of such events is re-enacted every year, thus contributing to creating a sense of continuity.[5]

To be true, ritual remembrance by hint of repetition contributes creating an air of timeless significance, at times even of sacredness. The Catholic church certainly played its part in this case. To the surprise of all those who consider the European Union humanly flawed, on 2 March 2004 Vatican officials confirmed that Robert Schuman was a candidate for beatification, the first step to sainthood. John Paul II considered that Schuman rightly perceived that the main cause of Europe's centuries of endless bloodshed was the rivalry between European countries. He had also been a practising Roman Catholic and an example to all those responsible for the construction of Europe.[6]

Ritual commemoration can also be the site for interplay between national and European institutions. It is not just at the European level that we have to look in order to see acts of collective remembrance that have some European implication. For instance, French President Mitterrand's last discourse as head of the state was a long plea in favour of European construction, and followed his participation in the fiftieth anniversary celebrations of the end of the Second World War. A clear symbolic link is made between these celebrations, ritually celebrated in London and Paris, and the discourse in favour of Europe, since he delivered his speech in Berlin, the city that symbolised the consequences of the end of the war.[7] In a parallel way, more that 10 years later, the newly elected Italian President Napolitano paid his first public visit to the island of Ventotene, where in 1941 Altiero Spinelli, together with other federalist militants, drafted the groundbreaking *Manifesto per una Europa libera e unita* while imprisoned on the island by the Fascists. Napolitano's appeal to revive the process of integration after the impasse due to the French and Dutch referenda assumes a particular connotation by being launched in one of the most significant *lieux de mémoire* of European federalism.[8]

Institutional remembrance is particularly crucial from our point of view because of its permanence in time and normative stabilising effects. This is however a fundamentally top-down process and may implicitly suggest that a homogeneous impact on identity-building necessarily follows from it. Yet, this cannot be taken for granted. Treaties die, policies change and official celebrations, such as Europe Day, may have only a very limited impact on citizens' identity.

With *public* remembrance, I mean the set of acts of remembrance that are carried out in public and for the public. Sites of public remembrance are, to name a few, newspapers, museums, fine arts, television programmes. Here I have tried to assess the presence of memories from the Second World War in relation to the EU through the analysis of newspapers. I searched eight newspapers from four countries (France, Germany, Great Britain, Italy) over the period 2000–2006.[9] Within this sample I then selected all the articles containing the two keywords 'Europe or European Union or European Community' and 'Second World War'. The analysis of these articles shows that the reference to the Second World War has been an important argument in the debate over European integration. Certainly it is not the only or even the most important argument (economic and social issues playing a greater role), but it has been one of them.

I then conducted another analysis on four of the newspapers (*La Stampa*, the *Guardian*, *Le Figaro*, the *Süddeutsche Zeitung*) with the keywords 'EU or European Union or European Community or Europe' and 'Second World War or WW2 or Holocaust or Shoah' on the days immediately before and after crucial dates: the celebration of Europe Day over the last seven years (2000–2006), the celebration of the sixtieth anniversary of D Day (6 June 2004) and the signing of the Constitutional Treaty on 29 October 2004.

The result of this research shows that there are few articles mentioning the Second World War or the Holocaust in connection with the dates analysed. However, more attention was paid to such events in the years of the failed ratification of the European Constitution. It is at times when people are called to express their opinion on the whole process that they are urged to reflect on their past. The data also confirm that it was in France and Germany that the debate was more animated (particularly in 2005), whereas the Italian newspaper was much more reluctant to engage in such a debate.

In the case of the British newspaper, it was on the occasion of the D Day celebrations that a conspicuous presence was registered.

The analysis of the content of the articles in both searches also confirms that what is at stake is how to interpret the whole process of European integration. Certainly, there remain a great many differences among Western countries, but it is revealing that even in a country traditionally eurosceptic, such as Britain, the overcoming of the war is often presented as the founding narrative of European construction.[10]

The experience of war, however, not only unites but also divides. In the case of Britain, this is not only evident in euroscepticism *à la* Thatcher, who argued that Europe brought Britain the disaster of the Second World War, but also in the memories of individuals and communities who cannot overcome personal and collective trauma. Together with articles celebrating the success of the EU in bringing about peace, there appeared articles remembering the most atrocious war crimes,[11] or lamenting a still vivid reciprocal suspicion between European citizens as rooted in war stereotypes.[12]

Recalling more or less directly the past is in both cases a powerful argument, perhaps even more powerful when it happens in an indirect and unmediated way. In 2006 a film was released by France 3, directed by Franck Appréderis and produced by Dominique Antoine. The film recounts the history of European construction by imagining an episode that occurred 5 years after the end of the Second World War. This historical moment is told in the story of Marie, a young French woman, and Jürgen, a former *Wehrmacht* soldier, now a reporter in Paris, where he is following the Schuman press conference. The producers declared that they would have liked the film to be released at the time of the referendum, because in their view many people in France do not know where the EU is coming from.[13]

Sometimes public and institutional remembrance can also overlap more patently. Clearly the levels that we have distinguished for analytical purposes are most of the time intermingled with each other in reality. An illuminating example is a long article that appeared on 6 May 2005 in the *Süddeutsche Zeitung* on occasion of the sixtieth anniversary celebrations of the ending of the Second World War. The article was written by the then *Bundeskanzler* Gerhard Schroeder and is a perfect example of a collective act of remembrance that combines the different levels we have distinguished so far. Here we also see how the European and the national levels of collective remembrance are at times mixed together, 8 May being both the day of the liberation from the horrors of the Nazi regime as well as the day that marked the end of the Second World War. It is from the division of the war that the unity of European citizens is said to derive, 'However much the memories of the European peoples may differ, they express the same thought: we want peace'.[14] The date 8 May represents the attempt to forge a new identity for the Germans as such and for the Germans as European citizens, an attempt that is explicitly grounded on a new culture of remembrance (*Erinnerungskultur*). It is a political identity that is said to be based on the values that emerged from the rejection of totalitarianism: democracy, rule of law, protection of minorities.[15]

It is only towards the end of the article that the political context of this long plea for European identity emerges. It is because we feel the relevance of the European past and we have learnt from it that the *Bundestag* and the *Bundesrat* should ratify the draft of the European Constitution, says *Bundeskanzler* Schroeder. The formula appearing in the Preamble of the draft of the European Constitution 'united in diversity' thus becomes the buzzword of a common European identity and should promote a sense of community and belonging among former enemies.

Analysis of the politics of remembrance taking place at the institutional level may suggest the image of a widely shared perception of the past. However, the debates that took place at the public level are much more complex. Furthermore, if we confront the image that we have reconstructed so far with that resulting from an analysis of the *pedagogical* level there emerges an even more complicated picture. By pedagogical remembrance I mean the work on the past that is carried out with the main objective of educating. This includes the work of a variety of people involved at all teaching levels: schools, university, cultural institutions broadly understood.

An analysis of Italian secondary school history textbooks from the 1995 to the present reveals that Europe is most of the times perceived as a mere economical and geopolitical project. Out of 13 textbooks,[16] only two – and very recent ones – give a primary role to the experience of war as the engine of the whole integration process (Bravo *et al.* 2006: 560; Della Peruta *et al.* 2003: 345). They only present the experience of the war as what enabled Europeanism to move from the abstract sphere of political thought to concrete reality.[17] The fact that they are all relatively recent, reflects the impact of the memory boom in historiography, but certainly also the more political development of recent years: it is at times when people raise questions about the meaning of European construction that they are driven back to history and construct a legitimating narrative out of it.

Quite different is the situation of German textbooks. An analysis of 17 history textbooks for secondary education and for the same period reveals a much greater role accorded to the experience of war as engine of the whole process.[18] The proportions are in this case reversed: only five textbooks out of seventeen accord a minor or no role to the experience of war (Brückner and Lachner 2005; Osburg and Klose 2003; Bernlochner *et al.* 1996; Hinrichs *et al.* 1998; Treml 1994). This is perhaps the consequence of the greater role that Germans accord to the memory of the war, also for their own national history, and of the greater importance given to the symbolic dimension of European construction. All those textbooks pay greater attention to images such as the myth of Europe raped by the bull, the image of Europe as the train not to miss at any costs, used sometimes in a celebratory way and sometimes as a satirical caricature.

For instance, the 2005 edition of *Zeiten und Menschen* opens the chapter on European integration with an impressive image of a war cemetery (Lendzian 2005: 314–15). In a similar way, a student opening the chapter on European integration of the 1999 edition of *Ansichten* does not even need to read the text of the section *Wie alles angefangen hat*: a collage of a desolating war cemetery together with pictures of war atrocities introduces the reader in the narrative 'Europe from the war' (Brokemper 1999). In a more evocative way, the 1996 edition of the *Geschichtsbuch* presents a cartoon from 1989 featuring grassland: above is a sign 'we are building the European house', and below statues of Hitler and Stalin still emanating a bad smell (Mütter *et al.* 1996: 179). Symbols can be the means for transmitting dominant views, but, at times, also the site for political critique.

More nuanced is the case of French history textbooks for secondary education. Half of the textbooks analysed present European integration as a merely economic and geopolitical project, whereas the other half accords a greater role to the experience of war. A detailed analysis of the image of Europe that comes out of textbooks in history and geography as well as civic education confirms this picture.[19] Even if Europe as both a geographical and a historical unity is given more attention, the teaching of the history of European integration remains a task carried out only by a minority of teachers (Baeynes 2003: 117ff.).

To conclude this point, the role of World War II in the making of the EU changes a lot according to the general image of the EU that one endorses: those who see in the European construction a purely economic and geopolitical process accords no or very little space to the experience of war. This holds true mostly for older texts: textbooks published after 2000 and even more after 2004 tends to give more space in general to the European construction and quite often also to the role of ideals such as the desire to guarantee peace. This, again, reflects the political changes through which Europe underwent in those crucial years. Still, there remain great differences between countries and sometimes also within the same country. This can be more clearly perceived in the case of Germany, which has regional education systems, but also in the case of France: it is significant that the only textbook published in a rural region (Dijon) and used for agricultural secondary schools accords a very minor role to the experience of war (Peltier 2001).

Finally, there is also a great variety of types of schools, this being again clearer in the cases of Germany and France, where often there are different editions of the same textbook according to the type of school. In particular, science and technology-oriented schools tend to have shorter textbooks that present Europe as an economic and geopolitical project. This does not imply a necessary connection between the recognition of the role of war and Europeanism. There are significant examples of textbooks that are euro-enthusiastic, but still see in the EU nothing more than a project of that kind (e.g. Camera 1996). The crucial point is the image of Europe that one endorses and recognises as significant for his or her own identity as a European citizen.

Even more explicit is the critical stance towards the narrative 'Europe out of the Second World War' among academics. The scepticism here is twofold. Together with those who see in Europe a purely economic project,[20] there are also those who emphasise the fact that other memories can be more relevant than that of the Second World War. A group of historians coming from different European countries have joined together in Paris to discuss the changing role of the memory of the Second World War and have concluded that the war cannot provide the founding narrative of a united Europe.[21] All the delegates at the conference agreed on the need for a Europeanization of the memory of the war – thus confirming our earlier observation that when people interact in the same social context they are also led to remember together. However, the conference emphasised the radical differences in the collective reception of the war, as expressed by the concept of divided remembrance or *geteilte Erinnerung*.[22]

In a similar vein, the historian Stefan Troebst recently discussed the possibility that memories of the dictatorships of the twentieth century can unite the European peoples. His conclusion is that no common European memory is possible: the experiences of the Gulag and the Holocaust divide Europe too radically into East and West. Between these areas, Troebst distinguishes further areas and concludes that in the foreseeable future nation-states will remain the primary area of reference for collective memory.[23]

Struggles over a divided past

What should we conclude? In the first place, it could be observed that what is important is not so much the negative answer that historians may give to the question of whether there exists a European collective remembrance of the war, but the fact that they raise the question in the first place. In virtue of raising the question in a European setting, they are already remembering together. The point is not to counterpoise history and remembrance as respectively faithful or unfaithful to the past. The past is always the site of struggles for the definition of the present. Historians are turned-back prophets, to use Schlegel's expression, no less than the people involved in the work of collective remembrance. Professional historians, too, are part of this work; however, not the only or the most important part (Winter 2006: 5). What interest us here is precisely to underline the politics of remembrance, i.e. the struggle for the definition of the past that is done in the perspective of the construction of an identity in the present and that, as we have seen, takes place at all levels.

From the set of activities that are part of the collective remembrance analysed in this work no univocal view of the legitimating narrative 'Europe born out of the War' emerges. This narrative certainly played a role and has been used at times to define a political project and a political identity otherwise perceived as too loose, but this has not been done in a homogeneous way. Struggles over the divided past of Europe and over its relevance for the contemporary European citizens take place both within and between the three levels that we have distinguished so far.

In the first place, as we have seen, there is a discrepancy between the institutional memory, which tends to present Europe as the land of democracy, rule of law and protection of minorities, which has been able to learn from its past, to use Schroeder's expression, and the image of Europe that comes out from the pedagogical and public memory. Whilst many professional historians transmit the image of the EU as a pure economic and geopolitical project, the public debates that emerge from an analysis of some European newspapers show an awareness of the role played by the experience of the war, but at the same time critically discuss its nature of founding narrative of the European identity.

If we consider the struggles that take place at all these levels, the institutional, at times triumphal, representation of the narrative 'Europe born out of the war' appears at best naive. An excess of triumphalism appears for instance in the Italian Minister of European Affairs Emma Bonino, who accompanying President Napolitano to Ventotene proposed to translate the *Manifesto di Ventotene* in Arabic in order to teach the nations of the Islamic world the route to peace and democracy.[24] This and similar celebrative acts of remembrance cannot but appear disproportionate to the human catastrophe represented by the Second World War and unable to correctly gauge the real impact of European federalism on the outside world.

At the same time, it can hardly be neglected that this narrative represented, and still represents, a powerful symbolic reservoir for European identity. As we have seen, this emerges with a particular emphasis in the critical moments of European construction, such as during the referenda over the Constitution. It is at times when the sense of European construction as a whole is at stake that people are induced to go back to their past. The experience of the war, and the willingness to avoid it, are used as an argument to show that there is meaning in the European project and that this meaning is positive. In this sense, it seems to provide a powerful, however minimal, core of meaning for the European identity.

To conclude, the politics of the past is something that situates itself between the past and the future. It is because the present but also the future of the European project is at stake that people are induced to mobilise their past. What they more or less consciously do is construct an identity in the present. The past does not automatically determine the present, but provides a series of arguments that can be used to legitimise it. The choice between all the potential arguments that history can potentially provide ultimately depends on the values and principles that individuals and groups decide to sustain and the context within which they operate.

Acknowledgements

This chapter connects the work carried out in the GARNET research project 5.2.1 with an ongoing research project on European identity and collective memory. I wish to thank all those who contributed to this enterprise with their helpful criticism and very lively discussions, in particular Camil Ungureanu, Marco Duranti, Gerdien Jonker, Bo Stråth, Karin Tilmans and Jay Winter, together with the other participants of this collective volume. Finally, I wish to thank the staff of the Georg Eckert Institute for International Textbook Research for their invaluable support in introducing me to the study of European textbooks and their help in the construction of my samples.

Notes

1 On collective memory and European identity, see in particular Eder and Spohn (2005).
2 On the collective elaboration of trauma from a sociological perspective see Alexander *et al.* (2004).
3 On the difference between the elaboration of the past as a triumph and the past as a trauma, see Giesen (2004).
4 For the official presentation of Europe Day, which appeared since 2002 among the other official European symbols, see the web history of the European Union at http://vlib.iue.it/hist-eur-integration/WebHistory.html (accessed 20 July 2007).
5 'Let us rejoice in the EU', *The Times*, 6 May 2006.
6 'Pope sets EU's founder on path to sainthood', *The Times*, 3 March 2004. On Schuman's cause for beatification see also http://www.catholique-metz.cef.fr/pages/dossiers/20040528_dossier_schuman/20040528_robert_schuman_03.pdf (accessed 20 July 2007).
7 'L'ultime plaidoyer de M. Mitterrand en faveur de l'Europe', *Le Monde*, 10 May 1995.
8 'Napolitano, appello per l'Europa "Impegno di tutte le forze politiche"', *La Repubblica*, 5 May 2006.
9 The newspapers surveyed are: *Il Corriere della Sera*, *La Repubblica*, the *Frankfurter Allgemeine Zeitung*, the *Süddeutsche Zeitung*, *Le Monde*, the *Guardian* through online archives and *La Stampa*, *Le Figaro*, *The Times* (including *The Sunday Times*) through the Lexis–Nexis database. In my approach, I have been inspired by Rosenzweig' and Thelen's *The Presence of the Past* (1998), though using newspapers instead of interviews.
10 See, for instance, 'Europe's coal engine of integration retires. The European Coal and Steel Community – a visionary attempt to prevent war and forge the EU – is finally about to expire. But it leaves an extraordinary legacy', the *Guardian*, 19 July 2002; 'D-Day: Lessons yet', the *Guardian*, 7 June 2004.
11 'Europe's forgotten war crime', *The Sunday Times*, 7 April 2002.
12 'For you British the war has never ended', *The Times*, 21 October 2004; 'It is time for our nations to look forward', *The Times*, 3 November 2004.
13 'L'Europe envers et contre tous', *Le Figaro*, 4 October 2006.
14 'Gedanken an den 8. Mai 1945', *Süddeutsche Zeitung*, 6 May 2005, translation mine.
15 'Gedanken an den 8. Mai 1945', *Süddeutsche Zeitung*, 6 May 2005.
16 The Italian secondary school textbooks analysed are: Benigno and Salvemini (2002); Bravo *et al.* (2006); Camera (1996); De Bernardi and Guarracino (1995);

Della Peruta *et al.* (2003); De Rosa (1997); Giardina *et al.* (2002, 2006); Lepre (1999); Marchese (2005); Polcri and Giappichelli (2000); Prosperi and Viola (2000); Villani *et al.* (1996).
17 Given that Italian textbooks are national, the sample has been constructed through a choice of the most important publishers for secondary education.
18 The German secondary school textbooks analysed are: Askani and Wagener (1997); Berger-von der Heide (2002); Bernlochner *et al.* (1996); Brokemper (1999); Brückner (1999); Brückner and Lachner (2005); Flues (1999); Funken and Koltrowitz (2003); Günter-Arndt *et al.* (1996); Hinrichs *et al.* (1998); Lendzian (2005); Lendzian and Schörken (1996); Mütter *et al.* (1996); Osburg and Klose (2003); Schmid and Wilms (1999); Treml (1994); Wollschläger (2000). The sample is representative of different *Länder* and different types of school. This also justify the higher number of textbooks analysed. Where the *Land* and type of school is not indicated this usually means that it is used in more than one *Land* and for different types of schools.
19 The French secondary school textbooks analysed are: Baylac (2004); Binoist *et al.* (2004a,b); Bourel (2004); Delouche (1997); Frank (1995); Lambin (1995, 1998); Marseille (1995); Le Pellec (2004); Peltier (2001). The various types of school are only occasionally different: most of the time the textbook is the same for all of them. Furthermore, they are the same for the whole country so the sample is representative of the different publishers.
20 See, for instance, the influential *The Age of Extremes* (Hobsbawm 1994: 239). As an example of more recent literature, which in contrast accords a greater role to the narrative 'Europe born out of the war', see Judt (2005).
21 In the German literature, the concepts of narrative (both historical and not) and that of myth often overlap. I have argued extensively for the need to distinguish between them in Bottici (2007).
22 'Eben war ich noch ein Nationalheld. Rollenwechsel im Kollektivgedächtnis: in Paris erörtern Historiker Variante der Erinnerung an den Zweiten Weltkrieg', *Frankfurter Allgemeine Zeitung*, 11 April 2006.
23 'Holodomor oder Holocaust? Von Professor Dr Stefan Toebst', *Frankfurter Allgemeine Zeitung*, 4 July 2005.
24 'Napolitano, appello per l'Europa "Impegno di tutte le forze politiche"', *La Repubblica*, 5 May 2006.

References

Alexander, J. C., Eyerman, R., Giesen, B., Smelser, N. J. and Sztompka, P. (2004) (eds) *Cultural Trauma and Collective Identity*, Berkley: University of California Press.
Askani, B. and Wagener, E. (1997) (eds) *Anno. Band 4. Das 20. Jahrhundert*, Braunschweig: Westermann.
Baeynes, H. (2003) 'L'Europa nei programmi e nei manuali scolastici francesi; verso una nuova comunità immaginaria europea?', in F. Pingel (ed.) *Insegnare l'Europa. Concetti e rappresentazioni nei libri di testo europei*, Turin: Edizioni Fondazione Giovanni Agnelli.
Baylac, M.-H. (2004) (ed.) *Histoire. Terminales Séries ES/L/S*, Paris: Bordas.
Benigno, F. and Salvemini, B. (2002) *Progetto storia. 1900–2000. Percorsi interdisciplinari*, Bari: Laterza.
Berger-von der Heide, T. (2002) (ed.) *Entdecken und Verstehen 3, Geschichtsbuch für die Klassenstufen 9/10 im Saarland*, Berlin: Cornelsen.
Bernlochner, L., Brack, H. and Brückner, D. (1996) (eds) *Treffpunkt Geschichte. Band 4*, Bamberg: Buchners Verlag.

Binoist, B., Bonneville, B. and Sirel, F. (2004a) (eds) *Histoire Tes ES et L*, Paris: Magnard.
——(2004b) *Histoire Tes S*, Paris: Magnard.
Bottici, C. (2007) *A Philosophy of Political Myth*, Cambridge: Cambridge University Press.
Bourel, G. (2004) *Histoire Tle S*, Paris: Hatier.
Bravo, A., Foa, A. and Scaraffia, L. (2006) *I nuovi fili della memoria. Uomini e donne nella storia dal 1900 AD oggi*, Bari: Laterza.
Brokemper, P. (1999) (ed.) *Ansichten 3. Arbeitsbuch für Geschichte-Politik an Hauptschulen in NordRhein-Westfalen*, Berlin: Cornelsen.
Brückner D. (1999) (ed.) *Das Waren Zeiten, Geschichte 4. Sekundarstufe I*, Bamberg: Buchners Verlag.
Brückner, D. and Lachner, H. (2005) (eds) *Geschichte erleben. Band 5*, Bamberg: Buchners Verlag.
Camera, A. (1996) *Storia contemporanea*, Milan: Principato.
De Bernardi, A. and Guarracino, S. (1995) *Storia del mondo contemporaneo*, Milan: Mondadori.
Della Peruta, F., Chittolini, G. and Capra, C. (2003) *Dall'Europa al mondo*. Volume 3, Florence: Le Monnier.
Delouche, F. (1997) (ed.) *Histoire de l'Europe*, Paris: Hachette.
De Rosa, G. (1997) *Il Novecento. Corso di Storia per le superiori*, Milan: Minerva Italica.
Eder, K. (2005) 'Remembering national memories together: the formation of a transnational identity in Europe', in K. Eder and W. Spohn (eds) *Collective Memory and European Identity*, Aldershot: Ashgate.
Eder, K. and Spohn, W. (2005) (eds) *Collective Memory and European Identity*, Aldershot: Ashgate.
Flues, H. (1999) (ed.) *Zeitreise. Rheinland-Pfalz 10*, Leipzig: Klett.
Frank, R. (1995) (ed.) *Histoire. Term L, ES, S*, Paris: Belin.
Funken, W. and Koltrowitz, B. (2003) (eds) *Geschichte plus. Augabe Sachsen. Gymnasium*, Berlin: Cornelsen.
Giardina, A., Sabbatucci, G. and Vidotto, V. (2002) *Storia dal 1900 a oggi*, Bari: Laterza.
——(2006) *Il mosaico e gli specchi. Percorsi di storia dal medioevo ad oggi. Volume 5B*, Bari: Laterza.
Giesen, B. (2004) *Triumph and Trauma*, Boulder, CO: Paradigm Publisher.
Giesen, B. and Junge, K. (2003) 'Historical memory', in G. Delanty and E. I. Isin (eds) *Handbook of Historical Sociology*, London: Sage.
Günter-Arndt, H., Hoffmann, D. and Zwölfer, N. (1996) (eds) *Geschichtsbuch. Oberstufe. Band 2. Das 20. Jahrhundert*, Berlin: Cornelsen.
Halbwachs, M. (1980) *The Collective Memory*, New York, Harper and Row [(1997) *La mèmoire collective*, Paris, Albin Michel].
Hinrichs, E., Müller, B. and Stehling, J. (1998) (eds) *Wir machen Geschichte. Band 4. Vom Ende des Ersten Weltkrigs bis zur Gegenwart*, Frankfurt am Main: Verlag Moritz Diesterweg.
Hobsbawm, E. (1994) *The Age of Extremes, 1914–1991*, London: Abacus.
Judt, T. (2005) *Postwar. A history of Europe since 1945*, New York: The Penguin Press.
Klain, K. L. (2000) 'On the emergence of memory in historical discourse', *Representations*, 69: 127–50.

Koselleck, R. (2000) 'Gebrochene Erinnerungen? Deutsche und polnische Vergangenheiten', *Jahrbuch der Deutschen Akademie für Sprache und Dichtung*: 19–32.
Lambin, J.-M. (1995) (ed.) *Histoire terminales*, Paris: Hachette.
——(1998) (ed.) *Histoire terminales*, Paris: Hachette.
Larat, F. (2005) 'Presenting the past: political narratives on European history and the justification of EU integration', *German Law Journal*, 6 (2): 273–90.
Lendzian, H. J. (2005) (ed.) *Zeiten und Menschen 2, Geschichte. Oberstufe*, Braunschweig: Schöningh.
Lendzian, H. J. and Schörken, R. (1996) (eds) *Rückspiegel. Woher wir kommen-wer wir sind*. Band 4, Braunschweig: Schöningh.
Le Pellec, J. (2004) (ed.) *Histoire. Terminales Séries ES/L/S*, Paris: Bertrand-Lacoste.
Lepre, A. (1999) *La storia del Novecento*, Bologna: Zanichelli.
Marchese, R. (2005) *Piani e percorsi della* storia, Milan: Minerva Italica.
Margalit, A. (2002) *The Ethics of Memory*, Cambridge, MA: Harvard University Press.
Marseille, J. (1995) *Histoire Term*, Paris: Nathan.
Mütter, B., Pingel, F. and Zwölfer, N. (1996) (eds) *Geschichtsbuch 4. Die Menschen und ihre Geschichte in Darstellungen und Dokumenten, Neue Ausgabe*, Berlin: Cornelsen.
Nora, P. (1996–98) (ed.) *Realms of Memory*, New York, Columbia University Press [(1984–1992) *Les Lieux de mémoire,* Paris, Edition Gallimard].
Osburg, F. and Klose, D. (2003) (eds) *Expedition Geschichte. Ausgabe G. Band 4. Von der Nachkriegszeit bis zur Gegenwart*, Frankfurt am Main: Verlag Moritz Diesterweg.
Peltier, C. (2001) (ed.) *Histoire du XXe siècle. 1res et term. agricoles*, Dijon: Educagri.
Polcri, A. and Giappichelli, M. (2000) *Percorsi di storia. Per i nuovi trienni delle scuole superiori. Il XX secolo 3*, Brescia: Editrice La Scuola.
Prosperi, A. and Viola, P. (2000) *Corso di storia. Il secolo XX*, Milan: Einaudi Scuola.
Ricoeur, P. (2000) *La mémoire, l'histoire, l'oubli*, Paris: Editions du Seuil.
Rosenzweig, R. and Thelen, D. (1998) *The Presence of the Past: popular uses of history in American life*, New York: Columbia University Press.
Schlegel, F. S. and Schlegel, A. W. (1992) [1798–1800] *Athenäum. Eine Zeitschrift von A.W. Schlegel und F.S. Schlegel*, Darmstadt: Wissenschaftliche Buchgesellschaft.
Schmid, H. D. and Wilms, E. (1999) (eds) *Fragen an die Geschichte. Das 20. Jahrhundert*, Berlin: Cornelsen.
Treml, M. (1994) (ed.) *Oldenbourg Geschichte für Gymnasien 13*, Munich: Oldenbourg.
Villani, P., Petraccione, C. and Gaeta, F. (1996) *Corso di Storia. Dall'Ottocento al Nocevento*, Milan: Principato.
Winter, J. (2006) *Remembering War. The Great War and historical memory in the 20th century*, New Haven, CT: Yale University Press.
Winter, J. and Sivan, E. (1999) (eds) *War and Remembrance in the Twentieth Century*, Cambridge: Cambridge University Press.
Wollschläger, A. (2000) (ed.) *Geschichte und Geschehen. Thüringen Regelschule Klasse 10*, Leipzig: Klett.

4 Identity and capital cities
European nations and the European Union

Göran Therborn

Capital cities make up a significant component of national identities: as locations of national power, as sites of representations of power, and as focal points of national cleavages, conflicts and cohesion. Whether seen negatively or positively, capitals have an important function in the legitimization and in the contestation of political power. By definition, capitals are political centres, and hence their making one aspect of centre formation.[1]

Capital cities and national history

Contemporary cities are usually made of layers of history: of building history, of economic history, of cultural and political history. In Europe they include legacies of Greco-Roman constructions, of the Middle Ages, the Renaissance, Counter-Reformation Baroque, the neo-Classicism of Absolutism, of nineteenth-century Historicism and spatial expansionism, of Modernist transformations and, more occasionally, of post-Modernist afterthoughts. The history of European cities bears witness to economic trends and cycles, to trade routes opened and closed, to the movements of herring in the Baltic and the North Sea, to colonial plunder and the slave trade, to manufacture, industrialization, and de-industrialization, to cycles of creativity and visitor attraction. Capital cities, in particular, are also made up of the vicissitudes of political history, of varying spatial extensions and organization of power, of different kinds and of different resources of power. They have travelled along different routes to and through national modernity, and they are currently differently located in the world of nation-states and of global flows. Even after the most vicious destruction, urban history tends to bounce back, as in Warsaw, Minsk or Berlin. Identities grow from historical experiences.

Capitals have a function of representing political power. As forms of representation, cities have five major dimensions.

1. A layout of streets, places, buildings, varying in form, size, interconnections and accessibility. In the national history of European capitals, the demolition of pre-modern fortifications and the military abandonment of

spaces previously used for defence provided important opportunities for a new urban layout. Linguistically, it was indicated by the shift from bulwark to boulevard, the Viennese move from the defensive *Glacis* to the ostentatious *Ringstrasse* providing the model example.
2. A set of buildings of political and of economic power, of culture, of popular well-being, of leisure, of consumption, varying in their relative size and frequency. In European history, the most significant national buildings were usually the parliament, the opera or main dramatic theatre, the palace of justice/supreme court and the national museum. The European capitals' later moments of popularity and globality added their own characteristic buildings.
3. Style, the architecture of buildings, the style of monuments. Most public European nationalism picked from the pre-modern repertoire of European architecture: neo-Gothic for the parliaments of London and Budapest, neo-Classicism in Athens and in the Viennese parliament, neo-Baroque for the German and the Swedish parliaments, neo-Renaissance for the Czech National Theatre and National Museum and for the Rijksmuseum of Amsterdam. In Paris, Haussmann imposed a disciplined French Classicism on the façades of the main boulevards, forming street-long horizontal lines, whereas in Central Europe a more irregular and decorative syncretism of the European repertoire, known as Historicism or Eclecticism, prevailed. The first architectural style breaking out of the old repertoire was known as *Art Nouveau* in Belgium and France, *Secession* in Central Europe, *Jugendstil* in northern Germany and Sweden, in Finland (sometimes at least) as National Romanticism, and in Catalonia as *Modernisme*. Around 1900 it was the preferred style of much of the national bourgeoisie, from Barcelona to Brussels, and from Budapest and Prague to Riga and Helsinki.

Monuments were mostly figurative, although they did include a number of obelisks, usually provided with inscriptions, sometimes in Latin, but more often in the national language. They were often allegorical, and the more important ones usually included an elaborate iconographic programme.
4. Toponymy or nomenclature, the naming of streets, places and buildings. A system of urban naming is a product of early modernity, decreed in Paris in 1728 (Farvacq-Kitkovic 2005: 5). Before the French Revolution the usual pattern consisted of a few *places* and streets of regal importance, whereas the rest were left as local landmarks. The French Revolution took nomenclature very seriously, turning *Place Louis XV* into *Place de la Révolution*, or *Place du Trône* into the *Place du Trône Renversé*, for example. The practice spread following the Napoleonic wars. In Stockholm, a (re-)naming programme was launched in 1885, replacing a lot of local medieval designations with patriotic or illustrious names (Stahre 1992: 17ff.).
5. Monumentality, the object and the form of celebration or commemoration. Public monumentality expanded enormously in the nationalist

nineteenth century. In Europe it was largely inspired by the Roman legacy, which also included the Egyptian obelisk, although the latter re-emerged in nineteenth-century Europe from direct French and British imperial contacts with Egypt. The medieval church sponsored monuments to Jesus, Mary and patron saints, and staged iconic processions. Plagues, or their ending, gave rise to columns of thanksgiving, e.g. in Vienna and Prague. Princely homages, coronations, weddings, baptisms or military victories often included temporary (mostly wooden) gates of honour. The princely equestrian statue was revived with the Renaissance.

The new national movement made its own use of the equestrian statue and the obelisk, it made permanent triumphal arches in stone, it moved the elaborate iconographic ensembles out of the palaces and the cathedrals into public places, while largely substituting secular, Greco-Roman or evolutionist allegories for Biblical ones. The national mode of monumentality was personal or allegoric, heroic or civilly celebratory of the nation's famous men. National flags, anthems and days came into being in the nineteenth century, intermittently also affecting the cityscape.

Capital cities and modernity

National capitals are modern social constructions. Medieval polities usually lacked a capital city, having itinerant emperors, kings and princes of variable mobility. Charlemagne, for example, had a preference for Aachen, and the area from Liège to Cologne, but was also very often in Worms in the southern Rhineland, and several times in Regensburg in south-eastern Germany. When capitals did become the norm, from the Renaissance onwards, they were not national, but princely *Haupt- und Residenzstädte* (capital and residence cities). The capital then represented his (occasionally her) power and glory, his/her identity. The prince had his power from God, not from the nation. An important tradition of medieval Europe was the urban representation of God and the Biblical narrative – in churches, sculptures, pictures – continued into modernity and was strongly reinforced by the embattled Eastern Orthodoxy after 1453 and by the Western Christian schism of the sixteenth century.

When nations rose, they had then to assert themselves against princes, with their aristocratic *pendants*, and against the worldly power of the church. This was especially important in the Catholic realms, given ecclesiastical state independence and the wealth of the Catholic Church, reaffirmed in the splendour of its Counter-Reformation.

The class character of nations has varied, but the rise of a nation, and thereby of a national capital, always involves a rise of other social forces than the nobility and the clergy. In Europe this new social force was usually, above all, the haute bourgeoisie, for whom the *Bourse* or the Royal Exchange was a major urban centre. But also significant was the growth and collective identity of petite bourgeoisies, of intellectual strata, of free farmers and of autonomous working classes. The emergence of national capitals also entailed a social transformation, from cities dominated by courtiers, clergy, domestic servants and soldiers, i.e. by servants of the king and God, to a society of economic and cultural relations. At the end of the eighteenth century, soldiers, civil servants and their domestic servants made up a good 40 per cent of the population of Berlin (Ságvári 1993: 169).[2]

A national capital, then, is a seat of sovereign national power, and a city representing the nation. In constitutional monarchies the political change can be gradual, and what is a national or a royal institution of power may be open to debate. With respect to capital cities, their representative function is crucial. To what extent is there a representation of the nation, its power, its sovereignty, its victories, its peaceful achievements, its ancestry, its culture? The seat of a body of national representatives, in other words a parliament building, is one significant indicator. Explicitly national or state institutions – theatres were often very important, monuments and street and place names referring to the nation and/or the state and its exploits are others. A full analysis should also look into the socioeconomic changes of the city, but the very possibility of a *décalage* of politics and economics has to be acknowledged too. The latter, then, had better not be used as a criterion for the character of the former.

The main European road, to modernity as well as to a national capital, was the road of internal battle between the nation, on one hand, and the prince and the church on the other (Therborn 2003). It was, of course, fought and travelled in varying ways, and we had better sort the latter into a few distinctive variants. However, the history of European capitals also includes two other routes, which should be singled out, although they did share the typical European experience of nation versus prince.

All along the east-central strip of Europe from Helsinki to Sofia, national capitals were established in a triangular conflict, pitting one ethnic nation against one or more other *ethnies*, and against a foreign prince. A third variant, on the western periphery of the continent, involved an emergent nation from old roots and a foreign prince or state, but without any stark cultural divide between them, as in the European colonies overseas. All the three roads have their revolutionary, ruptural, and their gradualist or accommodational variants.

No capital is like clay in the hands of the ruler. It is always a natural locale, in Europe usually with a history of its own, more often than not with significant local powers, *de facto* or *de iure*. City-shaping is then usually protracted and costly, and therefore subject to political vicissitudes of power and of resources. This norm certainly holds for European national capitals.

Now, the different historical relationships between the prince and nation do not constitute the only major axis of differentiation among European capitals. Attention should also be paid to state–city relationships. They may be looked at and interpreted in different ways, but for my purposes a perspective developed by Stein Rokkan seems to be the most fruitful (Rokkan and Urwin 1980; cf. Tilly 1992). As a kind of western European counterpart to the above-mentioned multiethnic eastern strip, there is what Rokkan called the 'city belt' of early and strong cities and weak states. It runs from central Italy to the Hansa cities of northern Germany, through (small-town) Switzerland, the Rhineland and the Low Countries.

Here, a particular conception of polycentrism and urban power *vis-à-vis* territorial states was reproduced in national modernity and has largely been maintained into current times. As an Italian politician (Ferrari) put it in 1864 in a parliamentary debate about the choice of a capital for the new Italian nation-state: 'The very idea of a preponderant capital has always been resolutely rejected by everybody. [...] We do not want an Italian Paris, we do not want an Italian London' (Djament 2005: 376n). Italy still has no one preponderant capital. Switzerland in the first half of the nineteenth century had six rotating capitals (Basel, Bern, Freiburg, Lucerne, Solothurn, and Zürich). After the religious civil war of 1847 and in turning the oligarchic confederation into a nation in the aftermath of the 1848 February revolution, the Swiss elected Bern their capital (over Zürich and the defeated Lucerne). But again, urban polycentrism has remained a feature of Swiss geography.

The Netherlands have opted for a unique solution, which is part of a post-revolutionary compromise between the dynasty of Oranie and the Amsterdam patriciate. Here we find an official capital (Amsterdam), which is not the seat of government and parliament, i.e. not the actual political capital; and an unofficial capital (The Hague), which is not the leading city of the country, demographically, economically or culturally.

After the Belgian secession, Brussels was brushed up to become national capital, with a national-cum-royal column higher than the classical Trajan column and with the biggest palace of justice in the world. But its important symbolic centre remained the *Grande Place* in the low city of the burghers, and there is no European capital which has paid as much lavish tribute to its mayors as Brussels, with its grand avenues and central *places* named after them.[3] The 1949 West German choice of Bonn, a modest city even within the Rhineland, continued the city belt tradition. Even in today's Berlin Republic, Hamburg and Bremen remain city-states of the Federal Republic, in a polycephalous urban system which also includes Munich, Frankfurt and Cologne as major players.

The time dimension: three moments of European capitals

This chapter will concentrate on national capitals/national identities and European capital/European identity, which seem appropriate comparisons – and a more than large enough topic for this occasion. However, I am, of course, also aware that capital city development does not end with an affirmation of the nation. Without subscribing to any determinist evolutionism, it seems that European national capital history may be analysed in terms of three developmental moments.

First, there was the national moment, the nation establishing its capital – with the three variants mentioned above – and the nation then defined as one by its leaders.

Second, there was a popular moment, when the popular (non-elite) classes of the nation manifested themselves – with recognized influence and/or with power. This popular moment, which usually dates from the aftermath of the First World War, paid homage to the Unknown Soldier, but also to peaceful labour and popular politics. The Belgian painter and sculptor Constantin Meunier turned to making sculptures of workers of different occupations in the late nineteenth century, which later spread to Copenhagen, Stockholm and other places. But his grand Monument to Labour, which he started working on in 1886, had its erection in Brussels blocked till 1930. Even though Meunier's art focuses on work and not on class conflict, for a long time there was a fear that the monument might become a rallying point for the socialists (Derom 2000: 144ff.).[4] The popular moment was also that of popular housing, distinctive features of post-First World War Social Democratic Vienna as well as of post-Second World War Social Democratic Stockholm and Helsinki.

Third, we have the global moment, when a national capital presented itself as/aspired to become a world city, seeing itself, and being allowed to see itself, primarily as a city in a global arena – of capital, tourism, creativity – and not as a capital worthy of the grandeur of the nation. Although this is an actual tendency, a certain caution may be due from an analytical point of view, as a result of the hype of some consultants and an academic trend. In 1991 the London Advisory Planning Committee with some other bodies launched a 'research project' on 'London World City', with a frank bluntness: 'So world cities are about concentrations of capital and the generation of wealth. But they are also about command and control' (Kennedy 1991: 6).

The top British architect Richard Rogers (Rogers and Eisher 1992: 218), in an influential publication of about the same time, put it differently, however: 'London must learn to see itself not just as a British capital but as a European city'. The office of the London Mayor, Ken Livingstone, added another perspective, the capital as the global agent of the nation:

> The case for London demonstrates that expenditure in London benefits the UK economy as a whole and helps the government achieve many of its national policy objectives [...]. On a global level, London is a world city and acts as a gateway for the international economy into the rest of the UK.
>
> (Mayor of London 2004: 6)

The most global of European cities clearly does not see itself as unrelated to or independent from the national polity and economy. And imperial cities have always had some kind of global vision, albeit often less than planetary. Baron Haussmann, the builder of the Western European paradigm of a national capital, saw his task as an 'immense enterprise which will make Paris a capital worthy of France, [...] almost said of the civilized World' (Hall 1986: 317).

Three European roads to a national power and to a national capital

National identities in Europe have developed in different ways and have been moulded in different forms. Interstate rivalries and wars, religious divisions of Christianity, ethno-linguistic differences have played a significant role in the emergence of a national awareness, of a consciousness of national differences. However, crucial to the modern political history of Europe is the rise and the assertion of the nation against the prince. In a way, this was a generalized version on the level of territorial states of the medieval conflicts of city burghers versus a local prince in the city belt of Europe. The only significant exception to this European road to political modernity, of nation versus prince, is the nation contra oligarchy form in Switzerland.

The national capitals resulting from the assertion of a nation indicate a topography of national identities. The mainstream of European nations asserted themselves against and/or above their princes. In this respect we have to distinguish three different constellations.

One nation versus one prince

This was the constitutive pattern of modern Europe. It was a road with two lanes. The fast lane was that of revolution, which was not always the fastest in the long run, because of the counter-revolutions it normally included. Paris – turned into a national capital by the Revolution, which ended the dynastic court at Versailles as well as other institutions of the *ancien régime* – was the paradigmatic case, the model and the most successful. The experiences of Madrid and Lisbon were much more convoluted, with the state armies and the dynasties both fractured by the Napoleonic incursion into Iberia. In both cases the nation–church conflict was central, and the national parliaments set up in the nineteenth century were housed in former monasteries in Lisbon as well as in Madrid.

The opposite pole to the revolutionary road was the gradual process of nationalizing monarchies. London was here the master copy, a theatre of revolution in the seventeenth century, but more religious than national, and its radical Enlightenment was kept low by the old English rival of France turning revolutionary. London had its small-state followers, in The Hague/Amsterdam, Copenhagen and Stockholm. The last one draped itself in predominantly royal iconography till the end of the First World War.

One nation, two or more princes

In the cases of Italy and Germany, the princes were too many and too small for the nation. Nation-building here was neither revolution nor reform, but 'unification'. In both countries the process was enduringly complicated by strong pre-national institutions refusing to go away – the princely rights of the Hohenzollern in Germany and the Papacy in Italy. German Berlin and Italian Rome had to accommodate both.

The fractured dynasties and warring princes of nineteenth-century Portugal and Spain had some structural affinities with Italy and Germany, but differed in that the warring princes as well as the proclaimed representatives of the nation laid claim to the same whole realm.

Two or more nations versus one prince

This configuration had three major sub-variants, all very different from each other.

In one sub-type there were parallel but non-synchronized conflicts, with a conflict between nation and foreign prince added onto the first nation versus prince constellation. Here, the foreignness, or rather the foreign base, of the prince was the issue. Brussels, Oslo, Dublin and Reykjavik emerged as capitals of new independent states. In the Nordic cases this was a negotiated peaceful process, whereas Brussels and Dublin had to come out of the pall of lethal gun smoke. In Brussels this was a swift operation, linked to the Parisian revolutionary cycle, whereas Irish national Dublin was born in the twentieth century through a protracted process of painful labour.

The second sub-type can be found in the east-central strip of Europe, from Finland to Bulgaria, with some elements also in Greece, where the conflict configuration was more complex and difficult. Here there developed different variants of conflicts between one nation, (an)other nation(s) and the prince. Ethnic change in (future) capital cities was a characteristic phenomenon of the nationalist modernization of what had been, in contrast to (religiously and linguistically) more totalitarian Western Europe, the multicultural region of Europe (Therborn 2006).

Russia is the third sub-variant, where the final battle against the prince was won by a force claiming to be both a universal class (a detachment of the world proletariat), and a union of nations, with only some nations on the north-western periphery of the former Romanov empire becoming independent (of the second sub-group).

These different national trajectories have left their traces in the urban iconography as well as in the history of debates and conflicts in the European capitals. Their character is spelt out in parallel publications from my ongoing project on the world's capital cities. Here they will provide a backdrop to the problematic of a capital of Europe, as part of the wider issue of European identity.

Brussels and capitals for Europe

Choosing and shaping a capital for Europe has been a complicated and protracted affair. As a project peacefully pursued by a number of sovereign nation-states, Europe had to have a negotiated capital. No natural one had emerged or was imposable, although de Gaulle may have thought otherwise. Models did exist, from the sixteenth- to seventeenth-century United Provinces of the Netherlands, from Switzerland and from the European settler states coming out of the British Empire. The United Provinces had selected a modest, powerless place, which they denied city rights but which had some symbolic historical significance as the late medieval seat of the Counts of Holland: The Hague. The Swiss cantons chose Bern in 1848 because of its relative accessibility in the mountainous country, and because of the bilingual character of the canton of Bern.

Where there were two major blocs of interest, the settler states decided to build a new capital in between: Washington, Ottawa, Canberra. There were also mobile solutions. Before 1848 the Swiss had rotating assembly sites. The short-lived kingdom of Netherlands and Belgium had two seats of government and court, between which the king and the royal government moved: The Hague and Brussels. The Union of South Africa had (and still has) two major capitals far apart, the government in Boer Pretoria and the parliament in Anglo Cape Town, with the supreme court in a third city, Bloemfontein, once capital of the Boer Oranje Free State.

The European project has groped its way, by much trial and error, through these models. The capital of Europe clearly had to be somewhere in the city belt interface between Germanic and Romance Europe, between France and Germany. Building a new city in this old, densely urbanized area was not much of a serious option, although there was a proposal of that sort floating around for a while, with a French painter and a German journalist canvassing together for a place between the former Maginot and Siegfried military lines: Bourg Blanc/Weissburg in Alsace.

The Council of Europe opted for Strasbourg, in now French, previously German Alsace/Elsass. But that Council was an interstate body, of which Britain was a founding member, although it came to develop a powerful suprastate court of human rights. The location of an embryonic potential European Union was another matter. For seating the High Authority of the Coal and Steel Union there were several candidates. At the time of decision, in July 1952, France, supported by Italy, officially fielded Strasbourg, the Dutch The Hague, and the Belgians Liège. The Christian Democratic government of Belgium, which was in the midst of a profound crisis – concerning the reign of King Leopold because of his accommodating Nazi Germany – pitting Catholic, Royalist Flanders against largely secular and anti-Royalist Wallonia, pushed for Liège rather than Brussels, presumably as a gesture of national reconciliation. Wallonian Liège was the centre of the Belgian steel industry, facing a difficult process of restructuring, and it was also the centre of the large and militant anti-Royalist opposition. To non-Belgians, smallish, old industrial Liège had no urban attraction.

There was also the idea of locating the new European institutions in a special federal district of Europe. Jean Monnet hoped for this though did not push for any particular site. The French Europeanist Foreign Minister Schuman advocated Saarbrücken. But the fate of Saarland was then unsettled, was it French? German? or European? (In the end, a referendum in l955 voted overwhelmingly for Germany, which ended all discussions of Saarbrücken as a federal district of Europe.) After several exhausting days of inconclusive negotiations, an offer from Luxembourg provided a provisional solution for the High Authority, with an (occasional) parliamentary assembly in Strasbourg, where there was a sufficiently large plenary hall in the new building of the Council of Europe. The Court of Justice, the second continuous institution of the Union, was quietly installed in Luxembourg in the wake of the High Authority. In the longer run, the tranquil little capital of the Grand Duchy of Luxembourg– where the lights went out early, as Jean Monnet (l976: 433ff.) points out in his memoirs – was clearly too small for European ambitions (Hein 2004: 40ff., 68ff.).

The 1957 Treaty of Rome broadened the European project, from coal and steel only to the economy as a whole. The European Economic Community (EEC) had the same institutional structure as the previous European Coal and Steal Community (ECSC): a Council of Ministers, a Commission (replacing the former High Authority), a (largely advisory) Parliamentary Assembly and a Court of Justice. For purposes of localization, the key institution was again the Commission. Ten applications were submitted in l958, four French – Strasbourg, Paris, Nice and the suburban department of Oise east of Paris – four Italian – Milan, Turin, Monza and Stresa – Luxembourg and Brussels. Well before 1990s 'globalization', Europeanization spawned urban foreign policy independent of national governments. Brussels had strong intergovernmental support – as a metropolitan city of a small country – for housing all the permanent institutions, and won the second parliamentary round in front of Strasbourg and Milan. However, the French government, now under de Gaulle, was not prepared to play ball. Brussels was accepted only as a provisional seat for the Commission, while Luxembourg and Strasbourg kept their judicial and parliamentary functions, respectively, for the time being (see further Hein 2004: 72ff.).

Provisional solutions have tended to prove enduring during the whole European project, and the Union still has a complex capital structure. For a long time the intergovernmental Council was itinerant, like the medieval courts, but now has a fixed headquarters in Brussels. The presidency rotates, and the powerful summits are mobile. Brussels is the seat of what in the Middle Ages was the Chancery, the actual political centre point of the European realm, where the bureaucracy is, and where the Parliament often meets, and would like to meet always. Strasbourg also sees the Parliament regularly, under powerful French governmental protection. Luxembourg corresponds to Wetzlar or Speyer in the Holy Roman Empire, the judiciary capital, and has also become endowed with investment banking, statistics and recurrent parliamentary sessions. Distances are short, but a nomadic active parliament is, of course, not very practical. The 'cultural capital of Europe' has become a roving roadshow, politically rational, but it is not the way a focus of cultural orientation and identity is made (Charle and Roche 2002).

Like some nation-states, even unitary ones like Sweden, the EU has located a set of agencies outside its capital(s). There are currently (late 2006) 25 such agencies, three for the pillar of foreign policy and security, three related to police and judicial matters, and 19 mainstream 'Community agencies'. The Defence Agency is in Brussels and the Translation Centre in Luxemburg, but the others are spread out, from Thessaloniki to Dublin, from Stockholm to Alicante. The Poles are guarding the eastern border, housing in Warsaw the European Agency for the Management of Operational Cooperation at the External Borders, but there are no other EU agencies yet in the 2004 member cohort, although in December 2006 Lithuania was promised a new gender equality agency. For some reason Finland is the only country among the EU15 left out of Union largesse.[5] Whatever their merits in jobs and subsidies, these agencies and their sites have very little capital function, and certainly no capital shine.

Socially and economically, Brussels has changed with its European role. By 1998, about a tenth of all employment in the Brussels Capital Region was due to European or international institutions – excluding employees of transnational corporations. While EU employment is growing much faster than the population of Brussels, the growth curves of city and EU office space are virtually identical, which may indicate that the former is driven by the latter (Commission and Belgian Presidency 2001: Part III). Brussels has become the favourite European location for US corporations. In the 1990s Brussels overtook Paris as the biggest host of international organizations. Media interest in the EU has given Brussels the second largest press corps in the world after Washington (Elmhorn 2001: 41ff., 68ff.). Brussels Capital Region has become the second most prosperous region in the EU in terms of GDP per capita, after inner London, but ahead of Luxembourg and the Ile de France, 235 per cent of the EU25 average in 2002, and 172 per cent of the second Belgian region (Antwerp) (Eurostat 2004).[5]

Economically and politically important as it is, its European capital function has a quite modest place in Brussels' geology of representation. European institutions have now expanded into a whole *quartier* of new buildings for the Council, the Parliament, parliamentary administration and a refurbished Commission building, free of asbestos and provided with new public transport access. On the other hand, this old fashionable neighbourhood is off-centre from the representative layout – sideways to Rue de la Loi heading to the *Cinquantènaire*, the Arch commemorating the fiftieth anniversary of Belgium, off the Parc de Bruxelles with the royal palace on one side and parliament on the other, and beyond the immense *Palais de Justice*, the *Mont des Arts* and the grand avenues. The layout of Brussels is still predominantly national – or pre-national, like the Grande Place.

As a sizeable *bon vivant* national capital, Brussels has seen no need for new representative buildings apart from those with a political or administrative function. Luxembourg was, of course, in a different situation, and has recently invested heavily in representative culture, with a concert hall by Christian de Portzamparc and an art museum by I. M. Pei. European Brussels has not produced any iconic architecture, at most some large-scale standard modernism. This is in contrast to Richard Rogers' Court of Justice in Luxembourg and the Strasbourg Parliament by the Architecture Studio. Brussels monumentality is still mainly Leopoldian, although new European buildings feature an E in some form or other. Some Europeanization of names has taken place. The Leopold Quarter is now referred to as the European Quarter – despite including the Leopold station –, while the Rond-Point de la Loi was named after Robert Schuman as far back as 1963. Berlaymont, the Commission building, however, was the name of the convent torn down for the new construction, and the new Council headquarters has been named after Justus Lipsius, a great Flemish sixteenth-century classical philologist and political theorist, who had a street there. Monumental projects for the Schumann Roundabout have been plenty, but have remained unrealized (Derom 2000: 264–65).

An inconclusive debate

In 2001, Romano Prodi, the then President of the Commission, and the Belgian Prime Minister Guy Verhofsdtadt – leading the Belgian Presidency in the second half of the year – organized two small, high-level meetings on the theme of 'Brussels, Capital of Europe' (Commission and Belgian Presidency 2001). Both the contents and the outcome of the initiative are symptomatically significant. The outcome was next to nothing. Most concrete and relevant was a proposal to arrange international architectural competitions for the *Quartier Européen*, and in an aside it was added that 'the realisation of a Museum related to the European project could be explored'.

Almost all the participants, beginning with Umberto Eco, agreed that 'the European capital should not follow the example of national capitals'. What that meant appears rather obscure from the official summary. Eco pushed the whole discussion in a peculiar direction, by contrasting 'two ideas of a capital city' in European history, that of Louis XIV and the urban networks of Italy and Germany (Commission and Belgian Presidency 2001: 10). Peculiar because Versailles was a dynastic, pre-national capital, against which the Parisians of the Revolution successfully revolted; peculiar also because it overlooked the national efforts of Rome and Berlin. The capital of Europe, it was said, should be 'light' but 'stable', promoting and respecting 'diversity' (p. 29).

Prodi pointed to the contrast between the Belgian nation-state symbolism in Brussels and the absence of anything similar representing Europe. But the participants were remarkably cool against monumentality: 'Constructing impressive buildings as symbols could be sending wrong signals' (p. 23). The Belgian prime minister was ecumenical and non-committal, European symbols could be 'a building, a monument, a song, a person' (p. 22).

In spite of this fear of a strong common European identity focus, the participants were far from smug and complacent. They concluded, *inter alia*, that 'the past experience of the European institutions in Brussels is not an example of best practice'. They pointed, as problematic areas, to: communication about Europe and its symbols, the meaning and quality of buildings in urban planning, the relations between the European institutions and Brussels' citizens, the participation of stakeholders in the decision-making process (pp. 29–30).

Most critical was the Dutch architect Rem Koolhaas, speaking his mind as always: 'Brussels today is a European capital by default, a curious aesthetic landscape sometimes generic and sometimes of such a scale that you can only talk about megalomania'. However, while deploring the lack of meaning of European buildings in Brussels, Koolhaas' critique remains intra-aesthetic – the buildings of the European institutions are not of the 'best ability' or the 'highest quality'. To accuse them of megalomania seems to me unfair, only feeding the insouciance of a 'light capital'. His concrete proposals were: either a radical refurbishment of the European Quarter with new buildings and a new 'conceptual framework' (unspecified), or a new start at another site, in northern Brussels by the canal harbour, the so-called 'Tour et Taxi' area (*Thurn und Taxis* in German), named after the (still existing) medieval German aristocratic family of Lombard origin (*Torre e Tasso*), which ran courier services in medieval Italy and then in the early seventeenth century was given the rights to organize the postal services of the Holy Roman Empire area. The family first organized this service from Brussels, before moving to Frankfurt in the early eighteenth century. In 2001, a *Thurn und Taxis* warehouse was turned into a cultural site for exhibitions and events of various kinds, but it remains a local, rather than a European, place.

There was also an intention to ignite a public debate around the capital issue. It was not very successful. As the official Final Report says, the European capital and its symbols 'drew relatively little attention from the press' (p. 128). The journal *European Voice* launched a competition about the best essay on the topic. The prize-winning one asserted: 'Europe needs a capital like a tree needs a chainsaw.' (The author was an American lecturer) (p. 129).

Brussels and Europe

Brussels may very well be taken as a metaphor of the European Union project. The EU project is in the shadow of still looming national legacies, increasingly afraid even to look at the latter. While they may be contained within the EU, ethnic divisions have not abated or disappeared. On the contrary, they have become more salient again. Between the Flemish and the Francophones, Belgium might well have fallen apart altogether, but for the EU. Brussels itself is very much part of this conflict, ignited in the 1960s, as it is a mainly French-speaking city surrounded by Flemish-speaking suburbs with contested boundaries, and is a contested prize among the two communities. Therefore, the Flemish region and the Flemish-speaking community have chosen to have their headquarters, and the former also its parliament, in Brussels. Furthermore, ethnicity in Europe is no longer only the old divisions. About one in eight inhabitants of Brussels is 'extra-communitarian'.

European Brussels has been built by political stealth and horse-trading, skilfully using and generously paying private capital interests. Most telling is the European Parliament building, which given the uncertainty of its location and the overt opposition of France and Luxemburg, could not officially have started out as such. Instead, it was launched, in 1987, as an 'International Congress Centre', financed by private investors given underhand guarantees. It met with vociferous local opposition, but went through to completion in 1995 (Elmhorn 2001: 219ff.; Hein 2004: 142ff.). Beneath the rhetoric, this, it may be argued, has also been a way of constructing the EU.

Located within the historical weak state-strong cities belt of Europe, on one of the two main cultural cleavages in Western Europe, the Germanic–Latin dividing line – and not far from the second between Catholicism and Protestantism –, Brussels is an excellent site for a Western European Union capital in terms of balance and fairness. If the EU were to split, like the Roman Empire, Vienna would be the most logical equivalent of Constantinople.

However, identities are made of other stuff. As Cavour said in the 1860s debate about the Italian capital: 'The question of capital is not decided […] by strategic reasons. […] The choice of capital is determined by great moral reasons. It is the sentiment of the people which decides questions pertinent to it' (Djament 2005: 372). Well, popular sentiment had nothing to do with the European choice of Brussels. Forty years after the Treaty of Rome, Brussels remains a second-tier European city. Peter Taylor (2004: 203) ranks it seventh in Europe in terms of 'global network connectivity', a league led by London and Paris. Brussels in Europe has the same rank as Washington DC in the USA. Zaventem, Brussels airport, only came in at number 18 among the European airports with respect to the number of passengers, coming in just after Dublin and Stockholm-Arlanda (Eurostat 2007).

In 1912, a Walloon MP told the new king about the situation in Belgium:

> There are Flemings and Walloons in Belgium, but, Your Majesty, there are no Belgians. […] A second sort of Belgian has been formed in the country, primarily in Brussels. But it is in fact of little interest. […]

This population of the capital is not a people: it is an agglomeration of mixed-bloods (*métis*).

(de Heusch 1998: 200)

The Walloon politician turned out to be prescient. Brussels is the capital of a failed nation-state. It is a functional European capital, but its contribution to European identity is confined to its rally of bureaucratic elites and lobbyists. So far, the city of Brussels has made little effort to resemble the role of Washington: 'When Americans make the pilgrimage to Washington they are trying to grasp the nation in its totality', a contemporary American analyst has said (Berlant 1996: 495). European Brussels rather seems to have, in a much lower key, the same distant ambivalence to European citizens that it has to both Flemings and Walloons. As stated by the Flemish writer Stefan Hertmans (1998: 81): 'Brussels is nobody's, and everybody's.'

Notes

1 Capital city history may thus be linked to Stefano Bartolini's (2005) different, more abstract-analytical conception of centre formation.
2 In the larger Vienna of the seventeenth century, the court, state functionaries, aristocracy and their servants made up a third of the population.
3 Anspach, de Brouckère, Buls, Max *et alii*, influential mayors of the nineteenth and early twentieth centuries.
4 In the early 1950s the monument was dismantled and shipped to the outskirts of Brussels, in order to make room for a bridge. Some years later, the famous *Maison du Peuple* by Victor Horta was also taken down.
5 While presumably good on safety, the Finns recently lost a match with the Food Safety Authority to the rich cuisine (and butchers) of Parma.

References

Bartolini, S. (2005) *Restructuring Europe*, Oxford: Oxford University Press.
Berlant, L. (1996) 'The theory of infantile citizenship', in G. Eley and R. G. Suny (eds) *Becoming National*, New York and Oxford: Oxford University Press.
Charle, C. and Roche, D. (2002) (eds) *Capitales culturelles. Capitales symboliques*, Paris: Publications de la Sorbonne.
Commission and Belgian Presidency (2001) *Brussels, Capital of Europe. Final Report*. Online. Available HTTP: < http://ec.europa.eu/dgs/policy_advisers/archives/publications/docs/brussels_capital.pdf > (accessed 6 June 2007).
Derom, P. (2000) *The Statues and Monuments of Brussels*, Antwerp: Pandora Publishers.
Djament, G. (2005) 'Le débat sur Rome capitale. Géohistoire d'une choix de localisation', *L'Espace géographique*, 4: 367–80.
Elmhorn, C. (2001) *Brussels. A reflexive world city*, Stockholm: Almqist & Wiksell International.
Eurostat (2004) *Regional statistics*. Online. Available HTTP: < http://epp.eurostat.ec.europa.eu/portal/page?_pageid=1335,47078146&_dad=portal&_schema=PORTAL > (accessed 6 June 2007).

——(2007) *Statistics in focus: Transport*. Online. Available HTTP: < http://epp.
eurostat.ec.europa.eu/pls/portal/docs/PAGE/PGP_PRD_CAT_PREREL/PGE_CAT_
PREREL_YEAR_2007/PGE_CAT_PREREL_YEAR_2007_MONTH_01/7-
19012007-EN-AP.PDF > (accessed 6 June 2007).
Farvacq-Kitkovic, C. (2005) *Street Addressing and Management of Cities*, Washington DC: World Bank.
Hall, T. (1986) *Planung europäischer Hauptstädte*, Stockholm: Kungl.
Hertmans, S. (1998) 'L'identité comme différence', in A. Pickels and J. Sojcher (eds) *Belgique toujours grande et belle*, Brussels: Revue de l'Université de Bruxelles.
de Heusch, L. (1998) 'Eloge de la bâtardise', in A. Pickels and J. Sojcher (eds), *Belgique toujours grande et belle*. Brussels: Revue de l'Université de Bruxelles.
Hein, C. (2004) *The Capital of Europe*, Westport: Praeger.
Kennedy, R. (1991) *London World City Moving into the 21st Century*, London: HMSO.
Mayor of London (2004) *The Case for London*, London: Greater London Authority.
Monnet, J. (1976) *Mémoires*, Paris: Fayard.
Rogers., R and Eisher, M. (1992) *A New London*, London: Penguin.
Rokkan, S. and Urwin, D. (1980) *Economy, Territory, Identity*, London: Sage.
Ságvári, A. (1993) 'Stadien der Hauptstadtentwicklung und die Rolle der Hauptstädte als Nationalrepräsentanten', in T. Schieder and G. Brunn (eds) *Hauptstädte in europäischen Nationalstaaten*, Munich: Beck.
Stahre, N.-G. (1992) *Stockholms gatunamn*, Stockholm: Stockholms stad.
Taylor, P. (2004) *World City Network*, London: Routledge.
Therborn, G. (2003) 'Entangled modernities', *European Journal of Social Theory*, 6 (3): 293–305.
——(2006) (guest ed.) 'Eastern drama. Capitals of Eastern Europe, 1830s-2006. An introductory overview', *International Review of Sociology*, 16 (2): 209–42.
Tilly, C. (1992) *Coercion, Capital, and European States: A. D. 990–1992*, Oxford: Blackwell.

Part III
Politics and ethics
The regulation of technology

5 Global warming and European political identity

Dimitri D'Andrea

The aim of this chapter is to assess if and to what extent the positions and policies of the European Union (EU) against global warming (GW) can help to define Europeans' political identity and to strengthen the legitimacy of the European institutions. To this end, after a brief description of the politically relevant characteristics of GW, I will assess, first of all, whether and to what degree European policies against climate change, which are described in section 2, are the expression of values and principles (sections 3 and 4); and second, the level of awareness among European citizens of what the Union is doing in this field and of the reasons and values underlying or implied in this action (section 5).

The true testing ground for checking the possibility of whether the EU's policies can boast legitimacy based on values and help consolidate the political identity of Europeans is nevertheless the ability of the European institutions to respect the commitments undertaken on the subject of reducing emissions (section 6) and the ability of the Union and its citizens to shoulder the costs that the policies to limit climate change (CC) will involve beyond Kyoto (section 7). The failure to achieve the Kyoto goals would have a delegitimizing effect on the European institutions, even if this only means their lacking in efficiency, while the inability of the Union and the European citizens to accept the costs that effective policies against CC will require after 2012 would debase all the claims of values and principles to date connected to this type of policy, making them little more than simple rhetoric.

Even before the *efficacy* of the institutions in respecting the commitments and the *effective* ability of Europeans to base their political choices on the values that inspire the anti-CC policies, the possibility that they help build the political identity of Europeans will however depend on the *relevance* that Europeans attribute to the threat of GW (section 8). Political identity is not produced by simply sharing values and principles, but by sharing the political response to the challenge that a particular group of individuals sees as decisive. The role that European policies against GW can have in deepening and *stabilizing* Europeans' political identity, depends, last of all, on recognizing the central importance of the CC challenge and the ability of

Europeans to keep up ethically correct policies when they lead to making sacrifices in terms of wellbeing.

Climate change: characteristics and political consequences

GW is the rise in the average temperature of the earth due to the increase in the concentration of greenhouse gases in the atmosphere. It is an anthropogenic change in the earth's climate due to the ability of some gases – mainly carbon dioxide, methane, nitrous oxide and fluorinated gases – to boost the atmosphere's capacity to maintain the heat that the earth's system receives from the sun. Connected to this phenomenon are some transformations in the environment that cause great damage to human beings' health and activities: from the rise in the average level of the sea due to the melting polar ice caps to the increase in extreme atmospheric events, from the polarization of the climate in the temperate zones to the loss of biodiversity, from the diffusion of pathogens and endemic diseases to the desertification of entire regions. If left to run its course, GW can cause radical damage to the interests of human beings and in the end wipe out the essential resources for human life on the planet (Intergovernmental Panel on Climate Change 2001: 8–13; De Marchi *et al.* 2001: 50–51). The measure of the damage will to a large extent depend on the degree of warming and how quickly it takes place; nevertheless, these factors do not only depend on human activities, but also on the potential domino effect, typical of complex systems, that an abrupt, substantial warming of the atmosphere may have on other variables in the ecosphere. In addition, GW is a phenomenon that does not progress in a linear manner and that possesses great inertia. Therefore, we are certain that the phenomenon causes harm, but we are not able to precisely pinpoint *how* and *when* the damaging events will take place, or the point of no return to use as the basis for calculating how long we can rationally go on 'as usual'. It is not possible to make a rational calculation to maximize the time left because it is impossible to say when the phenomenon may become uncontrollable and irreversible.

The warming of the planet's atmosphere can only be fought if everyone cooperates – citizens, states, supranational institutions, international organizations – but for the next few decades it will neither affect the planet's inhabitants without distinction or all in the same way, nor will it strike with such radical events as to prompt evaluations and concerns that are necessarily and absolutely the same for all (Stern 2006: VIII). And not just that: although the costs of the policies to limit GW must be paid by the present generations, the benefits in terms of damage avoided will only affect future generations. What present generations do in the next two decades will make very little difference to what will happen in the next 40–50 years, but it will definitely affect the condition of the planet's inhabitants at the end of this century and the into the next (Stern 2006: 1).

The Union's policy on climate change

The 1957 Rome Treaty did not explicitly lay down any sphere of competence for the Community on the subject of the environment and did not contain any reference to the protection of the environment and human health. A first development was recorded at the beginning of the 1970s, with the approval of the First Community Action Programme on the Environment (1973), which gave rise to quite an organized Community policy on the environment. In this first phase, the environmental provisions were approved as part of the Community's drive to harmonize the internal market as per Arts 100 and 235. The decisive shift took place in 1987 with the Single European Act (SEA), with the environment appearing for the first time under the specific competence of the Community in Title VII (see Krämer 2004: 54–55). On one hand, the SEA laid down that decisions concerning the environment were to be made by unanimous vote in the Council of Ministers upon proposal of the Commission and after listening to the opinion of the Parliament and the Economic and Social Committee (Art. 130s); on the other hand it transformed the provisions for the establishment and operation of the internal market into a topic that the Council could decide on with a qualified majority (Art. 100a). Therefore, the years immediately after the SEA saw a substantial amount of uncertainty on the legal basis for producing standards. In turn, this also led to an institutional conflict between the Commission, which defended the more 'communitarian' method of Art. 100a, and the Council, which defended the intergovernmental method of unanimity. The controversy was to be resolved by the European Court of Justice, which in case C-300/89[1] ruled Art. 100a as the legal basis for most of the provisions regarding the environment. The Maastricht Treaty was to take a further step in this direction, by explicitly setting down that for all provisions regarding the environment the co-decision procedure laid down in Art. 189c should be followed by qualified majority voting (QMV) in the Council,[2] except for the areas indicated in Art. 130s that require unanimity.[3]

The Union's attention to CC started to transform into concrete policies at the beginning of the 1990s, on one hand with the preparatory work for the Rio Conference (1992[4]), and on the other hand with the Council's decision of 24 June 1993 (Council of the European Communities 1993) which set up a community-monitoring system on greenhouse gas emissions and set the goal to stabilize emissions in 2000 at the same level as 1990. The development of European policies against CC was speeded up by the negotiations in view of the Kyoto summit and by the measures taken in view of respecting the commitments laid down in the protocol. The EU took part in building the international system of regulations for climate control as a separate entity from the member states: it was represented in negotiations by the country which held the term presidency and signed treaties as a party alongside the member states. After the Kyoto Protocol was signed (11 December 1997) and even before it was ratified[5] and came into force (16 February 2005), in 2000 the Commission launched the First European Climate Change Programme (ECCP) 2000–2004 and the Second ECCP in 2005. It is against this background that the main European policies against CC took shape (European Parliament and Council 2001, 2002b, 2003a,b, 2004a,b, 2006). Except for the ratification of the international agreements – which took place upon the unanimous decision of the Council – all the measures with the aim of meeting the Kyoto obligations were approved through QMV in the Council. Therefore, we are dealing with a strongly developed policy, clearly set apart from that of the member states, with a sizeable community dimension.

Climate change and future generations

In order to assess if the European policies against CC can be of any importance for Europeans' political identity, we need first of all to analyse if there are any values and principles, instead of mere converging interests, underlying their creation and/or their specific physiognomy. This and the next sections are devoted specifically to this analysis. Where there is interest *alone*, there is no identity. Political identity is a concept that points to the normative aspects deciding our belonging to the political body: it indicates all the values, principles and images of the world – how they are interpreted and ranked – which determine our sense of belonging to a political entity. The coherence – in the procedures or the outcomes – between these values and principles and the way a policy, a particular institutional set-up or a legal system as a whole works is the foundation of their legitimacy.

Even more than the declarations contained in the legal texts or in the official EU documents, it is the very nature of the phenomenon that testifies an ethical concern at the basis of European policies against CC. The negative consequences in terms of damage to health and human activities connected to GW will not significantly affect present generations. No matter how high they may be, the costs of the fight against CC will be borne by the present generations to the benefit of the future ones: at the present state in time, any cost–benefit calculations relating to CC must be made on an intergenerational basis. The preoccupation about CC cannot count on selfish motivations (boosting the wellbeing of present generations), or on functional imperatives of an economic kind (linked to a calculation of utility for the *same* party). It can only stem from ethical grounds: on the basis of attention to the consequences of our behaviour on other individuals. Limiting CC will certainly also avoid negative consequences for the present generations of the more advanced and more polluting countries, but the unequal spatial and social distribution of the effects of climate change and the uncertainty regarding their timing and extent make it impossible to find in self-interest a sufficient basis for the choice to limit the phenomenon.

This reference to future generations is also evident in the thinking behind European policies (see European Commission 1997: 3). The fight against CC is justified on the basis of recognizing future generations as holders of the same rights as present ones. The value of human dignity ruled in the EU's Charter of Fundamental Rights (2000), on the basis of which everyone has the right to life (Art. 2) and to the respect of their physical and mental integrity (Art. 3), does not only concern those people currently alive, but also future generations.

Besides, the interests of future generations is the notion that gives a meaning to two other central principles often used to justify the commitment against CC: sustainable development and the precautionary principle. With the Maastricht (Art. 2) and the Amsterdam Treaties (Arts 1 §7 and 3c), the idea of sustainable development was included among the principles at the basis of the Union. It is a regulatory principle that has been restated several times as the point of reference for all the EU's environmental policies (see Council of the European Union 2005b: 14) and the idea of sustainability in itself contains the idea of concern for future generations, of a rapport of intergenerational solidarity (Council of the European Union 2006: 4).

On the other hand, the precautionary principle has been one of the fundamental pillars holding up the policies against CC. Despite being recognized in the Union treaties, therefore making it legally valid,[6] it was only in 2000 that the Commission drew up its own clear definition (European Commission 2000: 10), at the same time setting the rules for applying it. The Commission placed its attention on laying down the conditions and methods for using the precautionary principle in defining policies that mainly deal with short- to medium-term risks. Despite this approach, the Commission did not fail to underline that 'the dimension of the precautionary principle goes beyond the problems associated with a short- or medium-term approach to risks. It also concerns the longer run and the wellbeing of future generations' (European Commission 2000: 18). The growing scientific evidence that CC is caused by human activities nevertheless makes it increasingly less necessary to use the precautionary principle while it favours use of an intergenerational prudence principle, for which there is sufficient knowledge of costs and benefits, though they are spread out over different generations.

Justice and intergenerational principles

The presence of values and principles in European policies against CC is nevertheless not limited to this 'foundational' level. In the Union's positions against GW, we can trace the presence of two different principles of justice that come into play in defining how the costs should be shared out in the fight against CC on an international level: the 'polluter pays' principle, and the 'common but differentiated responsibilities' principle. They are two principles that originate from different ways of looking at the idea of responsibility.

The 'polluter pays' principle, formulated for the first time in the 1970s, introduced the idea that the costs of damage caused to nature and human activities should be covered by those who had caused it rather than the taxpayers in general. It was formulated in the sphere of the Union's environmental policies for the first time in the First EC Action Programme on the Environment in 1973 and was explicitly included in the treaties with Art. 130r §2 of the SEA. As part of the Union's policies against CC, the 'polluter pays' principle is at the basis both of the European Emissions Trading Scheme (ETS), and the positions that give the more industrialized nations greater obligations in the fight against GW and in the efforts to mitigate its impact (European Commission 2001: 10) or to facilitate adaptation. In the 'polluter pays' principle, the responsibility is distributed in proportion to the role played in producing the damage: those who contributed more to producing a particular effect are more responsible (see also Council of the European Union 2006: 5).

Connected to the respect of this justice principle is the obligation of the richer countries towards the populations of the poorer ones. The populations of the less developed countries are much more exposed than those of more developed countries to the consequences of climate change. The polluters also possess the material, social and institutional resources that allow them to be to a large extent untouched by the negative consequences of the pollution that they have produced. In this first phase, the consequences of CC essentially affect those who are not responsible and have not gained any advantage by polluting (European Commission 1997: 3). What for rich countries is at most a debatable cost–benefit calculation, for poor countries is damage without advantage.

The other justice principle is instead 'common but differentiated responsibility'. Here the responsibility derives from being involved; the differentiation does not take into account the role played in generating the negative effects, but whether the party in question possesses the tools to take action. We are all responsible but the degree of our obligations is proportional to the power that we have. The 'common but differentiated responsibility' principle is explicitly mentioned in Art. 10 of the Kyoto Protocol and has been reconfirmed several times by the EU (Council of the European Union 2005b: 16, 2006: 8). The reference to power makes responsibility independent from the role played in producing GW, and binds it to possessing the tools needed to take effective measures to fight it. To date, in practice these two principles have given similar results because the countries more responsible for the phenomenon were the richer countries, but in the future these two criteria could clash if the countries with the greater greenhouse gas emissions were to be the less developed ones.

Public awareness and perception

A policy can possess legitimacy based on the values that it protects, and can help consolidate a political identity only if the citizens possess a sufficiently clear idea of its characteristics and its motivations and if they share the values behind it. As far as the EU's policies are concerned, this is anything but a case in point. Very often the Union's policies are hardly perceived by the citizens even when they play a fundamental role in issues that concern everyday life. After having analysed how the EU policies against CC appear in the Union's documents and laws, this section will try to assess the citizens' degree of perception. There are no specific studies devoted to establishing the level of knowledge and type of legitimacy that Europeans attribute to the policies to limit CC, in the same way that more generally there is no Eurobarometer survey specifically devoted to GW rather than generic environmental issues. From these premises, we can only formulate some general considerations based on the knowledge available and on a preliminary qualitative analysis of 3 years (1997, 1998 and 2006) of issues of some European newspapers. The dailies taken into account are *Il Sole 24 Ore*, the *Guardian*, *Le Figaro*, *El Pais* and the *Süddeutsche Zeitung*.

The first consideration concerns the perception of the EU's policies. From a recent Eurobarometer study it emerges that the EU's action on the subject of the environment 'is widely recognized, although it is often deemed insufficient' (Eurobarometer 2006a: 10). The interviewees were able to list many of the initiatives undertaken by the EU in this sector: from the directives on motor vehicle emission control to the signing of the Kyoto Protocol, through the support for the production of energy from alternative sources (Eurobarometer 2006a: 45–46). Greater awareness of the European anti-CC policies also emerges from a comparison between the way in which the EU's role in the fight against GW was carried in some daily newspapers in 1997–98 and how it emerges from the information provided by the same newspapers in 2006. In 1997 – the year of Kyoto – the EU mainly appears as an international player: there are descriptions of its conduct in negotiations, with the spotlight on its distance from US positions. Instead, little or nothing is said of the goals to reduce emissions that the EU had already set and the policies that it had already undertaken. In 2006, besides the increase in dedicated space, there is growing reference to policies on the construction of electrical appliances and automobiles, air transport, energy saving and alternative energies. A lot of space and attention is also devoted, and not just by the financial newspapers, to the National Allocation Plans (NAPs) under the Emissions Trading Scheme and to the European emission rights market. The emission-monitoring activity, the NAPs and the emission rights market have in fact aroused material interest, they have made the fight against CC enter the daily economic, political and administrative life of the single countries. There are still far-reaching differences in the attention reserved by the newspapers to GW, but this transformation of the type of information given by the press can be seen in all the countries under examination.

The second consideration concerns the existence of a generalized agreement over the values and principles behind the policies to fight CC. In the survey quoted above, it explicitly emerges that the EU needs '[...] to exercise pressure on the States – the United States in particular – who have refused to sign the Kyoto Protocol' to ensure 'the safeguard of future generations' (Eurobarometer 2006a: 46). According to another survey, 79 per cent of the public consider that 'passing on a sound environment to the next generation' will be very important for our society in ten years' time. Responsibility for future generations together with the precautionary principle are the references constantly given for justifying the EU's attention to the GW problem in the newspapers too, as it emerges from press analysis. Finally, the more economically advanced countries seem to substantially agree on a strongly regulatory approach to environmental problems centred around singling out binding objectives in view of sharing responsibility:

> 46 per cent of European citizens state that the most effective answer for solving environmental problems is 'making national or European Union regulations stricter, with heavy fines for offenders'. This was already the case during the survey in 2002.
>
> (Eurobarometer 2005a: 35)

The third consideration concerns the perception of the most suitable institutional level for resolving environmental challenges in general and CC in particular. On this topic there seems to be a large gap between those who consider the most appropriate level for dealing with and resolving environmental issues in general to be the Union, and those who instead place their trust in the nation-states: the percentages vary over time, but all in all the two groups balance each other out (Eurobarometer 2005a: 38). Nevertheless, these data need to be interpreted by bearing in mind that 72 per cent of Europeans respond that they are in favour of an increase in the role of the Union on the topic of the environment, whereas only 18 per cent declare that they are for a reduction in the importance of Community decisions on the environment (Eurobarometer 2006c: 40). In this perspective, the divide that emerges in singling out the most appropriate institutional level seems to conform to the need for both the levels to be present rather than a definite preference for one over the other.

Even though there is a lack of information on Europeans' assessment of the policies specifically aimed at limiting CC, emerging from these general considerations is a growing knowledge and awareness of what the Union has been and is doing in this field, and substantial agreement over the values and principles behind its actions.

Questions of efficacy and effectiveness

In order for a particular policy to possess a degree of legitimacy that goes beyond simple legality and to be able to have positive consequences on political identity, the simple presence of an ethical justification of the objectives and means used is not sufficient. It is also necessary on one hand that the institutions are able to effectively achieve the set objectives, and on the other that these objectives are in line with the general purpose and the values behind it. The inability to achieve the chosen objectives or the choice of unsuitable objectives due to the inability to pay the costs that would logically be imposed result in delegitimizing both the policy and the institution that expresses it. When the institutional instrument proves to be unsuitable or when the conflict between interests and values belies the normative foundation of a policy, no decisive contribution can be made to political identity.

In the case of the fight against CC, the question of *efficacy* concerns the respect of commitments undertaken, whereas the *effectiveness* of the ethical motivations concerns the congruence between the commitments that the EU and the citizens are able to make and the purpose pursued. As far as respecting the commitments undertaken is concerned, the EU has already proved able to achieve the objective that it had set itself in 1993 to stabilize CO_2 emissions by 2000 at 1990 levels (European Environment Agency 2006a: 12). With the Kyoto Protocol, the Union is bound to an overall reduction of 8 per cent in CO_2 emissions by 2012. However, in 2006, the emissions trend is anything but in line with the Kyoto objectives:

> By 2010, total EU-23 greenhouse gas emissions are projected to be approximately 2 per cent below 1990 level. This projection is based on member states' own estimates which take into account all existing domestic policies and measures. The projected decline is 5.6 per cent with additional domestic policies and measures.
> (European Environment Agency 2006b: 14)

If we are also to take into account the additional measures laid down, the 8 per cent reduction objective will only be achieved thanks to using the flexible mechanisms set out in the Kyoto Protocol (European Environment Agency 2005a: 18) and using carbon sinks for around 30 per cent of the total reduction laid down. In the pre-Kyoto talks, the EU had strongly opposed the introduction of flexible mechanisms, and the fact that today it is only able to achieve its reduction objectives thanks to these mechanisms is a partial political failure, because it shows the difficulty in operating in line with its strategies.

Further reason for scepticism derives from examining the emissions trends nation by nation. On the basis of the state of emissions in 2004 and the projections until 2010, only two member states (Sweden and the United

Kingdom) are in line with the objectives, whereas seven member states are predicted not to be able to achieve their objectives in any way (European Environment Agency 2006b: 18–19). If we are to assume that the measures will be fully respected and perfectly efficient, the overall objective set for the Union will only be achieved thanks to the fact that some more virtuous countries will fill in the gaps and insufficiencies of others. Around half of the member states will not be able to fulfil the commitments they have taken on even by using the flexible mechanisms allowed for in the Kyoto Protocol. Therefore, even in the rosiest of hypotheses, the Union's success in respecting the international commitments will not be retraceable to an evenly shared effort or political culture.

But the most important question for being able to argue that the European policies against CC are identity-building concerns the capacity of the EU and its citizens to achieve reductions of greenhouse gas emissions that are effectively sufficient to prevent future generations paying the cost for our wellbeing with a drastic reduction in their chances of wellbeing or even the possibility of their survival. The Kyoto Protocol has had an extraordinary political meaning, but it is hardly believable that a 5 per cent reduction will be enough to effectively limit GW. The general goal that the EU has set itself is to avoid an increase in the earth's temperature of more than 2° Celsius compared to the pre-industrial era. In the Sixth Environment Action Programme, the goal of 2° Celsius was judged compatible with a level of concentration of CO_2 of less than or equal to 550 ppm (European Parliament and Council 2002a: 3). More recent studies have made a correction to this estimate in an utterly more pessimistic direction, making it more or less impossible for the goal of an increase in temperature of 2° Celsius or less to be guaranteed by limiting the concentration to around 550 ppm (see Council of the European Union 2005a: 4; Stern 2006: III; European Commission 2005: 3). In light of this, emission cuts in the most developed countries that would be sufficient to achieve the 2° Celsius goal take on huge dimensions: 15–30 per cent by 2020 and 60–80 per cent by 2050. The conclusions of the Union Council of 22–23 March 2005 move in this direction (Council of the European Union 2005b: 16), but what shows an even more definite shift is the position taken by the European Parliament, which proposes setting a goal to make a reduction of '60–80 per cent by 2050' (European Parliament 2005: 4).[7]

Interests and legitimacy

In this perspective, the costs issue becomes crucial. For the European policies against GW to have an effect on the EU's identity they must have a normative dimension. However, whether this is the case will first become clear in the capability of Europeans to sacrifice part of their wellbeing if their principles require them to do so. If respect for the chances of wellbeing for future generations is one of the values shared by Europeans and a possible way of creating a more solid political identity, Europeans must show that they can make this value their criterion for political action even when this means making a sacrifice to their material interests.

It is a question which can only be given a definite answer in the next 10–20 years. Nevertheless, it is possible to formulate some cautiously sceptical considerations by interweaving the difficulties met by the Union in fulfilling the partial and limited commitments set by the Kyoto Protocol with the huge amount of effort that the Union will have to make to curb CC by the amount indicated by its own institutions. In a situation of linear progress, from a technological point of view, an 80 per cent reduction in CO_2 emissions by 2050 means totally upsetting our way of life in a way that goes far beyond merely economic costs and implies totally rewriting social forms, images of wellbeing and production methods. It would mean questioning some fundamental structures of modern Western subjectivity: the absence of limits in using natural resources, the 'more consumption = more wellbeing' equation, maximum exploitation of the possibilities of the technical tools available, the acceleration of consumption and our whole social life.

This cautious scepticism as to the ability of Europeans to stick to a value or a principle when this imposes sacrifices is also somewhat confirmed on a decisively more empirical and by no means conclusive level by the results of a Eurobarometer survey that asked Europeans if they were willing to pay more to have energy produced from renewable sources. Beyond the far-reaching differences from one country to another, the result highlights the difficulty found by Europeans in accepting the economic costs of the fight against CC: 66 per cent of the citizens in the 10 new member states, 51 per cent of the 15 old member states and an average of 54 per cent for the 25-member state EU are not willing to pay more to have energy produced in a sustainable manner. The percentage of those who would be willing to bear economic costs goes down to 24 per cent at the mention of how much would have to be spent, i.e. 5 per cent more compared than current prices. Despite the percentage being higher (+3 per cent) than in a previous survey, only one-quarter of Europeans would be willing to pay 5 per cent more to have energy from renewable sources (Eurobarometer 2006b: 19).

Europeans have been able to promote policies aimed at fighting CC, and they seem able to respect the commitments that they have undertaken, even though the methods used reduce the significance of EU identity because they do not bear proof of a totally generalized agreement over the principles and values behind them. Nonetheless, the disproportion between what has been done and what should be done nourishes a certain scepticism as to the ability of Europeans to maintain a position so imbued with ethical meanings and values, and to coherently follow a path in fighting CC whose costs in economic terms – but not only economic terms – are forecast to be sizeable. The values and principles that are at the basis of the fight against CC can form a significant segment of European political identity only if Europeans show their effectiveness by accepting the costs of various kinds

88 *Dimitri D'Andrea*

connected to the by-now – inevitably – drastic reductions in emissions for an effective response to GW. Europeans can make respecting the right to life of future generations and protecting their right to equal chances of wellbeing one of the elements of a substantial and not rhetorical identity only if they show that they effectively believe in these values by paying the necessary costs. Should Europeans be incapable of paying these costs, the whole justification behind the policies against GW would essentially become mere rhetoric, even though this does not necessarily mean that there would be no positive effect on the political identity of Europeans, as identities are nourished to an extent by rhetoric as well as by deeds.

The question of relevance

Even more than by the possible inability of Europeans to stick to the values and principles at the basis of their policies on CC, the contribution of the policies against GW to the construction of the European identity is invalidated by its scarce *relevance*. In order to be able to carry out a role in building political identity, a particular policy must not only show a credible and solid reference to values and principles, but it must also relate to a problem perceived as central to defining the boundaries of the political body. In order for the sharing of values and principles expressed in a certain policy to lead to the consolidation of a political identity, that particular regulatory core must relate to the fundamental challenge that the individuals have to face. Political identity is consolidated and stabilized when there are common values and principles in relation to a threat that is considered imminent and to the political plan thought to address it.

Can we single out CC as a threat that Europeans consider central? One of the threats that gives a meaning to their being together and decides which political entity they belong to? Though we may not be able to say anything definite on the ethical ability of Europeans to make great sacrifices in terms of wellbeing, we can make some more precise considerations of how Europeans rank GW among the challenges bearing down on the present day. Since the end of the last century, the importance of GW among the environmental risks has progressively increased. In 2002 GW only appeared in eleventh place and only 38 per cent of those interviewed declared that they were very worried about this phenomenon (Eurobarometer 2002: 9–10). The Europeans' perception of environmental risks was still focused on traditional industrial risks, air and water pollution and only secondarily on global risks such as the thinning of the ozone layer and CC. In 2005 the results were very different: CC was put in third place among Europeans' environmental worries (45 per cent), and it was the environmental risk considered most serious by the citizens of the 15 oldest member states (Eurobarometer 2005b: 8–10).

This growth in the relative importance of CC among the environmental risks is also confirmed by the greater attention that the press pays to this topic. In 2006, the number of articles that appeared in the six newspapers analysed here referring to GW in connection to the EU's actions or positions more than doubled compared with 1998 (from 179 in 1998 to 366 in 2006). There are still great differences from country to country (both in absolute terms and in terms of the increase), but it is without doubt a topic that not only has conquered space, but has also taken on a more political dimension, that is, it is increasingly dealt with in connection with concrete choices of policy and with the negotiations for National Allocation Plans as part of the Emissions Trading Scheme.

Despite this quantitative and qualitative change, the threats that model Europeans' expectations and demands from the Union seem to continue to be different. That is, the relative importance of GW among the environmental risks has increased, but the latter are still not at the top of the Europeans' list of worries (Eurobarometer 2006a: 7–8). The main threats that Europeans see weighing down on their future are mainly of an economic and social nature, and principally concern the impact of globalization on crucial aspects of social life such as employment (49 per cent) and the economic situation in general (18 per cent), the solidity of public health systems (18 per cent) and immigration (14 per cent) (Eurobarometer 2006d: 7–8). It is as if the perception of risks connected to climate change were 'suffocated' by more immediate or urgent worries (Eurobarometer 2006a: 18).

At this point, we can draw some conclusions and trace some possible scenarios. Despite the lack of relevance of the problem, the European policies against GW have a legitimacy that outweighs their legality and are justified not just by the fact that they are created in line with the accepted rules of law production. They are policies that at this time possess legitimacy because they pursue aims with ethical foundations that are substantially shared by Europeans. So long as the next steps in the fight against CC do not challenge the solidity of the Europeans' principles, there is a public that has a positive perception of the EU's initiatives in this field and even wants more of Europe. The existence of shared values and principles can bestow strong – not merely legal – legitimacy on the EU policies on GW, but, as GW is coupled with a modest degree of relevance in the citizens' perception, it is not from the anti-CC policies that a significant effect in promoting identity can be expected. In other words, under these conditions it is not agreement over the values and principles created in the fight against CC that is going to trigger a sense of belonging together among Europeans capable of legitimizing the whole European political construction.

The scenario could however change in the near future. As we have seen in the former section, the policies on CC that the EU will have to take up if it wants to stick to its commitment to protect future generations will require vast amounts of money and, what is more, involve increasingly vast spheres of social life. The relevance and visibility of the problem is destined to increase in the same scale as the regulations that it will require. If Europeans keep an ethically oriented approach to the problem, addressing both the interests of the present generations in the poorer countries and those of future generations in all countries, the solution to the problems of employment and social cohesion now perceived as more urgent will enter a string link to the choices made to limit CC. The dramatic character of those choices, the necessity to make hard collective sacrifices in order to save the planet for posterity would then push the questions involved in a more radical policy on CC into the centre of attention for Europeans.

Notes

1 Commission of the European Communities versus Council of the European Communities on the legal basis of the directive on waste from the titanium dioxide industry, Case C-300/89. Judgement of the European Court of Justice of 11 June 1991.
2 Arts 251 and 175 §1 and §3 of the consolidated version of the Treaty establishing the European Community.
3 Art. 175 §2 of the consolidated version of the Treaty establishing the European Community.
4 The EU signed the Convention on climate change on 12 June 1992 at the end of the Conference proceedings and approved the Convention upon decision of the Council on 15 December 1993 (Council of the European Union 1994).
5 See Council of the European Union (2002) – the Community's approval of the Kyoto Protocol.
6 See Art. 174 §2 of the consolidated version of the Treaty establishing the European Community.
7 Similar substantial cuts are forecast by the European Environment Agency (2005b: 35).

References

Cerutti, F. (2001) 'Le sfide globali e l'esito della modernità', in D. D'Andrea and E. Pulcini (eds) *Filosofie della globalizzazione*, Pisa: ETS.
Commission (1997) *Communication: 'Climate Change: the EU approach of Kyoto'*, COM (97) 481 final, Brussels, 1 October 1997.
——(2000) *Communication on the Precautionary Principle*, COM (2000) 1, Brussels, 2 February 2000.
——(2001) *Communication on the Sixth Environment Action Programme of the European Community 'Environment 2010: our future, our choice'*, COM (2001) 31 final, Brussels, 24 January 2001.
——(2005) *Communication: 'Winning the Battle against Global Climate Change'*, COM (2005) 35 final, Brussels, 9 February 2005.
Council of the European Communities (1993) *Council decision of 24 June 1993 for a monitoring mechanism of Community CO2 and other greenhouse gas emissions*, (93/389/EEC), Luxemburg, 24 June 1993.
Council of the European Union (1994) *Council decision 94/69/EC of 15 December 1993 concerning the conclusion of the United Nations Framework Convention on climate change*, Brussels, 15 December 1993.

——(2002) *Council decision of 25 April 2002 concerning the approval, on behalf of the European Community, of the Kyoto Protocol to the United Nations Framework Convention on climate change* (2002/358/CE), Brussels, 25 April 2002.
——(2005a) *Climate Change: medium and longer term emission reduction strategies, including targets. Council conclusions*, 7242/05, Brussels, 11 March 2005.
——(2005b) *European Council, Brussels, 22 and 23 March 2005. Presidency conclusions*, 7619/1/05 REV 1, CONCL 1, Brussels, 23 March 2005.
——(2006) *Review of the EU Sustainable Development Strategy (EU SDS) – Renewed strategy*, DOC 10117/06, Brussels, 9 June 2006.
D'Andrea, D. (2004) 'Rischi ambientali globali e aporie della modernità', in D. Belliti (ed.) *Epimeteo e il Golem*, Pisa: ETS.
De Marchi, B., Pellizzoni, L. and Ungaro, D. (2001) *Il rischio ambientale*, Bologna: Il Mulino.
Eurobarometer (2002) *The Attitudes of Europeans towards the Environment. Standard Eurobarometer 58.0*, European Commission, Public opinion analysis, Brussels. Online. Available HTTP: < http://ec.europa.eu/public_opinion/archives/ebs/ebs_180_en.pdf > (accessed 24 June 2007).
——(2005a) *The Attitudes of Europeans towards the Environment. Special Eurobarometer 217*, European Commission, Public opinion analysis, Brussels. Online. Available HTTP: < http://ec.europa.eu/public_opinion/archives/ebs/ebs_217_en.pdf > (accessed 24 June 2007).
——(2005b) *Social Values, Science and Technology. Special Eurobarometer 225*, European Commission, Public opinion analysis, Brussels. Online. Available HTTP: < http://ec.europa.eu/public_opinion/archives/ebs/ebs_225_report_en.pdf > (accessed 24 June 2007).
——(2006a) *The European Citizens and the Future of Europe. Qualitative study in the 25 member states*, OPTEM, European Commission, Public opinion analysis, Brussels. Online. Available HTTP: < http://ec.europa.eu/public_opinion/quali/ql_futur_en.pdf > (accessed 24 June 2007).
——(2006b) *Attitudes towards Energy. Special Eurobarometer 247*, European Commission, Public opinion analysis, Brussels. Online. Available HTTP: < http://ec.europa.eu/public_opinion/archives/ebs/ebs_247_en.pdf > (accessed 24 June 2007).
——(2006c) *The Future of Europe. Special Eurobarometer 251*, European Commission, Public opinion analysis, Brussels. Online. Available HTTP: < http://ec.europa.eu/public_opinion/archives/ebs/ebs_251_en.pdf > (accessed 24 June 2007).
——(2006d) *Standard Eurobarometer 65. First Results*, European Commission, Public opinion analysis, Brussels. Online. Available HTTP: < http://ec.europa.eu/public_opinion/archives/eb/eb65/eb65_first_en.pdf > (accessed 24 June 2007).
European Environment Agency (EEA) (2005a) *Annual Report*, Copenhagen: EEA.
——(2005b) *European Environment Outlook*, Report 4/2005, Copenhagen: EEA.
——(2006a) *Annual European Community Greenhouse Gas Inventory 1990–2004 and Inventory Report 2006*, Report 6/2006, Copenhagen: EEA.
——(2006b) *Greenhouse Gas Emission Trends and Projections in Europe 2006*, Report 9/2006, Copenhagen: EEA.
European Parliament (2005) *Resolution on 'Winning the battle against global climate change'*, 2005/2049 (INI).
European Parliament and Council (2001) *Directive 2001/77/EC on the promotion of electricity produced from renewable energy sources in the internal electricity market*, Brussels, 27 September 2001.

—— (2002a) *Decision no. 1600/2002/EC laying down the Sixth Community Environment Action Programme*, Brussels, 22 July 2002.
—— (2002b) *Directive 2002/91/EC on energy performance of buildings*, Brussels, 16 December 2002.
—— (2003a) *Directive 2003/30/EC on the promotions of biofuels or other renewable fuels for transport*, Brussels, 8 May 2003.
—— (2003b) *Directive 2003/87/EC establishing a scheme for greenhouse gas emission allowance trading within the Community and amending Council Directive 96/61/EC*, Luxembourg, 13 October 2003.
—— (2004a) *Decision no. 280/2004/EC concerning a mechanism for monitoring Community greenhouse gas emissions and for implementing the Kyoto Protocol*, Strasbourg, 11 February 2004.
—— (2004b) *Directive 2004/101/EC amending Directive 2003/87/EC establishing a scheme for greenhouse gas emission allowance trading within the Community, in respect of the Kyoto Protocol's project mechanisms*, Strasbourg, 27 October 2004.
—— (2006) *Regulation (EC) no. 842/2006 on certain fluorinated greenhouse gases*, Brussels, 17 May 2006.
Intergovernmental Panel on Climate Change (IPCC) (2001) *Climate Change 2001: synthesis report. Summary for policy-makers*. Online. Available HTTP: < http://www.grida.no/climate/ipcc_tar/vol4/english/pdf/spm.pdf > (accessed 24 June 2007).
Krämer, L. (2004) 'The roots of divergence: a European perspective', in N. J. Vig and M. G. Faure (eds) *Green Giants? Environmental policies of the United States and the European Union*, Cambridge, MA: MIT Press.
Stern, N. (2006) *The Economics of Climate Change. Executive summary*. Online. Available HTTP: < http://www.hm-treasury.gov.uk/independent_reviews/stern_review_economics_climate_change/stern_review_report.cfm > (accessed 24 June 2007).

6 EU food safety policy and public debate

Elena Acuti

This chapter aims to reconstruct European Union (EU) food safety policies by investigating if and how they can help to strengthen the legitimacy of the Union as well as its citizens' sense of belonging together.

It is important to state that this study considers food safety policies as a whole, without making any differentiations between actual food scandals (relating mainly to the cases of bovine spongiform encephalitis (BSE) in the UK in 1996 and dioxin in Belgium in 1999) and the controversies revolving around the use of green biotechnology (in particular genetically modified organisms (GMOs), which affect food safety only indirectly.

There are two main reasons for this choice. First of all, rather than their technical details, what interests me about these particular policies are the specifically European values in the notion of safety behind them.

Second, I am interested in the institutional conditions in which the specifically European set of principles in this policy area was shaped, setting the EU apart from other international players, in particular the USA.

The research starts off with a historical and political presentation of how Europe has dealt with food risk over the past 30 years. The aim of this first section is to highlight the progressive centralization of food safety policies, with a shift from the member states to the European institutions. Following on from this is a description of the current EU food risk policy as well as the principles that influence it (the precautionary principle and the freedom of choice principle). I will then concentrate on the specific nature of EU food risk policies in relation both to the member states and the other international players, such as the USA, by taking the dispute over GMOs as a brief case study. In the final part of the chapter I will underline the importance of these EU policies in the process to build a European political identity and strengthen its legitimacy.

The European Union and food biotechnology: a 30-year debate

The following reconstruction of the last 30 years of historical and political events concerning food biotechnology shows the influence that the institutional evolution of the European Community/Union (EC/EU) has had on the structure of food safety policies and on how they are perceived by the citizens. Indeed, factors such as the perception of food risk, the development of a public debate and the trust between citizens and institutions can at least in part be linked to reactive post-crisis attitudes and to the immaturity of the EU institutions in particular periods of their history.

From 1973, when the recombinant DNA technique was successfully used for the first time in the USA, almost until the beginning of the 1990s, the European states were split between the *forerunners* (which made a set of rules based on a scientific approach), including Great Britain, Sweden, France, Switzerland and Germany, and the *latecomers* (which merely adopted a 'wait and see' approach), including the Mediterranean countries, Ireland, Finland, Austria, Belgium, Luxembourg and Norway.

This first phase was characterized by an almost total lack of public debate and a notion of risk assessed only according to criteria of the scientific community. In 1978 a second phase began, with Great Britain revising its legislation on recombinant DNA. As a consequence, it was put in the new category of low-risk technology regulated by more flexible standards. This decision was linked to the gradual introduction of biotechnology to the commercial and industrial sphere which attracted the interest of new political and social players (non-governmental organizations (NGOs) and consumers, largely in favour of the adoption of a precautionary approach). As a result, the topic entered the public sphere.

In the 1980s a Europe-wide shift in the political landscape towards conservative governments favoured a widespread competitive economic mentality that strongly encouraged the commercialization of biotechnologies. On the other hand, a public debate was slowly opening up which would lead to an evolution in the very notion of risk, to also include social and moral elements, such as worries about the irreversibility of change in the ecosystem as a consequence of releasing GMOs into the environment.

The need for a legal definition of the industrial activities in the biotechnological field and the risk of the market breaking up because of the differences in national legislation caused the European Commission to intervene. After the failure of some proposals in 1979 and 1986, the EC issued two directives on GMOs in 1990, the year marking the beginning of the third phase in the evolution of the EC attitude. They were the Contained Use (of GMOs) Directive (90/219/EC, 1990) and the Deliberate Release Directive (90/200/EC, 1990), which guaranteed permission to trade GMOs within the EC, while the decisions on releasing them remained under the competence of the national governments (European Parliament and Council 1990a,b). The two directives were a compromise between the requests to regulate the field that had emerged during the debate, and the tendency to establish a notion of risk strongly concentrated around scientific aspects only.[1]

At the same time, there was a decrease in the public debate, also because of the differentiation between agricultural and medical biotechnologies.

Therefore, even though the former may have met with great opposition, the public was more willing to accept the therapeutic possibilities opened up by the latter.[2]

A fourth phase was inaugurated as a consequence of the BSE emergency. The first case of BSE in Great Britain was seen in 1982, and at the end of the 1980s it led to a ban by some states against meat from British cattle. This was followed by bans by the EC (Decision no. 89/469 of 28 July 1989 issued on 18 July 1998 and Decision no. 90/200 of 9 April 1990) that were withdrawn, along with an inspection programme, between 1990 and 1994 following the intensification of British checks on meat put on the market (Lezaun and Groenleer 2006). On 20 March 1996, the British government admitted that there was a possible link between the BSE that affected cattle and a new strain of Creutzfeldt–Jacob disease. The scandal that followed was characterized in public opinion by a 'growing distrust in scientific experts and political regulators in matters of food safety, since they had been reassuring the public for a long time that there was no evidence for such a link' (Torgersen et al. 2002: 62).

The arrival of genetically modified (GM) soy and corn from the USA just a few months after the 'mad cow' scandal was met with great scepticism by European consumers. Despite the lack of scientific grounds, citizens tended to assimilate the BSE crisis with the risks connected to GMOs, grouping them together under the category of unexpected consequences stemming from excessively forcing the traditional agricultural production and breeding processes (Torgersen et al. 2002). As a result, the problem became a commercial as well as a political one.

In the following years, two new crises concerning food safety helped strengthen European food risk regulations: the case of dioxin in the chicken industry in Belgium, discovered in 1999, and the introduction of a type of GM corn (Bt10) not authorized for release in the environment, which was discovered in 2005. Indeed, these scandals encouraged the adoption of joint standards (such as the ones collected in the White Paper on Food Safety, see Commission 2000a). As a result, the differences between the member states' provisions were reduced, new consultative bodies specifically devoted to risk assessment (among which the European Food Safety Authority in 2002) were set up, and the Commission was made to gradually return to a food risk management method not simply based on scientific risk assessment (Lezaun and Groenleer 2006).

The Bt10 crisis seems to have been particularly relevant because it underlined the will of the EU to present itself as a unitary political actor on the international scene. In 2005 this variety of transgenic corn not authorized for release in the environment had been put on the US market and, given the intense exchanges between the USA and the EU, had probably reached European markets. This case was characterized by a sense of a lack of urgency in taking action, since the threat concerned substances (GMOs) that had already been studied by teams of scientists and 4 years had passed since the suspected marketing had begun. This meant that, from a scientific point of view, the advisory committees had already stated that there was a potential risk linked to GMOs. From a practical point of view, since these substances had been imported 4 years before, their hypothetical dangerous effects were probably already in action. The member states, brought together by the Commission in a meeting of the Standing Committee on the Food Chain and Animal Health, were almost in total agreement (with 22 out of 23 votes in favour) about the adoption of emergency measures, even if this was more significant as an act of dissent from the policies followed by the USA than as a technical measure concerning a *fait accompli*.

According to Javier Lezaun and Martijn Groenleer (2006), the provisions adopted by the European institutions mainly show the desire to appear as *a single political player*, with a specific legislative structure concerning food safety. As it concerned actions taken against an external country, the USA, and placed the same obligations on all the European member states, it led to quite a homogeneous reaction and helped strengthen the idea of unity within the EU.

Lastly, the episodes distinguishing the last decade of European food risk management are particularly important due to the emergence of two guiding principles, the precautionary principle and the freedom of choice principle, which will be dealt with in the following section.

Food safety in Europe: principles and values

The European food risk policies feature a particularly precautionary attitude and attention to protecting the consumer's freedom of choice.[3]

The *precautionary principle* (first mentioned in the Maastricht Treaty, Art.130/2, 1993) became increasingly important in Europe after the BSE food scandal. Such a principle can be applied in cases in which 'potentially dangerous effects deriving from a phenomenon, product or process have been identified, [when] scientific evaluation does not allow the risk to be determined with sufficient certainty' (Commission 2000b: 4).

From a theoretical point of view the precautionary principle seems to present some similarities with Jonas' *The Imperative of Responsibilities* (Jonas 1984), even though Jonas does not use those actual words (Sandin 2005; Van den Belt 2003). His argument is based on the fact that technology's scope is greater than ever before, and that our technological decisions are prone to having vast consequences for the future of humankind (Sandin 2005). Environmentalists often hold that modern biotechnology has 'apocalyptic potential' because it tampers with the basic processes of life. If we release GMOs into the environment, the ultimate consequences for the natural flora and fauna are extremely hard to predict but may well be irreversible. So the precautionary principle is conceived as the basic rule for dealing with fundamental scientific uncertainty (Van den Belt 2003).

From a more empirical point of view, the precautionary principle marks a great innovation in risk management strategies and has several functions (Christoforou 2004). The most important of these functions is that it obliges[4] the authorities dealing with risk to adopt political provisions in the absence of a positive estimate of the certainty and degree of the damage. As expressly shown in EC Regulation no. 178/2002,

> it is recognised that scientific risk assessment alone cannot, in some cases, provide all the information on which a risk management decision should be based, and that other factors relevant to the matter under consideration should legitimately be taken into account including societal, economic, traditional, ethical and environmental factors and the feasibility of controls.
> (European Parliament and Council 2002, Art. 19)

Therefore, the precautionary principle was adopted with the twofold aim to 'ensure health protection in the Community' (Art. 20) and 'to regain the trust of the general public and consumers in the European institutions' regulations' (Art. 22).

The desire to regain the citizens' confidence can also be seen in the establishment of a politically *neutral scientific authority*, the European Food Safety Authority (EFSA), and in the transparent labelling policy. Indeed, with the establishment of the EFSA in 2002, a division was made between scientific assessment and political management of the risk. As a consequence, the assessment processes can be more transparent, and it is also possible to involve an informed but not necessarily expert public during the decision-making stage. In addition, it also guarantees that information really is available (the actions of the EFSA must be made public), making it easier to trace political responsibility.

Furthermore, consumers are guaranteed the freedom to choose using the information given on labels[5] (EC Regulations 1829/2003 and 1830/2003, see European Parliament and Council 2003a,b). Attention to the traceability of foodstuffs and transparent labelling seems to underline an anti-paternalistic attitude within the European institutions (unlike in the USA) which places the freedom of choice principle on the same level as consumer protection (Anderson 1999; Teitel and Wilson 1999). The provisions relating to labels have obtained a very large degree of consensus among the European public, even though this has not been sufficient to overcome the sceptical attitude relating to the consumption of GMOs (see below).

What values can be made out behind the creation of the two principles described? On the one hand, the precautionary principle seems to allude to a particular conception of science and technology. Indeed, 'its growing popularity in Europe reflects the perception that scientific knowledge is an insufficient guide to regulatory policy' (Cameron 1999). On the other hand, investment in science[6] is the main tool in order to achieve the goal of the

Lisbon strategy (Commission 2001b). Let us also note that the notion of science put across by the European elites seems to be in line with the notion defined by the European Group on Ethics in Science and New Technologies (EGE). According to EGE, 'science and technology must increase – and not decrease – freedom and choice for everyone' in the context of a European civilization where any replacement of any element of 'nature or tradition' by scientific or technological means must depend on the capacity 'to show more active generosity than nature or tradition show' (European Group on Ethics in Science and New Technologies 2000: 3).[7] On the whole, rather than expressing scepticism towards science, the EU institutions are interested in promoting risk management policies that also include values such as respect for human dignity, the freedom of choice principle and public participation (Commission 2002).

Opinion surveys also seem to confirm that European citizens have a similar positive view of science: 38.13 per cent think that science will improve our living conditions against 12.4 per cent who claim that it may make them worse (European Values Survey 2000b). This goes alongside the Europeans' clear preference for the co-habitation of man and nature rather than the domination of man over nature: 91.8 per cent in the EU versus 84.6 per cent in the USA favour *co-habitation*; 6.15 per cent in the EU versus 14.5 per cent in the USA favour *domination* (European Values Survey 2000a).[8]

This attitude can be assumed to be one of the roots of the Europeans' sceptical attitude concerning the use of biotechnology in agriculture, whereas the use of these techniques is more accepted in the medical and therapeutic field (Eurobarometer 2005c). Another root can be traced to, as Ian Welsh puts it, 'values relating to the exercise of choice and control over food consumed, which in Europe has centuries of cumulative cultural codes codified in "consumer protection" legislation' (Welsh 2006: 63–64). A final reason is probably the fact that the European public cannot clearly see the positive results of food biotechnology on health. Even if eating GM foods were assessed as sufficiently 'safe', the absence of immediately recognizable benefits would leave the consumer with a feeling of scepticism.

The legitimization of the EU policies on biotechnology relies on the citizens sharing their philosophical premises but also being ready to accept their social costs. These costs include an increase in the price of food, due to traditional but more expensive agricultural techniques, and to the implementation of a traceability policy through labelling. This is exactly the case in the EU, where 53 per cent of the public would be willing to pay a higher amount to buy food that is not genetically modified (Eurobarometer 2002). This is despite the fact that the principles behind European food safety policies might conflict with the solidarity principle, when forcing African countries to refuse GM seeds sent by the USA for fear that the European market would refuse agricultural products deriving from these (Patterson and Josling 2005; Tsioumani 2004).

Recent history, institutional assets and diverging principles: explaining transatlantic differences on GMOs.

Whether or not the EU can be regarded as *one* player in biosafety policy can be analysed by looking at the EU–US dispute on GMOs.

Since 1998, the opposition in Europe to GM food has become increasingly tough (Torgersen *et al.* 2002). On the occasion of the European Council of Ministers for the Environment (June 1999), France, Denmark, Greece, Italy and Luxembourg declared that they would not authorize imports of GMOs until suitable measures had been taken to ensure transparency and information by reviewing labelling standards.[9] Austria, Belgium, Finland, Germany, Holland, Spain and Sweden declared that they would maintain a widely precautionary attitude, without placing an actual ban. As a result, the outcome of this meeting was a *de facto* moratorium on GM products. Then the EU negotiated new rules on the protection of food safety relating to GMOs (European Parliament and Council 2002) that also included a reform of the labelling standards (April 2004), and in May 2004 the moratorium was withdrawn.

The main argument used to explain this step was that such an extreme interpretation of the precautionary principle (closure of an entire market to a product whose safety could not be scientifically documented) could not only be accused of protectionism – an accusation brought by the USA against the EU in the dispute at the World Trade Organization (WTO) in 2003 – but could also damage the freedom of choice principle. To all appearances, the EU proved to be adamant to carry on with its own regulatory model, that is, it did not withdraw the moratorium until a suitable law had been drawn up to regulate the internal GMO market.

Therefore, the EU appears on the international stage as a *unitary player* with its own strategy:[10] the authorization for imports given by the Union was an indication of the Commission's ability to take political responsibility (Lezaun and Groenleer 2006) and to approve a product in spite of the lack of consent by some member states, notably Denmark, Greece, France, Luxembourg, Austria and Portugal (Tsioumani 2004). So, it can be concluded that within the EU polity there is a tendency towards a progressive unity of action, despite the differences that still persist between the member states (for example, the degree of involvement of the public in decision-making processes, the influence of NGOs and consumers, the role of 'green' parties, the production capacity of the biotechnology and chemical industries, the various approaches to agriculture and the different ways of looking at the technological risk) (Torgersen *et al.* 2002; Patterson and Josling 2005).

The relationships between the member states themselves, and between them and the EU highlight three main factors.

First of all, there is a *common basis* of culture and values underlying the perception of food risk, even if this does not cancel out the differences described above (Assemblée des Régions d'Europe 2006).

Second, the member states might diverge in their position on a specific GMO issue, but there is a strong effort on the EU's part to apply its biosafety principles in the *whole* European area. Divergences among the member states might be regarded as obstacles to the emergence of a European political identity on this issue, but can also be regarded as fruitful components of a European public debate in which not only citizens but also member state governments take part.

Third, the existence of a European internal market adds a further element to this public debate: how is it possible to guarantee effective *protection* for this market? Are the European institutions able to guarantee it? In other words, trust in the EU also results from its ability to deliver this new type of good.

The GMO dispute is also significant because it highlights differences and similarities between the EU and USA in their risk regulation models. As we have seen, these differences can be regarded as the expression of different cultural, social and political identities. However, where do such differences come from? How important is recent social and political history? How important are institutional structures? I would argue that two facts have contributed to the transatlantic differences in normative preferences: the crises that Europe has experienced since the 1990s, and the different institutional structures of the two main actors. Before dealing with these explanatory factors, let me introduce a core difference in the European and US biosafety models.

The current European model (Patterson and Josling 2005) is a *process-based*, 'horizontal' and precautionary paradigm. This means that it pays more attention to the process through which the product is obtained than to the actual characteristics of the product itself. The regulations adopted are drawn up *ex novo* and are applied across the board (*cross-cutting regulations*) to different goods obtained using the same procedure. In addition, the precautionary attitude also involves a pro-active approach with the aim of avoiding hypothetical environmental damage that has not yet been detected, but could reasonably be expected to happen.

On the other hand, the current US *product-based* model pays more attention to the product rather than the production process and is 'vertical' (Patterson and Josling 2005). Therefore, the finished object alone is assessed for risk. This means that GM products are subject to the same laws as 'natural' crops, depending on the specific sector that they belong to, for example, fertilisers or food. What is more, the preventive approach is also mainly reactive and aims at reducing environmental damage as much as possible once it has scientifically been proven (Patterson and Josling 2005).

The division between the European 'precautionary' model and the American product-based one (Patterson and Josling 2005) became relevant at the beginning of the 1990s. In the previous two decades, aspects of both models played a significant role in biotechnology management both in Europe and in the USA. Let us remember that from the middle of the 1960s

EU food safety policy and public debate 101

to around the middle of the 1980s, the environmental and consumer protection standards in the USA were stricter and more innovative than those of the EU and of each of its member states. However, since the 1990s environmental law in Europe has become much stricter and more precautionary than in America (Vogel 2005). A large part of the explanation for this trend has to do with Europe's food crises, as we have seen above. Not only has the USA not had to deal with serious food crises in recent years, but the type of public debate, nourished by the media, generated in the USA, has mainly paid attention on the beneficial effects for the environment and for human health that can stem from genetic manipulation techniques (Gaskell *et al.* 2002). On the contrary, the European media has nourished scepticism towards biotechnology, constantly highlighting the uncertainty and exposure to risk factors.[11] Furthermore, the green parties have played a much more active role in Europe than in America (Patterson and Josling 2005).

Alongside the reaction to the food crises and their coverage by the media, a further factor which explains transatlantic differences has to do with the different institutional *decision-making structures* in the USA and the EU. When the USA started to become increasingly sensitive towards ecological topics around the middle of the 1960s, it was of course a sovereign state with all the constitutional, institutional, economic and political requirements needed to come up with a coherent political strategy to protect the environment. When the technology relating to genetic modifications started to be developed, the USA had a well-structured regulatory system (Vogel 2005) which was more open to suggestions from the scientific community (Torgersen *et al.* 2002), circumstances which favoured a more flexible response and a more tolerant attitude towards new technology in the agricultural and food sectors. This clearly could not be the case in Europe.

To sum up, there are now clear divergences between the USA and the EU, but rather than being grounded on long-term cultural differences, they seem to be the result of a more recent reinterpretation of core social principles in light of a response to specific crises within an immature institutional context. This reinterpretation has involved both EU institutions and the European public, as we will see from the analysis of opinion polls in the next section.

What the Europeans think about food safety

In reviewing the European press I selected the three events I have referred to in this chapter: the BSE scandal in Britain, the dioxin case in Belgium and the introduction of the Bt10 variety of transgenic corn.

For the first event I considered *The Times* (along with *The Sunday Times*), the *Guardian*, *La Stampa*, *Il Sole 24 Ore*, *Le Figaro*, *Libération*, *El Pais*, *El Mundo*, the *Süddeutsche Zeitung* and *Die Welt*, as well as the weekly *Der Spiegel* in the period March–June 1996 plus a sample of British newspapers (the *Daily Mirror*, the *Independent*, the *Telegraph*, *The Financial Times*, the *Evening Standard*, the *Herald* and the *Observer*) in the month of March 1996. In both cases there were on average 1.2 articles per day. However, the articles where the BSE food scandal was linked to the EU constituted 11.36 per cent of the whole amount, i.e. less than one out of four. On comparing the continental European newspapers with the British newspapers, two different views of the EU became evident. The former group of newspapers considered the EU a positive actor that guaranteed application of the controls required to protect the EU internal market (ban on British beef), whereas the latter claimed that the EU made the UK market pay too high a price by forbidding the exportation of meat. In both cases, the EU was perceived as a unitary actor with technical and 'neutral' competences.

The dioxin scandal (in the period June–August 1999) was given less coverage in the European newspapers (less than 0.7 articles per day on average). However, the trend was much the same as for the BSE scandal. European newspapers contained quite an ambiguous message: on the one hand, the EU was seen as putting strict controls on the national interest (remember that the Belgian authorities did not immediately inform the EU of the dioxin emergency because they feared a EU ban on the sale of their chicken meat), while on the other hand, there was an overall lack of trust in the European institutions as they usually intervened once the damage had already been done. The EU institutions did not seem to perform well during the preventive phase.

The importation of Bt10 transgenic corn (March–April 2005) is an important case study because it belongs both to the food scandal issue and the GMO debate. Owing to the lack of urgency, it was not a true food scandal like in the previous cases and the European press gave it less relevance (0.1 article per day on average). However, this event helped to revitalize the debate on GMOs, which has since remained more or less constant. In addition, it was also a very important period because it was immediately before the French referendum on the EU Constitutional Treaty, so the debate on GMOs was very often linked (92 per cent) to the EU and sometimes (46.15 per cent of cases) in the French press the GMO debate and agricultural policy were explicitly linked to the referendum vote.

It is relevant to state that from 1996 until 2005, in relation to food safety policy, the EU was increasingly regarded abroad as a unitary actor also having a clear role on the international scene. As a unitary actor, the EU was seen as a *quasi-polity* that should have the technical skills (availability of advisory boards, a body of laws) to guarantee food safety within its borders. At the same time these potentials were not considered fully developed: the EU was seen as slow in reacting and not very strict in its controls during the prevention phase.

In general, food safety issues (including both food scandals and the GMO debate) are present in the European press even in times of no crisis.

The member states where these issues are more debated in the press are the ones that have been involved in a food scandal, such as the UK, and the ones with an old, strong cultural food tradition, such as Italy and France. The same issue is seen differently by Italy and France and the UK: in the UK the focus is more on the institutional aspect, whereas in France and Italy the EU is seen more as the defender of typical culinary traditions and of safe lifestyles.

Conclusion

Although the Europeans do not mention past food crises among the main sources of risk (Eurobarometer 2006), the reticence shown towards the consumption and production of GMOs seems to prove that the latter are a perceived risk. Furthermore, the press review in particular shows that the GMO topic underwent intensive debate precisely because the threat is perceived in quite a similar manner in the various member states. As already noted, the Europeans do not link the perception of the risk related to GMOs to a widespread lack of trust in science, towards which they profess a feeling of optimism. In fact, the sceptic attitude concerning the use of biotechnology in the agricultural and food sectors also seems to be linked to doubts in the citizens' minds towards European institutions, which were developed following failures to regulate risk in past food crises.

If it is true that a specific European way of seeing science and the man–nature relationship can be identified behind the EU's and the Europeans' attitude towards green GMOs, it is also true that this attitude is based on pre-existent values that have been restyled because of a new perception of risk. The message as far as European political identity and EU legitimacy are concerned is clear: crises are crucial moments in the formation of trust and in the condensation and institutionalization of guiding principles. The current policies within the EU are the result of the recent crises and of the multilevel system of governance that exists within the EU and which makes decisions and their implementation highly complex enterprises. Although the effectiveness of EU regulation depends greatly on the member states' capacity to implement its rules, the failure to '[protect] the European consumers market' will be regarded as inadequacy on the part of the EU, thereby having a negative impact on the EU's legitimacy as a political actor and as a space of identity formation.

Today, the feeling of confidence in the European political authorities, which weakened during the past food scandals, could be regained by developing a debate with European citizens that gives civil society a more influential role in the decision-making processes. Involving civil society in the decision-making process was taken into consideration by the EU Commission during a meeting held in Brussels in June 2002 (European Convention 2002) among the European institutions[12] and some organizations,[13] but this kind of participation needs to be further improved. Indeed, wider involvement of the public in decision-making processes would in turn require an improvement in the information available and more transparency in allocating responsibility to the various actors.

Acknowledgements

For their useful suggestions, I wish to thank Luigi Pellizzoni, Javier Lezaun and Wynn Grant as well as the other participants in this collective research, in particular Renata Badii and Dimitri D'Andrea.

Notes

1 Nevertheless, the latter aspect was modified in part in the amendment to Directive 94/15/EC (European Parliament and Council 1994).
2 See also the following section and Renata Badii's chapter in this volume.
3 Art 5.7 of the SPS (Sanitary and Phytosanitary) Agreement and TBT (Technical Barriers to Trade) Agreement; see World Trade Organization (1994, 2001).
4 See *Treaty of Amsterdam, amending the Treaty on European Union, the Treaties establishing the European Communities and related Acts*, Art. 174 (2).
5 'One basic condition is that the GM food (or feed) must be labelled. This is to give consumers a choice: either to buy the product in question or to choose something else'; speech by Commissioner David Byrne, see Byrne (2001).
6 Consider also the proposals to bring science closer to the needs of civil society: see Commission (2001b).
7 The EGE probably uses the term 'generosity' to refer to the capacity to produce more benefits relating not only to the economy, but to the whole quality of life. The European Group on Ethics in Science and New Technologies (set up in 1991) is a neutral, independent, pluralist and multidisciplinary body whose task is to examine ethical questions arising from science and new technologies. On this basis, the EGE provides the European Commission with opinions in connection with the preparation and implementation of Community legislation or policies.
8 See also Eurobarometer (2006, 2005a).
9 That is by reviewing the Directive 90/220/EEC.
10 This attitude was also perfectly evident to the other players involved: the USA, Argentina and Canada (Tsioumani 2004).
11 Think of the exposure given in the European press and TV networks to symbolic anti-GMO events organized by anti-globalization icons such as José Bovet.
12 Represented by David Lawrence, Director of Directorate-General A: Sustainable Development and Policy Support of the Commission's Environment DG, who presented the projects of the Environment Directorate-General.
13 Statements were then made by representatives of the following organizations: the Eurogroup for Animal Welfare, European Agricultural Convention, European Landowners' Organization, European Women's Lobby and the European Environmental Bureau.

References

American Corn Growers Foundation (ACGF) (2001) *2001 ACGF Corn Producers Survey GMO's & Markets.* Online. Available HTTP: < http://www.acgf.org/programs/GMO2001Survey/GMO2001Survey.htm > (accessed 18 June 2007).

Anderson, L. (1999) *Genetic Engineering, Food and our Environment – A brief guide*, Devon: Green Books.
Assemblée des Régions d'Europe (2006) 'Les OGM n'ont aucune frontière', *Libération*, 6 April, 2006.
Byrne, D. (2001) *The Right to Know about Genetically Modified Food*, 25 July 2001. Online. Available HTTP: < http://ec.europa.eu/food/fs/gmo/biotech07_en.pdf > (accessed 18 June 2007).
Cameron, J. (1999) 'The precautionary principle', in G. Sampson and W. B. Chambers (eds) *Trade, Environment, and the Millennium*, Tokyo, New York and Paris: United Nations University Press.
Chang, H. F. (2003) *Risk Regulation, Endogenous Public Concerns, and the Hormones Dispute: nothing to fear but fear itself?* Research Paper no. 03–25, Institute for Law and Economics, University of Pennsylvania Law School. Online. Available HTTP: < http://papers.ssrn.com/sol3/papers.cfm?abstract_id=432220#PaperDownload > (accessed 18 June 2007).
Christoforou, T. (2004) 'The precautionary principle, risk assessment, and the comparative role of science in the European Community and the US legal system', in V. J. Norma and M. G. Faure (eds) *Green Giants? Environmental policies of the United States and the European Union*, Cambridge, MA: MIT Press.
Commission (2000a) *White Paper on Food Safety*, COM (1999) 719 final, Brussels, 12 January 2000. Online. Available HTTP: < http://ec.europa.eu/dgs/health_consumer/library/pub/pub06_en.pdf > (accessed 18 June 2007).
——(2000b) *Communication on Precautionary Principle*, Brussels, 2 February 2000.
——(2001a) *Communication: 'Towards a Strategic Vision of Life Sciences and Biotechnology'*, COM (2001) 454 final, Brussels, 4 September 2001. Online. Available HTTP: < http://ec.europa.eu/biotechnology/pdf/doc_en.pdf > (accessed 18 June 2007).
——(2001b) *Communication: 'Science and Society Action Plan'*, COM (2001) 714 final, Brussels, 4 December 2001.
——(2002) *Communication: 'Life Sciences and Biotechnology – A Strategy for Europe'*, COM (2002) 27 final, Brussels, 23 January 2002.
——(2005) *Response Statistics for Community Action Plan on Animal Welfare and Protection: welfare and protection of farmed animals*. Online. Available HTTP: < http://ec.europa.eu/food/consultations/action_plan_farmed_background_en.htm > (accessed 18 June 2007).
Confederation of the Food and Drink Industries of the EU (CIAA) (2002) *Europeans Are Satisfied With Their Food*. Online. Available HTTP: < http://www.ciaa.be/pages_en/press_area/pressrel_list.asp?pressrel_id=191&year_crit=2002&search_crit=survey&search_where=in%5Ftitle > (accessed 18 June 2007).
Eurobarometer (2002) *Europeans and Biotechnology in 2002. Special Eurobarometer 177. Eurobarometer 58.0*, European Commission, Public opinion Analysis, Brussels. Online. Available HTTP: < http://ec.europa.eu/public_opinion/archives/ebs/ebs_177_en.pdf > (accessed 18 June 2007).
——(2005a) *Europeans, Science & Technology. Special Eurobarometer 224. Eurobarometer 63.1*, European Commission, Public opinion Analysis, Brussels. Online. Available HTTP: < http://ec.europa.eu/public_opinion/archives/ebs/ebs_224_report_en.pdf > (accessed 18 June 2007).
——(2005b) *Social values, Science and Technology. Special Eurobarometer 225. Eurobarometer 63.1*, European Commission, Public opinion Analysis, Brussels.

Online. Available HTTP: < http://ec.europa.eu/public_opinion/archives/ebs/ebs_225_report_en.pdf > (accessed 18 June 2007).
——(2005c) *Risk Issues. Special Eurobarometer 238. Eurobarometer 64.1*, European Commission, Public opinion Analysis, Brussels. Online. Available HTTP: < http://ec.europa.eu/public_opinion/archives/ebs/ebs_238_en.pdf > (accessed 18 June 2007).
——(2006) *Europeans and Biotechnology in 2005. Special Eurobarometer 244b. Eurobarometer 64.3*, European Commission, Public opinion Analysis, Brussels. Online. Available HTTP: < http://ec.europa.eu/public_opinion/archives/ebs/ebs_244b_en.pdf > (accessed 18 June 2007).
European Convention, The Secretariat (2002) *CONV 120/02, Information note*, Brussels, 19 June 2002.
European Group on Ethics in Science and New Technologies (EGE) (2000) *Citizens Rights and New Technologies: a European challenge*, European Group on Ethics in Science and New Technologies, Brussels.
European Parliament and Council (1990a) *Directive on the Deliberate Release into the Environment of Genetically Modified Organisms*, 90/200/EC, 8 May 1990.
——(1990b) *Directive on the Contained Use of Genetically Modified Micro-Organism*, 90/219/EC, 8 May 1990.
——(1994) *Amendment to Council Directive 90/200/EC1990, Directive 94/15/EC, According to Technical Progress*.
——(2001) *Directive 2001/18/EC*, 12 March 2001.
——(2002) *EC Regulation 178/2002*, 28 January 2002.
——(2003a) *EC Regulation 1829/2003*, 22 September 2003.
European Values Survey (2000a) *Human and nature. B009*, 1999–2000.
——(2000b) *Opinion about scientific advantages. E022*, 1999–2000.
Gaskell, G., Thompson, P. and Allum, N. (2002) 'Worlds apart? Public opinion in Europe and the USA', in M. W. Bauer and G. Gaskell (eds) *Biotechnology. The making of a global controversy*, Cambridge: Cambridge University Press.
Jonas, H. (1984) *The Imperative of Responsibility: in search of an ethics for the technological age*, Chicago: University of Chicago Press.
Lezaun, J. and Groenleer, M. (2006) 'Food control emergencies and the territorialization of the European Union', *European Integration*, 28 (5): 437–55.
Patterson, L. A. and Josling, T. (2005) 'Regulating biotechnology: comparing EU and US approaches', in A. Jordan (ed.) *Environmental Policy in the European Union*, London: Earthscan.
Sandin, P. (2005) 'The precautionary principle and food safety', *Journal of Consumer Protection and Food Safety*, September 2005: 1–4.
Teitel, M. and Wilson, K.A. (1999) *Genetically Engineered Food: changing the nature of nature*, Rochester: Park Street Press.
Torgersen, H., Hampel, J., von Bergmann-Winberg, M.-L., Bridgman, E., Durant, J., Einsiedel, E., *et al.* (2002) 'Promise, problems and proxies: twenty-five years of debate and regulation in Europe', in M. W. Bauer and G. Gaskell (eds) *Biotechnology. The making of a global controversy*, Cambridge: Cambridge University Press.
Tsioumani, E. (2004) 'Genetically modified organism in the EU: public attitudes and regulatory developments', *RECIEL*, 13 (3): 279–88.
Van den Belt, H. (2003) 'Debating the precautionary principle: "Guilty until proven innocent" or "Innocent until proven guilty"?', *Plant Physiology*, 132: 1122–26.

Vogel, D. (2005) 'The hare and the tortoise revisited: the new politics of consumer and environmental regulation in Europe', in A. Jordan (ed.) *Environmental Policy in the European Union*, London: Earthscan.

Welsh, I. (2006) 'Values, science and the European Union', in S. Lucarelli and I. Manners (eds) *Values and Principles in European Foreign Policy*, London: Routledge.

World Trade Organization (WTO) (1994) *Technical Barriers to Trade Agreement*. Online. Available HTTP: < http://www.wto.org/english/tratop_e/tbt_e/tbt_e.htm > (accessed 18 June 2007).

——(2001) *Sanitary and Phytosanitary Agreement*. Online. Available HTTP: < http://www.wto.org/english/tratop_e/sps_e/spsagr_e.htm > (accessed 18 June 2007).

7 EU red biotechnology regulation and European values

Renata Badii

The aim of this chapter is to assess if and to what extent the European Union's (EU) policy regulating the medical biotechnology sector can contribute to form a common sense of belonging and loyalty legitimizing the EU as a political project.

In order to tackle this theme, I will first try to outline the ethical, social and economic implications connected to regulating the biotechnology sector in general and medical biotechnology in particular. Second, I analyse the European strategy on life sciences and biotechnology drawn up by the Commission in 2002 with specific regard to the European biotechnology regulation model, and then I examine whether it can be considered an expression of values and principles with an important role in defining a common European identity. Finally, I will assess how European citizens perceive this specific policy.

The biotechnology challenge for democratic societies

Since first appearing in the 1970s, biotechnology has raised many questions in Europe. On one hand, it seems to offer incredible opportunities both to improve the quality of life and to develop a strategic economic sector, especially in present-day knowledge-based economies. On the other hand, the scientific community and public opinion have progressively shown deep preoccupation over the possible risks connected to the application and marketing of biotechnology, both for the environment and for human beings. But beyond the uncertainty over possible risks connected to the development of the biotechnology sector, especially in terms of its use in biomedicine, the problem that is felt to be most critical when it comes to drawing up legal regulations consists of the fact that some biotechnological techniques (for example, using stem cells or genetic screening) raise ethically controversial questions and *moral dilemmas*, with the very concept of human life and its dignity at the centre of completely diverging interpretations and beliefs.

In order to outline the ethical, social and economic implications connected to medical or red biotechnology, as well as the problems in regulating it, one needs to consider that red biotechnology entails a continual reclassification of the relations between the public–political sphere and the personal–private sphere. Indeed, red biotechnology leads to the *politicization* of events and aspects of existence that to date had been considered the most intimate and private *par excellence*, as they are situations that by their very nature escape authoritative regulation. Issues related to procreation, death and care, as well as to the perception of our bodies and our personal identity, have become a public question since the development of medical biotechnology because they are subject to political resolutions (on research, health, the economy, etc.) progressively disciplined by institutions, medical protocols and legislative decisions.

In the sphere of medical biotechnology, the difficulties in creating regulations depend first of all on the fact that the public authorities, on both a national and a European level, need to somehow come to a compromise between the requests of different subjects – biotechnology industries, scientific communities linked to the academic world and the private sector, patients associations, citizens – in a context characterized by a deep-set moral pluralism and by contrasting interests. In this sphere of problems, it is not just a matter of identifying the right allocation criteria for such scarce commodities as those of the biomedical sector, but also of reaching a compromise between ultimate conceptions of good and evil, as well as what is considered a 'good life'.

Thus, biotechnology places two different fields of closely connected political problems at the centre of attention. First, biotechnology regulation highlights the need for democratic societies to rethink the relationship between science and society: when the scientific community is not able to express a certain and unambiguous position (as in the case of biological and genetic knowledge and the impact of medical biotechnology on natural and social systems), and the new scientific knowledge stirs up moral dilemmas as to how it should be applied, the political decisions pertaining to scientific issues of public importance cannot be legitimately based only on the authority of scientific specialists. With respect to the science–society relationship, it is important to note that the final report of the Biotechnology Consultative Forum promoted by the EU and the USA in 2000 openly recognized that 'the biotechnology debate is also a debate over the role of the citizen' (European Union and United States of America 2000: 6). In a democratic context, the legitimacy of the political regulation of biotechnology depends increasingly on the ability of institutions to open up the decision-making process itself to representatives of civil society. This means that in order for the political decision-making process on scientific issues of public importance to be socially acceptable, institutions must implement more transparent regulation procedures, which should be more accessible to the citizens and above all more inclusive of the different interests and moral points of view (Funtowicz *et al.* 2000).

The problem of the social acceptability of biotechnology also reveals the economic implications of this sector: the political institutions' attempt to open up the governing of biotechnology to a greater number of representatives of civil society is not only due to the will to respect democratic values and principles, but also dictated by reasons of economic pragmatism. The citizens are also consumers. Their *trust* in new technologies and in the capability of their institutions to guarantee acceptable regulation, both in terms of safety for human health and the environment and ethical standards, is a fundamental component in allowing the development of such a strategic sector as biotechnology in the national economies (Salter and Jones 2002b).

Thus we can see the second challenge that regulating biotechnologies, and medical biotechnology in particular, creates for democratic societies: the difficulty in reconciling market logics and protecting individual rights in the application and marketing of the new biological and genetic knowledge. Owing to its enormous positive potential in the sector of care and prevention of illness, medical biotechnology has a strong 'emancipating' implication, with its promise to free us from pain, illness and our biological destiny. But one also needs to consider that in absence of clear legal guarantees, the marketing of processes and products deriving from the new scientific knowledge could become the source of new inequalities and new forms of discrimination and 'disciplining'. For example, the possibility to collect and file the genetic information of entire populations, thanks to predictive genetic tests, is a serious threat to the right to privacy and the most fundamental criteria of equality among citizens. The knowledge of the genetic heritage of individuals could be transformed into a factor of discrimination in terms of access to collective services, in particular, health, work, and illness and life insurance. Similar problems are raised by the issue of patents for biotechnological inventions: although on the one hand the guarantee of intellectual property is without doubt an important tool for encouraging scientific research and allowing the development of biotechnological enterprises, on the other it risks making the products or processes deriving from research inaccessible for those less well-off in our society, and, above all, the populations of poor or developing countries.

Towards a policy-related view of science?

The issue of how to conceive the relationship between science and society in relation to both factors of biotechnology regulation (improving the democratic quality of the decision-making processes, and promoting the development of the biotechnology industry while observing fundamental liberties) became a central part of the life sciences and biotechnology strategy promoted by the European Commission in 2002 to relaunch Europe's regulation policy for this sector.

The need to rethink the relationship between science and society was prompted by several factors: in the first place, after the food emergencies and scandals in the 1990s the European institutions had to regain the citizens' trust in the opinion of experts and in the capabilities of the national and European institutions to regulate science. Furthermore, the EU greatly feared that the clear opposition of European public opinion towards genetically modified organisms (GMOs) could condition the all-round social acceptance of biotechnology (Torgersen et al. 2002). In fact, from the 2005 Eurobarometer on the perception of biotechnology it clearly emerges that the vast majority of Europeans do not intend to encourage the GMO food market, which is seen as not useful, morally unacceptable and a risk for society. But, on the whole, a slight majority of Europeans (52 per cent) now appear optimistic towards the use of biotechnologies, with the greatest advantages expected to be gained precisely from medical biotechnology, this trust depending on the one hand on its 'moral acceptability', and, on the other, on the guarantee of a high level of control over this kind of technology by the political authorities (Eurobarometer 2006). The growing attention of the EU, and the Commission in particular, to the Europeans' social perception of science and especially biotechnology[1] can therefore be explained as an increasing awareness of the need to rethink European policy in the sphere of biotechnology regulation.

Besides, the EU is aware of the many disadvantages connected with failing to achieve an avant-garde position in the biotechnology sector. On presenting its strategy on the topic of *Life Sciences and Biotechnology* in 2002, the European Commission strongly underlined that the desire to become a leading player in the field of biotechnology is not only due to strictly economic reasons (to remain competitive against other actors, such as the USA, India and China; to exploit the economic potential and employment opportunities of this sector). Indeed, the Commission is aware of the fact that only by achieving a leading position in the sector, and first of all in research, will it be possible to assert its own biotechnology management model, compatible with European ethical and social values (Commission 2002).

With respect to these goals, the Commission explicitly recognizes that 'without broad public acceptance and support, the development and use of life sciences and biotechnology in Europe will be contentious, benefits will be delayed and competitiveness will be likely to suffer' (Commission 2002). In relation to this particular need, since the 2000 *White Paper on Governance* the EU has been trying to develop a set of rules based on principles and values shared within the EU which promotes an idea of *policy-related science*. This conception sets apart policy-related science, used in addressing and resolving policy issues, from pure and applied science, and recognizes the political effect of social decisions on science, which must be founded on criteria of *transparency* and *participation* in order to be able to gain legitimacy (Funtowicz et al. 2000). The science regulation model therefore becomes part of a general strategy to improve the democratic quality of European governance, making it more transparent, more participative, and giving a clearer definition of the responsibility of the political and non-political actors involved in the decision-making processes (Commission 2001a).

By analysing the biotechnology strategy preparatory documents presented by the Commission in 2002, it would seem that the EU refuses a technocratic view of medical biotechnology regulation, recognizing that the application of biotechnology implies moral dilemmas, and that the will to regulate the market involves having to face up to the moral pluralism characterizing Europe. But this is difficult for EU law to mediate, as we know from national legislations. According to the Commission, the European and national political authorities should therefore make use of a multidisciplinary consultation system, open not only to all scientific opinions, but also to counselling from other types of experts. At the same time, there is also an awareness of the need to promote dialogue between the scientific community and society, in response to the requests for more information and transparency, while citizens should be given the possibility to express themselves in the appropriate assemblies, and to participate in the forming of regulations (Commission 2001c). The central importance given to the principles of transparency, responsibility, information and participation is confirmed by the *User Guide to European Regulation in Biotechnology*, a manual recently published by the Commission to provide information to biotechnology enterprises and workers in the sector, but also to explain the guiding principles of the European strategy on biotechnology to the whole European public. For example, the Commission affirms that 'public engagement – including access to information and participation in decision-making – is a continuing priority for biotechnology' (Commission 2006).

Therefore, it seems that the European biotechnology regulation system is heading towards a model based on a *policy-related* conception of science, with transparency, information and public participation as its regulatory principles, above all due to the ethical implications of developing biotechnology. From this point of view, according to some authors, we can see how the European model differs from the *science-based* regulation model adopted in the USA, which sees scientific knowledge in a neutral and technical light, and is therefore more strictly and objectively shaped by scientific advancements. In reality, this model also is critical of the technocratic regulation of public issue-related science, but here the social control over science is carried out above all by courts, whose opinion prevails over that of the scientific experts within the regulation process (Tallacchini and Terragni 2004).

European principles and the political role of bioethics

In order to be able to assess if the European policy on regulating red biotechnology is important in promoting a sense of belonging together among the Europeans, one needs to consider whether this policy can be said to express values and principles that are shared within the European space to such an extent as to become a normative element. At the moment there are quite sizeable differences between the various national legislative systems in the sphere of medical biotechnology, from the viewpoint of the ethical principles inspiring the legislation, of the institutions involved in the decision-making processes and the decision procedures themselves (Ager 1999). When we speak of 'shared' European values and principles in the field of red biotechnology, we can only refer to the attempt to establish a common ethical perspective. This minimum moral consensus cannot be considered definitive, nor can it eliminate the moral disagreement on medical biotechnology arising from the plurality of ethics, religions and philosophies present in European societies, but it can at least come up with a *modus vivendi*.

Precisely because of the great moral disagreement on the forms of research considered ethically acceptable, and on which developments and industrial applications of biomedical research to promote, on a European level we constantly risk ending up with no common ethical lexicon, and seeing the proliferation of contrasting national legislative tendencies within the communitarian space. Hence, it is difficult to design a unitary European strategy. As regards this problem, the EU has strongly backed the action taken by the Council of Europe to draw up a framework convention in order to identify and guarantee some fundamental bioethical principles and values within the EU. The *Convention on Human Rights and Biomedicine*, more commonly known as the Oviedo Convention (Council of Europe 1997), also made it possible to draw up additional protocols on specific issues of clinical practice (medical research, organ transplants, embryo protection, cloning and genetics). Particularly attentive towards the social, legal and ethical implications connected to the development of biomedical sciences since the beginning of the 1980s, in 1989 the Council of Europe set up its own committee of experts on the progress of biomedical science (CAHBI), which worked closely with representatives of the EU, the World Health Organization, UNESCO (United Nations Educational, Scientific and Cultural Organization) and the OECD (Organisation for Economic Co-operation and Development) in preparing the text of the Convention. The Council of Europe has tried to avoid imposing rigid and uniform solutions, and has instead attempted to stimulate the member states to reform their respective legislations in pursuit of greater harmonization (Galloux *et al.* 2002).

Although the Oviedo Convention was not signed or ratified by all the EU member states, it can nevertheless be considered a document proving the political will of many European states to single out some common ethical principles and to guarantee the protection of human rights in biomedical regulation. In addition, it also indicates some guidelines for research on human beings and clinical practice. In particular, the Convention of Oviedo:

1. places the interests and well-being of the individual before those of society and science, favouring the protection of freedom and human

dignity rather than market logics (ban on marketing the human body, its products and functions; protection of privacy for data concerning genetic make-up and health; assertion of the principle of free and informed consent; ban on cloning);
2. underlines the value of solidarity, which means guaranteeing access to qualified medical care for all and defence of the weakest subjects;
3. asserts the need to promote an interdisciplinary debate within the signatory states on the medical, social, economic, ethical and legal implications of medical biotechnology.

In terms of promoting a common moral lexicon on a European level, it is important to remember that the fundamental principles of the Oviedo Convention were included in the *Charter of Fundamental Rights of the European Union* proclaimed in Nice in 2000. Indeed, article 3, which lays down the right to the integrity of the person, explicitly mentions the fields of medicine and biology, banning marketing of the human body, its parts and products; prohibiting eugenic practices and cloning human beings; and giving the right to free and informed consent. Article 35, concerning medical care, directly reflects the indication in the Oviedo Convention which asserts the principle of equal rights to medical services for all European citizens.

Second, the Oviedo Convention can be interpreted as an indication to the EU member states on how to deal with dissent on ethical issues, as it has helped to legitimize the role of bioethical assessment in the European policy on medical biotechnology (Salter and Jones 2002a). The Oviedo Convention gave a great boost to the credibility of the European Group on Ethics (EGE): an independent, pluralist and multidisciplinary agency that refers directly to the chairman of the European Commission on the ways in which the ethical values of European societies must be taken into account in EU policies on scientific and technological development. Since 1991, the EGE (known until 1997 as the Group of Advisers to the European Commission on the Ethical Implications of Biotechnology) has produced opinions on many issues relating to biotechnology, bringing together national ethical committees on a European level. Especially since 1998, when the EGE helped include the agenda on human genetics in the Fifth Framework Programme, the agency has made a name for itself as an important political mediator in the field of EU regulation on biotechnology. Its official recognition is present in Directive 98/44/EC on the legal protection of biotechnology inventions, in which article 7 states that: 'The Commission's European Group on Ethics in Science and New Technologies evaluates all ethical aspects of biotechnology' (European Parliament and Council 1998). This recognition helped to assert the importance in Europe of the mediation carried out on a national level by the ethical committees, affirmed by Directive 2001/20/EC on good clinical practice (European Parliament and Council 2001).[2]

However, some authors strongly underline that institutionalizing the bioethical approach in Europe, which is what happened when ethical committees were set up, has gone against the original spirit with which bioethics came about. In other words, it has promoted comitology rather than an open and interdisciplinary dialogue on ethical issues, involving different social players (Bunton and Petersen 2005).

The European biotechnology strategy and the promotion of a European political identity

Can the European model for regulating biotechnology be considered a policy capable of promoting a common sense of belonging and loyalty among the Europeans and towards the European institutions? In order to assess the contribution of a specific policy to promoting political identity, it is not sufficient for this policy to be recognized as legitimate because it is an expression of shared principles and values. Three other elements are equally as necessary: there must be a sufficiently defined perception of the policy and its normative reasons; this policy must be effective, that is the institutions must really be able to achieve the set goals; and the issue must be politically important, or rather, medical biotechnology must be perceived as a central political issue for defining the European political body as a common 'challenge' that brings the European societies closer together despite their differences.

As far as the first element is concerned, that is the Europeans' perception of the European policy for regulating medical biotechnology, let us look at the Eurobarometer *Europeans and Biotechnology in 2005*, even though this study does not specifically refer to medical biotechnology, but takes into account the whole spectrum of advanced biotechnology. By analysing the collected data and comparing it with the previous series of surveys on this issue (conducted in 1991, 1993, 1996, 1999 and 2002), the Eurobarometer editors argue that in 2005 the Europeans appeared more optimistic towards biotechnology, more informed and confident towards the European regulation system, both as regards safety and ethical standards. Considering the actors involved with different regulatory functions in the 'biotechnology system' (scientists, biotechnology enterprises, national governments and the EU), it is interesting to note that in all the member states, with the exception of Austria, Denmark, Finland and Sweden, those interviewed declared that they have more confidence in the regulatory action concerning biotechnology promoted by the EU than in the action promoted by their own national governments (on a European level, the percentage of public confidence in the EU reaches 74 per cent, against 68 per cent in national governments; cf. Eurobarometer 2006). The EU's role in relation to this policy therefore seems to be perceived and appreciated by the European citizens. At the same time, one however needs to consider that the Europeans' level of information and attention relating to biotechnology is still quite low:

most of those interviewed declare that they do not have a clear idea of biotechnology (40 per cent), 35 per cent have formed their opinion on the basis of news in the media, 15 per cent have a very basic knowledge of the topic, and only 10 per cent of Europeans have had an 'active' attitude, reading up about it and/or taking part in public and scientific initiatives (Eurobarometer 2006). Therefore, it still seems that only a small minority of Europeans actively pay attention to the topic of biotechnology; this means that the way the Europeans perceive the political implications of this field and the specific role played by the EU remains volatile, subject as it is to unproved opinions on biological matters that may come up in the media.

As far as medical biotechnology in particular is concerned, the perception of the European regulatory policy however varies considerably on the basis of the type of actor taken into consideration. When considering the stakeholders in the field of red biotechnology, such as the European Association of Biotechnology Industries (EuropaBio), and patients' associations such as the European Platform for Patients' Organizations, Science and Industry (EPPOSI) or Rare Diseases Europe, the European association of patients affected by rare diseases (Eurordis), one is faced with actors who are aware of the importance of regulation on a European level, and, therefore, of the efforts aiming at harmonizing the various national legislations carried out by the EU. The Union appears fundamental for promoting the industrial and pharmaceutical sector, for coordinating scientific research on a European level, and for guaranteeing equal opportunities of medical care and prevention to all citizens in the Community area. However, these stakeholders often express criticism as to the true capacity and political will of the European institutions and member states to implement what is stated in official documents. According to Andrea Rappagliosi, the chairman of the EuropaBio Healthcare Council, what prevents progress in medical biotechnology in Europe is '[the] lack of political leadership at EU level that is needed to put innovative healthcare biotechnology at the top of the policy agenda to ensure that a strategic sector, which could dramatically improve growth and competitiveness, is supported and promulgated' (EuropaBio 2006).

The inability to achieve the set goals in the medical biotechnology sector would therefore seem to threaten the positive effect of this European policy on promoting political identity. In the same way, it seems to weaken the legitimacy of the EU, whose emphasis on promoting a knowledge-based economy (central goal not only of the European biotechnology strategy, but of the whole Lisbon strategy) risks ending up as simple political wishful thinking. It is interesting to note that this criticism was raised by representatives of different European parliamentary groups on occasion of the first parliamentary discussion for the approval of the Seventh Framework Programme (13 June 2006): the inability to increase the European research budget as promised (55 billion euros earmarked against the 73 initially proposed by the Commission), despite the continual reference of the European institutions to the central importance of the Lisbon strategy, reflects the crisis of Europe, 'which wants to act but cannot succeed, has targets and goals but also enormous difficulties in funding them'.[3]

Another method to weigh up the public perception of the European regulatory policy in the medical biotechnology sector is to examine a sample from the European press, by analysing the newspapers' attention to two particularly important events in the history of this policy.

The first event considered was the signing of the Oviedo Convention on 4 April 1997: this piece of news is only present in the British (two articles in *The Times*), Spanish (two articles in *El Pais*) and German press (two articles in the *Süddeutsche Zeitung*), whereas the Italian and French press examined did not cover the event.[4] It is interesting to note that the UK press highlights the importance of the document from an international point of view, quite rightly presenting the Convention as the first international document that singles out guidelines in biomedical research and clinical practice;[5] the Spanish press mainly underlines the Council of Europe's attempt to harmonize the various national laws,[6] and the will to single out a minimum moral sense common to all the European countries;[7] on the other hand, the German press only concentrates on the position of Germany, which never signed the Oviedo Convention, considering it insufficient in terms of the guarantees offered to patients with regard to medical experiments and the issue of embryo protection.[8]

The discussion on the EU funding of stem cell research is the second event used to analyse the public debate. The discussion took place as part of the process to approve the Seventh Framework Programme. On 15 June 2006, the European Parliament approved the amendment in favour of EU funding of adult and embryo stem cell research proposed by the ITRE (Industry, Transport, Research and Energy) Commission: this will also allow funding of embryonic stem cell research in the national legal systems where this is already allowed, with each scientific proposal examined for approval case by case. Upon the first reading, the position adopted by the European Parliament was confirmed by the EU Competitiveness Council of European Research Ministers meeting held on 24 July 2006. This meeting managed to avoid a ban on all forms of European public funding of stem cell research because of the opposition of the member states who do not allow this form of experimentation. During the Council, a majority was reached thanks to the guarantees given in the amendment already approved by the European Parliament concerning embryo protection: while repeating the ban on cloning for reproductive ends and activities to modify the genetic heritage of human beings that could make these modifications inheritable, the approved document also specified that studies to create human embryos exclusively for research purposes or for supplying stem cells will not be funded (European Parliament 2006a, Art. 6).

As far as the European press examined is concerned, except for *El Mundo*, all the newspapers in the sample (see note 4) covered the ethical issue central to the process to approve the Seventh Framework Programme, and the decision within the Council in particular. In addition, several articles were also devoted to analysing the compromise reached.[9] Ten years on from Oviedo, it seems that the press of the five European countries examined almost unanimously perceives the political importance of the EU's role in regulating medical biotechnology, as well as the very political importance of this topic, which has become progressively more familiar to the European public.

All the press examined starts off by acknowledging the range of differing ethical positions in Europe as well as the differences between the legislations of the 25 member states, also underlining the transversality of the parliamentary vote in bioethical matters across the political spectrum. The route to a compromise therefore seems the only reasonable path that can be followed in what the *Guardian* presented as a passionate debate 'between liberal and conservative positions' on the topic of biomedical research.[10] Above all, from the analysis of the British, Spanish and French press, what emerges is a positive view of the compromise reached, interpreted as an example of European pragmatism, capable of bringing together the needs of research and the market with the desire to guarantee ethical standards in regulations. Therefore, it is shown that the only possible way of respecting common ethical standards is to respect a multi-speed European system in biomedical legislation,[11] and to recognize the need to examine cases one by one as regards the sticky issue of stem cell research.[12] It is also interesting to note that the British, French and Spanish press underline the importance of the ability shown by the member states to mediate compared with the 'rigid' position on public research funding adopted in the USA: during the week before the EU Council vote, President Bush used his power to veto the Senate's decision to use federal funds to finance embryonic stem cell research.[13]

On the other hand, if we consider the German press, which stands out in terms of quantity as it dedicated the highest number of articles to the European funding of stem cell research, a different image emerges of the compromise reached by the member states. Although some articles strongly underline that the agreement reached represents the lowest possible denominator in Europe on the ethical issues raised by red biotechnology,[14] other articles present the European compromise in the most detrimental meaning of the word. A multi-speed European biomedical legislation is thus presented as the synonym of a lack of clarity on common ethical principles; rather, what lies behind the European compromise and the decision to consider the funding projects case by case is the member states' renunciation of the search for true agreement on ethical principles due to the need to nevertheless reach a compromise in an economically important sector.[15]

The split in the German press is related to the position adopted by the German research minister, Annette Schavan, during the EU Council of 24 July 2006: like Italy, Germany had decided to back down from the six-state line-up promoting the so-called 'ethical declaration', with which, in

November 2005 during the EU Competitiveness Council on the preparation of the Seventh Framework Programme text, Germany, Italy, Austria, Malta, Poland and Slovakia had declared their common commitment not to promote European funding for research activities involving the destruction of embryos, thus encouraging funding for research on adult stem cells only.

Beyond the national differences, the German press casts light on a fundamental aspect of the European panorama, that is the difficulty of being able to speak of *full* European consent on ethical issues regarding the regulation of medical biotechnology. Thus, in the case of ethical issues it is not easy to think that those who come out 'defeated' on a European level can consider the position adopted by the majority fully legitimate: despite starting off from common European values (such as respect for human life), the decisions within the EU that take up a stance on a specific interpretation of those values risk turning out to be temporary agreements rather than the expression of real consent over common principles. In this connection, it is interesting to note the comment given after the EU Council of 24 July 2006 by the Polish research minister, Michal Sewerynski, who, despite the guarantees in the final document of the amendment, refused the compromise together with the ministers of Lithuania, Malta, Slovakia and Austria, and declared, according to *Le Figaro*, 'Mon gouvernement, mon opinion publique et ma propre conscience m'obligent à m'inscrire en faux face à cette proposition', refusing to 'battre en brèche les principes d'éthique les plus fondamentaux'. Equally, the Maltese minister Censu Galea asserted that the text approved during the Parliament and Council 'permet des recherches qui vont au-delà de nos principes et des valeurs de nos concitoyens'.[16]

As regards the importance of the medical biotechnology regulation policy in promoting a sense of belonging together among the EU citizens, it would therefore appear right to adopt a cautious stance: European regulation of medical biotechnology is an extremely delicate field, because in this political decision-making process ethical issues (with theological, philosophical and cultural implications) challenge a polity that is not yet fully defined. These very issues are destined to remain controversial in the identity formation of a regional actor like the EU, considering that the member states themselves have difficulty in defining shared normative criteria for their own national legislation in the biomedical sector. Moreover, in a historic moment in which the national political elites seem to be having great difficulty in relaunching the EU as a political project, it is hard to think that in such a controversial and complex policy field as this the member states can find motives for overcoming national differences and implementing greater political integration on a European level.

On the other hand, without doubt there is a Europe-wide debate on bioethics, and it has found a place not just in the press or academia but in EU institutions as well. To a certain extent, this debate is but a new manifestation of the traditional variety of opinions, schools of thought and religious beliefs, a quintessential feature of European history. The existence of an institutionalized EU-wide debate on bioethics is a sign that the EU is a precarious, fledgling polity rather than simply a new market regulator. If the EU cannot define a common position on this matter, it cannot stop debating or seeking a compromise either. This is in itself a contribution to the formation of a European political identity.

Acknowledgement

I wish to thank Monica Toraldo di Francia (University of Florence) who introduced me to the study of bioethics, Ian Welsh (University of Wales) for his precious comments on previous versions of this work, as well as the editors and the other participants in this collective research for all their notes and criticisms.

Notes

1 Think of the numerous surveys on biotechnology carried out in 1991, 1993, 1996, 1999, 2002 and 2005, and the recent Special Eurobarometers dedicated to the perception of science and technology (see Eurobarometers 2005a,b).
2 See also Commission (2001c: 18ff.).
3 Speech by David Hammerstein Mintz for the Greens/EFA group; similar criticisms were levelled by Umberto Guidoni (GUE/NGL), Umberto Pirilli (UEN) and Vittorio Prodi (ALDE/ADLE); see European Parliament (2006b).
4 The press analysis was carried out through the Lexis–Nexis database, using 'Oviedo' and 'biomedicine' as keywords. The period of time analysed covers the month of April 1997, and the newspapers examined were *The Times* (along with *The Sunday Times*) and the *Guardian*, *Le Figaro*, *La Stampa* and *Il Sole 24 Ore*, the *Süddeutsche Zeitung* and *El Pais*.
5 'European Nations Sign Ban on Human Cloning', *The Times*, 5 April 1997.
6 'Una venteina de paises firman hoy el convenio sobre biomedicina', *El Pais*, 4 April 1997.
7 'Europa, los derechos humanos y la biomedicina', *El Pais*, 4 April 1997.
8 'Bonn tritt Bioethik-Konvention nicht bei', *Süddeutsche Zeitung*, 5 April 1997.
9 The period of time under analysis covers the months of June to October 2006, and thanks to the availability of several archives within the Lexis–Nexis database, in addition to the newspapers quoted previously, I also analysed *Libération*, *El Mundo*, *Die Welt* and *Der Spiegel*. The keywords were: 'biotechnology or stem cell or biomedicine' and 'Europe or EU or European Union or European Community'. In quantitative terms, one article came up in *The Times*, two in the *Guardian*, none in *El Mundo*, four in *El Pais*, three in *La Stampa*, four in *Il Sole 24 Ore*, one in *Libération*, two in *Le Figaro*, nine in the *Süddeutsche Zeitung*, six in *Der Spiegel* and 12 in *Die Welt*.
10 'US Faces Science Brain Drain after Europe Backs Stem Cell Funding. Debate Divides Members but Ends in Compromise', the *Guardian*, 25 July 2006.
11 'Staminali, dall'UE sì alla ricerca', *Il Sole 24 Ore*, 16 June 2006.
12 'Europäische Wissenschaftler dürfen bei EU-Fördergeldern mitbestimmen; Interview mit dem EU-Forschungskommissar Janez Potocnik über neue Schwerpunkte der europäischen Forschung', *Die Welt*, 20 April 2006.

13 See the articles 'EU Deal on Stem Cell Research', *The Times*, 25 July 2006; 'Embriones: luz àmbar', *El Pais*, 28 July 2006; 'L'Europe favorable à la recherché sur les cellules souches', *Le Figaro*, 26 July 2006.
14 'Europas Ethik. Die EU hat bei der der Förderung der Stammzellforschung einen tragbaren Kompromiss gefunden', *Süddeutsche Zeitung*, 25 July 2006; 'Vielfalt ist Kapital, aber auch Bedrohung', *Die Welt*, 26 July 2006.
15 See 'Schwieriger Kompromiss. Mehrheit für Forschung mit überzähligen Embryonen. Debatte im Eu-Ministerrat', *Süddeutsche Zeitung*, 25 July 2006; 'Von Fall zu Fall. Die EU-Einigung zum Embryo verändert das Bild vom Menschen', *Süddeutsche Zeitung*, 28 July 2006; 'Eizellen als Handelsware', *Die Welt*, 1 August 2006 – article by Hitrud Breyer, Green Party MEP.
16 'L'Europe favorable à la recherché sur les cellules souches', *Le Figaro*, 26 July 2006.

References

Ager, B. (1999) 'The regulation of biotechnology in Europe', in V. Moses and R. E. Cape (eds) *Biotechnology. The science and the business*, 2nd edn, London: Harwood Academic Publishers.

Bunton, R. and Petersen, A. (2005) 'Genetics and governance: an introduction', in R. Bunton and A. Petersen (eds) *Genetic Governance. Health, risk and ethics in the biotech era*, London: Routledge.

Commission (2001a) *European Governance. A White Paper*, COM (2001) 428 final, Brussels, 25 July 2001.

——(2001b) *Communication – Towards a strategic Vision of Life Sciences and Biotechnology*, COM (2001) 454 final, Brussels, 4 September 2001. Online. Available HTTP: < http://ec.europa.eu/biotechnology/pdf/doc_en.pdf > (accessed 16 June 2007).

——(2001c) *Communication – Science and Society Action Plan*, COM (2001) 714 final, Brussels, 4 December 2001. Online. Available HTTP: < http://eur-lex.europa.eu/smartapi/cgi/sga_doc?smartapi!celexplus!prod!DocNumber&lg=en&type_doc=COMfinal&an_doc=2001&nu_doc=714 > (accessed 16 June 2007).

——(2002) *Communication – Life Sciences and Biotechnology. A strategy for Europe*, COM (2002) 27 final, Brussels, 23 January 2002. Online. Available HTTP: < http://eur-lex.europa.eu/LexUriServ/site/en/com/2002/com2002_0027en01.pdf > (accessed 16 June 2007).

——(2006) *Users Guide to European Regulation in Biotechnology*. Online. Available HTTP: < http://ec.europa.eu/enterprise/phabiocom/docs/user_guide_biotech.pdf > (accessed 16 June 2007).

Council of Europe (1997) *Convention for the Protection of Human Rights and Dignity of the Human Being with regard to the Application of Biology and Medicine: Convention on Human Rights and Biomedicine*, Oviedo, 4 April 1997, ETS no. 164. Online. Available HTTP: < http://conventions.coe.int/treaty/en/treaties/html/164.htm > (accessed 16 June 2007).

Eurobarometer (2003) *Europeans and Biotechnology in 2002. Eurobarometer 58.0*, European Commission, Public opinion Analysis, Brussels. Online. Available HTTP: < http://ec.europa.eu/public_opinion/archives/eb/ebs_177_en.pdf > (accessed 16 June 2007).

——(2005a) *Europeans, Science and Technology. Special Eurobarometer 224*, European Commission, Public opinion Analysis, Brussels. Online. Available

HTTP: < http://ec.europa.eu/public_opinion/archives/ebs/ebs_224_report_en.pdf > (accessed 16 June 2007).

——(2005b) *Social Values, Science and Technology. Special Eurobarometer 225*, European Commission, Public opinion Analysis, Brussels. Online. Available HTTP: < http://ec.europa.eu/public_opinion/archives/ebs/ebs_225_report_en.pdf > (accessed 16 June 2007).

——(2006) *Europeans and Biotechnology in 2005: patterns and trends. Eurobarometer 64.3*, European Commission, Public opinion Analysis, Brussels. Online. Available HTTP: < www.ec.europa.eu/research/press/2006/pdf/pr1906_eb_64_3_final_report-may2006_en.pdf > (accessed 16 June 2007).

EuropaBio (2006) 'Chairman of EuropaBio Healthcare Council calls for effective and timely patient access to innovative medicines: beyond the subsidiarity principle', *EuropaBio Press Statement*, Brussels, 30 May 2006. Online. Available HTTP: < http://www.europabio.org/articles/PR_healthcare300506.doc > (accessed 16 June 2007).

European Parliament (2006a) *Legislative Resolution on the Proposal for a Decision of the European Parliament and of the Council Concerning the Seventh Framework Programme of the European Community for Research, Technological Development and Demonstration Activities* (COM(2005)0119 – C6–0099/2005 – 2005/0043 (COD)), *Text Approved by the Parliament* (15 June 2006) P6_TA(2006)0265.

——(2006b) 'Programma di ricerca a favore della crescita, nel rispetto delle questioni etiche', *European Parliament News-Press Service*, 13 June 2006. Online. Available HTTP: < http://www.europarl.europa.eu/news/expert/infopress_page/052-8884-164-06-24-909-20060608IPR08812-13-06-2006-2006-false/default_it.htm > (accessed 16 June 2007).

European Parliament and Council (1998) *Directive 98/44/EC on the Legal Protection of Biotechnological Inventions*, 6 July 1998.

——(2001) *Directive 2001/20/EC on the Approximation of the Laws, Regulations and Administrative Provisions of the Member States Relating to the Implementation of Good Clinical Practice in the Conduct of Clinical Trials on Medicinal Products for Human Use*, 4 April 2001.

European Union and United States of America (2000) *EU-US Biotechnology Consultative Forum Final Report*, Washington, D.C. Online. Available HTTP: < http://ec.europa.eu/external_relations/us/biotech/report.pdf > (accessed 16 June 2007).

Funtowicz, S., Shepherd, I., Wilkinson, D. and Ravetz, J. (2000) 'Science and governance in the European Union: a contribution to the debate', *Science and Public Policy*, 27 (5): 327–36.

Galloux, J. C., Gaumont Prat, H. and Stevers, E. (2002) 'Europe', in M. W. Bauer, G. Gaskell and J. Durant (eds) *Biotechnology in the Public Sphere: a European sourcebook*, London: Science Museum.

Salter, B. and Jones, M. (2002a) 'Human genetic technologies: European governance and the politics of bioethics', *Nature Reviews Genetics*, 3 (10): 808–14.

——(2002b) 'Regulating human genetics: the changing politics of biotechnology governance in the European Union', *Health, Risk and Society*, 4 (3): 325–40.

Tallacchini, M. and Terragni, F. (2004) *Le biotecnologie. Aspetti etici, sociali e ambientali*, Milan: Bruno Mondatori.

Torgersen, H., Hampel, J., von Bergmann-Winberg, M.-L., Bridgman, E., Durant, J., Einsiedel, E., *et al.* (2002) 'Promise, problems and proxies: twenty-five years of debate and regulation in Europe', in M. W. Bauer and G. Gaskell (eds) *Biotechnology. The making of a global controversy*, Cambridge: Cambridge University Press.

Part IV
Social and civil Europe

8 The European social model(s) and the self-image of Europe

Vaïa Demertzis

Introduction

During the 1990s a vigorous debate emerged in the EU over social policy. First enounced as a 'European social dimension', the debate rapidly turned to another concept: the 'European social model' (ESM). It appeared in the European political debate promoted by the European Commission in the mid-1990s, and has since become a successful catch-all concept for European as well as national politicians and institutions to deal with current socioeconomic challenges in the EU.

This contribution suggests that, rather than a reality to be discovered, the ESM is a social and political construct promoted by the EU institutions (mainly the Commission and the Council) trying to define a European supranational social policy, depending on actors and times. Indeed the content, the references and the uses of the ESM in political and public debates have evolved from its creation by the European Commission in 1994 to its institutionalization operated by the European Council since 2000. These variations are here analysed through their links with the broad discussion on EU identity and legitimacy since it is assumed that the conceptualization of the ESM constitutes a tool for the policy-makers to tackle the problematic issues of EU identity and legitimacy.

To what extent does the conceptualization and institutionalization of the ESM manifest the EU institutional attempts to build a European social bond as the core of the EU identity? And in which ways does the introduction of the ESM respond to EU legitimacy problems? To answer these questions, three dimensions of the ESM are investigated in the three sections of this chapter: its origins (the historical dimension, in the first section), its policy content (the factual dimension, in the second section) and its occurrence in public debate (the public dimension, in the third section). First, the political and scientific roots of the ESM are helpful to evaluate its emergence in the EU agenda in terms of EU (self-)identification and legitimacy. Second, illustrating the policy content of the concept of ESM highlights how peculiar the 'EU social policy' is in contrast to national welfare states and to what extent it is relevant for

EU identity and legitimacy. Lastly, the status of the ESM in public debates and the way(s) the European citizens perceive it is submitted to a contrasted analysis of the political institutional debate, the media coverage and the citizens' attitudes towards the ESM. The results of the three-sided analysis are gathered in the concluding section to assess the political role of the ESM in the definition and construction of EU identity and in the search for EU legitimacy.

The conceptual roots of the ESM

The ESM is a normative and political concept that arose recently on the European agenda. Both political and scientific discourses have been referred to the ESM but did not succeed in agreeing on a precise and unique definition. Loosely defined, the ESM has then become a catch-all concept for European as well as national policy-makers and researchers to deal with the problematic relationship between national and European levels of socio-economic matters. This section presents how the conceptualization of the ESM, both in political and in scientific terms, is concerned with the European search for EU identity and legitimacy.

The political emergence of the ESM

The concept of the ESM first emerged on the official agenda of the DG V (Directorate-General for Employment, Industrial Relations and Social Affairs) in a consultative document (Commission 1993a) before its celebration in two broad documents shaping the political vision of the whole Commission of the European Communities: the White Papers *Growth, Competitiveness and Employment – The Challenges and Ways forward into the 21st Century* (Commission 1993b) and *European Social Policy – A Way Forward for the Union* (Commission 1994). Such an emergence of the ESM on the European political agenda was correlated with the Delors' presidency of the European Commission (1985–95); it gradually replaced the term 'European social dimension' to evoke the European experience of simultaneously promoting sustainable economic growth and social cohesion. The ESM appeared as a result of a reflection engaged by Delors' cabinet about the social dimension of the European Community to accompany the achievement of the internal market, the main goal of the Maastricht process and treaty (1992). In that perspective, the ESM was first defined at the political level as a set of European values[1] shared by the national social systems of the EU member states (the European welfare states): the commitment to democracy, individual rights, free collective bargaining (social dialogue), market economy, equal opportunities for all, social welfare and solidarity (Commission 1994: 4). According to Jacques Delors himself (Delors 2004: 403) – a French socialist with a Catholic background – the emergence of the ESM was influenced by Social-Democratic thought and

Keynesian theory. It acknowledged solidarity, a core value of the Social-Democratic identity (Telò and Magnette 2001; Stjernø 2005), as a European value to be preserved. Socialist, Social Liberal and Christian thoughts influenced this definition since it recognized a positive relationship between wealth, freedom, social justice and the social market economy as the normative framework of national welfare states.

By referring to European social values, the ESM was broadly characterized by a historical *acquis* of values and social institutions to preserve[2] rather than actions to be taken and promoted. Founding the ESM on a *European heritage* made less specific claims about the detailed organization of social policy. It marked the impossibility for EU social policy to supplant national social policy and highlighted the process by which member states were at the same time building a European social space based on common fundamental values while maintaining their own dynamic in the organization of their social policies. The ESM has thus not been conceived by its promoter as a European project by itself – building a European welfare state as a distinctive supranational mode of socioeconomic regulation – but rather as an attempt to discern common values and goals for a political purpose. Therefore the ESM was neither a descriptive concept nor an analytical one, but a normative concept that has been created at the European level by the European political elite (mainly the president's cabinet) with a view to offset the harmful consequences (first objective) and ensure popular acceptance of the advent of the enlarged market (second objective). Such a proclamation of European social values revealed the necessity faced by the EU institutions to obtain a large social consensus with a view to implement the single market and mobilize supporters from among European elites to coordinate and communicate this project (Wincott 2003: 289).

The conceptual dimensions of the ESM

Created in the political realm, the concept of the ESM has been widely deployed within the scientific literature but has remained a rather polysemic term. There is no commonly agreed definition, but a number of different meanings that have been frequently mixed up. According to Maria Jepsen and Amparo Serrano Pascual (2005), one can identify four understandings of the ESM in the scientific debate: the ESM as an entity, as an ideal type, as a European project and as a political project.

First, the most common definition of the ESM highlights the socioeconomic features (principles or institutions) shared by the EU member states. Indeed the ESM has grown out of a particular historical context characterized by the emergence and development of the European welfare states during the post-war period. In a second round of definitions – based on comparative research (e.g. Esping-Andersen 1990; Ebbinghaus 1999; Scharpf 2002) – specific national socioeconomic models are identified as various 'ESMs'. The plural form stresses the diversity of national social systems in Europe, notably concerning the role of the state, market and family in providing social protection.[3] A third definition emphasizes the dynamic process that would lead to the constitution of a distinctive ESM as a European project of a supranational mode of socioeconomic regulation. Finally, the ESM is also regarded as a particular political way to deal with socioeconomic problems that have been politically constructed as common references and would then be characterized by a set of agreed policy objectives (Hemerijck 2002).

However, despite the variety of references to the concept in the scientific literature, the scholarly definitions of the ESM do share common assumptions. They all refer to a European 'model', but 'model' means either a conceptual representation of some phenomenon to enable reasoning within a theoretical and normative framework – with a set of variables and logical relationships between them – or a set of policies and institutions to be imitated. Therefore, mobilizing a European social 'model' in the EU discourse develops the *self-image* of Europe by defining one specific kind of relationship between the economic and social realms and by building the ESM in contrast to other socioeconomic models.

On the one hand, the ESM is enounced in terms of a 'unique blend of economic well-being, social cohesiveness and high overall quality of life which was achieved in the post-war period' (Commission 1994: 1a) that should be developed to 'provide a new synergy between the welfare and wealth-creating functions of society' (Commission 1994: 35). Social and economic dimensions are thus related. But the interpretation of the functional link between both components of the ESM may differ from one period to another, depending on predominant ideological referents. On the other hand, the debate about the ESM is based on the implicit reference to a dichotomy between the American and the European socioeconomic model. An analysis of the political conceptualization of the ESM at the EU level would emphasize the changing self-image of Europe conveyed by the concept of the ESM.

First, the emergence of the ESM manifested a new approach to European socioeconomic integration, considering social matters as means for economic integration. From the onset, the idea was to put social policies back in accordance with economic policies because the institutional delay in the development of the social field could be an obstacle to economic integration: European social integration was seen as a productive factor for economic integration, capable of ensuring European cohesion by reducing regional disparities. This balance between social and economic concerns is hugely controversial, since it raises the question to what extent member states of Europe actually share and agree on common socioeconomic foundations.

Second, in a global context, Europeans share a certain amount of common identity vis-à-vis the USA, Japan and China. Originally, the identification of a ESM implied an external confrontation with alternative regional models – such as the relatively deregulated American one and the more developmental Southeast Asian one (Hay *et al.* 1999) – from which the EU socioeconomic dimension has to be distinguished. This contrasting statement referred to the fact that EU member states have welfare systems that the USA does not.

The policy content of the ESM

Having exposed the conceptual roots of the ESM and their impact in terms of EU identity and legitimacy, the existence of a concrete ESM must be studied. The identity marks of the ESM have been based on the institutions of the national welfare states, which rely on social regulation of the economy and generous welfare state transfers and services. This section thus aims at analysing to what extent the ESM has a policy content, that is to say to what extent a peculiar EU social policy does exist and has evolved. In that perspective, it is important to question the claim that a distinctive transnational ESM would emerge at the EU level, describing the supranational and transnational mechanisms implemented at the EU level during the last 50 years: can we identify tendencies towards the emergence of a coherent transnational ESM or expect a further Europeanization of national welfare policies? Are the national welfare states converging or are the various models of social protection still prevailing? These questions are raised having in mind the possible production of a supranational identity, investigating

> whether EU membership is likely to result in the modification of existing welfare institutions to bring them more in line with a transnational ESM (existing or emergent) and whether the development of pan-European social institutions implies the replacement of national welfare provision by that at a supra-national level.
> (Hay *et al.* 1999: 16)

Most often, when people are debating the need to modernize the ESM, they are referring to institutions and policy processes of either the national welfare states or the European social dimension. But the EU social legislation is far from the traditional social policy of domestic welfare states. Beyond the reality of the various European welfare states, the expression of the ESM designates a set of common values and features shared by all the European welfare states. Within the context of this distinctive ESM, a variety of rather more specific national models of social provision have been identified (the British, the Swedish and the German perhaps being paradigm cases) as distinctive ESMs. Social security systems in the individual EU countries thus reflect specific traditions, social advances and cultural heritage. As a consequence (of the diversity of national welfare states), uniform European legislation in the social policy field has not, and could not, progress beyond the level of relatively *low minimal standards* that are acceptable to all member states. European social integration has been characterized by a 'constitutional asymmetry of economic policy and social protection policy' (Scharpf 2002: 646). Indeed economic policies have been progressively Europeanized, while social policies have remained at the national level and have been constrained by the supremacy of European rules of economic integration, liberalization and competition (Scharpf 2002: 666).

EU social policy does not include any social redistribution (Majone 1996; Hix 1999) between citizens, between employers and workers or between rich and poor people. The core redistributive powers of the domestic welfare states – responsible for the supply of social goods and services (social insurance, health care, education, housing, etc.) – still remain under the control of national states, although the EU undertakes some direct redistributive policies in other areas. Social policy at EU level is thus social regulation aimed at addressing the effects of market failures rather than at redistribution (Hix 1999: 223). Besides, treaties as well as policy processes also recognize the role of European social partners in designing and implementing certain parts of European law and policy objectives. The method of social dialogue between workers and employers at a European supranational level, launched by the President of the European Commission Jacques Delors in the 1980s and 1990s, legitimates at EU level the practice of negotiation between social partners in which unions oppose their collective power as social organizations (that is to say their solidarity as a mean of collective action) to the power of private ownership wielded by employers (Telò and Magnette 2001: 78–79).

However, EU member states are increasingly facing a common institutional environment and common challenges (globalization, post-industrialization, ageing). The demographic trends and the process of globalization produce a variety of common pressures (economic, technological, social) that are presented as inevitable (Ferrera *et al.* 2000; Scharpf and Schmidt 2000). A *common agenda of reforms* for a social and institutional 'modernization of the European social model' (structural reform, training for new technologies, knowledge-based society, etc.) is then proposed. Thus, an overall need has emerged to elaborate strategies and tools that ensure consistency and convergence of policy outcomes and at the same time respect diversity. The member states have been cooperating through various European policy processes, including the European Employment Strategy (EES), Broad Economic Policy Guidelines (BEPG), the Cardiff (1998) and Cologne (1999) Processes, which aimed at promoting the idea of active and socioeconomically sustainable welfare policies.

In this perspective, the Lisbon strategy (2000–10) has designed a new strategic socioeconomic goal for the EU: 'to become the most competitive and dynamic knowledge-based economy in the world, capable of sustainable economic growth with more and better jobs and greater social cohesion' (Council 2000a: §5). In contrast with the Commission approach considering the social dimension of the single market as a condition of its success, the

Lisbon strategy assesses that economic performance and social cohesion are mutually supportive objectives, thus reciprocal conditions, with a view to create a virtuous and sustainable cycle of economic and social progress: economic, employment and social policies are not treated as separate elements but as three sides of an equilateral triangle forming a mutually supportive and balanced policy mix. The strategy focuses on the transition to a knowledge-based economy and society (through technology, innovation, education and formation), investment in people and fighting against social exclusion as well as sustaining healthy and favourable economic growth. First, the strategy defined ambitious quantitative targets in both fields: it called for a 3 per cent growth rate and 70 per cent employment rate on average by 2010 (with a specific rate of 60 per cent for women). Second, more policy coordination at EU level between economic and social fields was required. In this perspective, the Broad Economic Policy Guidelines, sectoral economic policies, tax policies and employment and social policies were intended to be coordinated in order to avoid competition and contradiction between their objectives.

A new model of cross-national policy-making has also been inaugurated to respond to the issue of national diversity, promoting a convergence by objectives rather than by policies: the so-called Open Method of Coordination (OMC), whereby domestic policy actors respect national differences while accepting commonly agreed guidelines, that is to say common objectives decided at the EU level. This new method does not attempt to achieve common policies but rather at sharing policy experiences and practices through monitoring and benchmarking. Policy choices remain at the national level, but specific policy problems are defined as common concerns and national governments agree to be compared and evaluated in an organized iterative process (Telò 2002; Radaelli 2003; Goetschy 2006). First the OMC appears as a way to improve the coordination between the member states towards a better convergence of national social policies, through the definition of targets on a European level and the mechanisms of benchmarking and policy learning. Second the OMC also tries to improve the coordination between economic and social policies and then to create a better interdependence between European economic integration and persisting different national social models. The production of European statistics (Eurostat) or the promotion of benchmarking in EU social policy developing a number of indicators (through the OMC) are intended to stimulate EU member states to 'share common problems – by which they are "threatened" – and to produce similar key recipes to fight against these (socially constructed) common problems' (Jepsen and Serrano Pascual 2005: 241). The EU member states would thus share an advantage in facing these collective challenges in common, and this might induce a feeling of belonging to the same community and foster the construction of a common identity. EU identity is thus expected to develop by putting European values at work in specific policy paradigms and national social reforms.

However, both the continuing national fragmentation of European social policy and the absence of a centralized social protection at the European level – which are at the core of the need for the OMC – generate a more competitive economy that pushes towards rethinking the European idea of social solidarity (Streeck 1999). Thus, compared with the ordinary ingredients of a national social model (well-structured social stakeholders, social law, collective bargaining, worker representation, right to strike, social protection and redistributive policies, public service policies), the ESM is more fragmentary and does not form a coherent entity (Goetschy 2006), yet it remands to a series of interpreted values around which a new cognitive convergence is achieved.

The ESM in political and public debates

Although the ESM has no concrete policy content, it is often referred to in political and public socioeconomic debates as a European reality. Discussing the status of the concept in different levels of debates enables us to evaluate the possible gap between political discourse, media coverage and the way it is perceived by the European citizens.

The political debate about the ESM at the EU institutional level

The ESM has a fundamental *legitimating function* in EU integration. The analysis of its political definitions and uses by the Commission and Council emphasizes two conceptions of EU legitimacy: the first one exploring the European essence (values or features), while the second one requiring a European response to common challenges. Nevertheless both approaches are often presented as complementary (as underlined by calls for reform of the ESM in order to preserve it).

First coined in the White Paper *Growth, Competitiveness, Employment – The Challenges and Ways forward into the 21st Century* (Commission 1993b) but only defined in the White Paper *European Social Policy – A Way Forward for the Union* (Commission 1994), the concept of the ESM remained a 'matter of thought' in the Commission's quarters until the extraordinary European Council in March 2000 that adopted the Lisbon strategy for the socioeconomic modernization of Europe. Indeed the European Presidency Conclusions of Lisbon (Council 2000a), Feira (Council 2000b) and Nice (Council 2000c) put the 'modernization of the ESM' on the agenda of the European Council and defined the European socioeconomic strategy, called the Lisbon strategy, by three interrelated objectives: growth, employment and social cohesion. Such a goal of 'modernization' supports the view that the ESM is now defined by the common challenges threatening the member states rather than by values intrinsically shared by them. The national welfare states are seen as challenged by both international and domestic factors, facing the ongoing globalization pressures and internal socioeconomic challenges (demographic changes, shift to post-industrial economies). The notion of the ESM has thus become a mobilizing concept intended to point to the favoured approach to cope with these new challenges, so to orient economic and social renewal at the national level and thus to legitimize difficult national social reforms. This political function explains why even those who so far have been considered rather reluctant to engage in further social integration, e.g. the British government, have begun to refer with greater ease to a concept such as the ESM (e.g. the Hampton Court informal EU summit organized by the British EU Presidency in October 2005).

Since 2000, the discussions on the ESM have been restricted to the Spring Councils devoted to socioeconomic questions (set up by the Lisbon Extraordinary European Council). Europe's political leaders have tried to specify the characteristics (and not only the underlying values) of the ESM, considering that it 'is based on good economic performance, a high level of social protection and education and social dialogue' (Council 2002: §22) and moreover on 'full employment and greater social cohesion' (Council 2005: 29). Nonetheless, since 2004 an interpretation of the Lisbon strategy that stresses the economic dimension has challenged the original Lisbon Strategy's three dimensions (economy, employment, social cohesion): the Kok report (High Level Group on the mid-term review of the Lisbon strategy, 2004) that influenced the Spring European Council of March 2004 (Council 2004: §17), the Commission Communication to the Spring European Council 2005 (Commission 2005) that influenced the Spring 2005 Presidency Conclusions (Council 2005) and the Spring European Council of March 2006 (Council 2006: §69) have pointed out the necessity for the ESM to be 'sustainable'. In contrast, the Spring 2007 Council (Council 2007) has seemed to reaffirm the initial three sides of the equilateral triangle (growth, employment and social cohesion). Indeed, its Presidency Conclusions (Council 2007) dealt with 'boosting employment, modernizing and reinforcing the ESM' (points 18–20) and stressed the importance of the social dimension of the EU: 'in order to ensure the continuing support for European integration by the Union's citizens, (. . .) the common social objectives of Member States should be better taken into account within the Lisbon agenda' (§19).

The concept of ESM has never been quoted by the EU treaties – which does not mean that there was no reference to social issues before (see the Amsterdam Treaty). And the Treaty establishing a Constitution for Europe (2004) did not evoke the ESM either, what should be related to the conflict that opposed the President of the Convention to some of its members about the creation of a working group on social issues. Indeed, none of the initial working groups that had been constituted since June 2002 (European Convention 2002a) did include a social reflection. Social issues have thus been first discussed in Group VI on economic governance. In December 2002 a reluctant Giscard d'Estaing finally agreed to set up an additional policy-related working group XI – the last one – on 'social Europe' (European

Convention 2002b: §5). Under the presidency of M. Katiforis, this working group did not succeed in developing a coherent approach leading to the inclusion of the ESM in the Treaty establishing a Constitution for Europe. Its final report (European Convention 2003) hardly mentioned the ESM:

> several members were of the view that the definition of the objectives of the Union should contain a reference to the ESM. In this respect, some members pointed to the need to be clear on the interpretation given to this concept
>
> (European Convention 2003: §17)

Eventually, the final draft of the Constitutional Treaty did not incorporate the ESM in the definition of the Union's values and objectives (Part I, Title I, Arts I-2 and I-3) but included the objective of a

> sustainable development of Europe based on balanced economic growth, a social market economy, highly competitive and aiming at full employment and social progress, and with a high level of protection and improvement of the quality of the environment.
>
> (Treaty establishing a Constitution for Europe, Part I, Title I, Art. I-3, §3)

If the institutional debate about the ESM has been limited to the socio-economic discussions, how much did the issue of an ESM appear in public debate and in which terms?

The media coverage of the ESM in national newspapers

On the basis of database research gathering from two national newspapers from each of Italy, Great Britain, France, Spain and Germany,[4] and referencing the articles citing the keywords 'ESM' or 'social Europe' from 2001 to 2006,[5] one can notice particularities in the national debates in comparison to either the EU political debate and events or debates in other member states.

The analysis of the headlines referring to the ESM and social Europe emphasizes a progressive interest of the national media for the concept of the ESM and particularly a chronological variation of its occurrence. Indeed, though each newspaper has its own ideological standpoint, and beyond their national specificities in the coverage of the ESM, they all share a common evolution in coverage of the ESM. From 2001 to 2003, the ESM was almost not quoted in the newspapers. In 2004 the concept emerged more frequently in the articles. And in 2005 a lot of articles were devoted to the ESM while in 2006 the ESM was again less covered by national newspapers. The choice of the EU political events to be covered by the media, which depends on the particular national concerns of member states and their populations, explains this evolution. The European elections of 2004 and the enlargement in May 2004, when 10 new countries joined the EU, followed by the treaty of adhesion of Bulgaria and Romania in April 2005 and the opening of official discussions on Turkish membership in October 2005 have affected the occurrences of the ESM in the national media. The threat of the 'Polish plumber' and the general debate on possible social dumping inside the enlarged EU have activated the queries about the definition of the ESM to be submitted to the new countries. The other main events that induced great coverage of the ESM were the French and Dutch referenda on the European Constitution in May 2005 and the following Hampton Court informal EU Summit hosted by the British Presidency in October in order to face socioeconomic euroscepticism. Since the lack of social Europe has been at the heart of the criticism, on the left wing of the French electorate, the definition of the ESM and especially its ideological content became the main focus of the French campaign, as relayed by the media.

But beyond the chronological variation of the occurrences, the quotations about the ESM have varied nationally. A comparison of the national newspapers that largely referred to the ESM in the database reveals that the ESM was mostly quoted in French – *Libération* (310 references from 2001 to 2006) and *Le Figaro* (405 references) – and Spanish newspapers – with 460 references in *El País*.[6] The French case is particularly relevant since French and English newspapers were hugely diverging when it came to the ESM. If the *Guardian* and *The Times* first handled the ESM during the campaign for the British referendum on the Euro in 2002, the French *Libération* and *Le Figaro* had already been discussing the ESM and social Europe since 2001 with regard to the future of the French Left confronted with the emergence of the British Third Way. They also covered the international dimension of the ESM differently: if British newspapers put the stress on the comparison with the American socioeconomic model (especially in October and November 2004), there was almost no reference to the social dimension of the transatlantic comparison in the French ones. It reflects how French and British welfare states differ in their social principles and their proximity with the American model: the French welfare state is often considered as conservative whereas both the British and the American social systems are part of the liberal ideal type (Esping-Andersen 1990). However, both French and British newspapers were converging in referring to the 'ESM' or 'social Europe' in the media coverage of the French European Constitution referendum in 2005. In that particular case, the ESM has been related to euroscepticism, expressing the 'idea of contingent or qualified opposition, as well as incorporating outright and unqualified opposition to the process of European integration' (Taggart 1998: 366). Do public opinion surveys confirm that the ESM is negatively perceived and mainly presented as an argument in favour of euroscepticism?

Citizens' attitudes towards the ESM

Although the European regulatory social policy does not redistribute resources or constitute a 'European welfare state' (Majone 1996), it has a powerful indirect redistributive impact since it

> reflects a particular welfare compromise at the European level that constrains existing welfare compromises and choices at the domestic level (...) [towards] downward pressure on states with high labour market standards and upward pressure on states with low labour market standards.
>
> (Hix 1999: 231)

Indeed social policy does produce a reallocation of values in European societies by choosing values that are preferred by some citizens and not others. The most helpful surveys to evaluate both fears and expectations of EU citizens are the qualitative study on *The European Citizens and the Future of Europe* (OPTEM 2006) and the Special Eurobarometer 251 about *The Future of Europe* (Eurobarometer 2006), which both took place in February–March 2006 in the 25 member states.

The findings show that the EU has a positive social image and is regarded as a protective and cohesive Union. EU citizens' spontaneous declarations about the EU mentioned both unification and solidarity as the core notions in their positive perception of the EU (OPTEM 2006: 9). However, EU citizens express a perceived *gap between this positive image and the actual reality*: many citizens of the EU are pessimistic and express great concerns about a general climate marked by uncertainty, and particularly the insecurity related to the emergence of new social risks (OPTEM 2006: 8–9). The main concerns are of a socioeconomic nature, and are related primarily to employment issues in an economic situation that is perceived as unstable and to the weakening of social protection system contributing to the sense of precariousness. In these specific areas, Europeans from both old and new member states deem that the EU social performance has been poor and constitutes a major failure of the EU (Eurobarometer 2006: 60). The EU should be more convincing in order to increase its credibility and thus its legitimacy (Eurobarometer 2006: 41). The impact of globalization on this social decline – associated with the notion of competition from new member states and their workers, and more generally to the opening up of the world economy – is mentioned spontaneously in several of the older member states, but also in some of the new ones (Malta, Cyprus and Latvia in particular) (OPTEM 2006: 17).

The expectations of European citizens for the future of the European Union are primarily social and remarkably converging. In social issues, Europe seems to be in charge of a specific mission, notably removed from the North American system: EU citizens expect the EU to support economic development and put it at the service of an egalitarian and generous social policy. More than one out of two interviewees considers that comparable living standards are the key element for the future of the EU. However, one must emphasize that the results obtained in the 15 old member states (47 per cent) and those in the 10 new member states (74 per cent) differ by 27 points (Eurobarometer 2006: 37). The citizens of the new member states are thus considerably most concerned with social levels whereas in the old member states social concern is focused on the consequences of EU enlargement for the national employment market. On the one hand, a European social initiative is perceived as favourable to increase national social standards. On the other hand, a European social action is perceived as necessary to face the fear of social dumping inside the EU that threatens Europeans.

The vast majority of EU citizens would like more common European action in social areas on condition that it does not bring about social regression compared with the current system or that time is left (or support given) for the less advanced countries to adapt. In a context where each member state has its own social welfare system, 62 per cent of respondents are in favour of the *harmonization* of these systems within the EU whereas 28 per cent are against the idea (Eurobarometer 2006: 43). This desire for social harmonization seems to be stronger in the 10 new member states (81 per cent) than in the 15 old member states (58 per cent) (Eurobarometer 2006: 43). And for almost a third of participants, the harmonization of social protection systems would be a good way of strengthening European citizenship, with a difference of 23 percentage points between new and old member states: 52 per cent of citizens in the new member states against 29 per cent of citizens in the 15 old member states would feel more like European citizens with European supranational social protection (Eurobarometer 2006: 45–46).

Conclusion

Both the conceptual construction and the discursive evolution of the ESM in the EU political debate have demonstrated that the concept of the ESM is a mobilization term for policy-makers, especially when it comes to envisaging, constructing and implementing (or not) a common social and employment policy agenda at the European level and to legitimize the necessity of national social reforms on the EU scale. The ESM then appears to be an issue of political relevance for European integration in terms of both legitimacy for the EU and identity for Europeans.

On the one hand, the concept of the ESM needs to be understood rather as a political project by means of which EU institutions are seeking to increase first the legitimacy of European economic integration and then the legitimacy of national social reforms (keeping in mind that the conceptual construction of the ESM also enhances the legitimacy of EU institutions and above all the Commission's legitimacy). The ESM discussion shapes EU legitimacy either on a European essence or on common challenges to be faced and tackled: the ESM was first used in the 1990s as a historical *acquis* to be preserved and then mobilized in 2000 to build a consensus on the way to dealing with current challenges. On the other hand, the ESM has great potential for deepening European identity within the context of globalization while at the same time revealing the difficult attempts to build EU identity on stable foundations: these are shifting from the identification of shared social values between European welfare states to the preservation of national social diversity. The singular expression (the ESM) puts the stress on what unites the member states on social matters and would constitute a distinctive ESM, whereas the plural form stresses what distinguishes the member states in social matters and constitutes distinct ESMs. The ESM has thus been politically built up as a common concept symbolizing an identity shared by national social systems and relevant to European citizenship.

The findings have showed that the ESM is a controversial concept with varying policy content, depending on the political actors enacting it. It has been associated with the new socioeconomic strategy of the EU since 2000, the Lisbon strategy, which is a matter of conflict between different political interpretations, given the external context of liberal globalization and the internal pressures for social protection. In that perspective, the ESM does not aim at replacing national welfare states by a European welfare state. On the contrary, the ESM aims at respecting the national diversity of the different paths that the social systems have historically followed (*path dependency*[7]). In the current EU institutional debate on the ESM, it is not a question of harmonization but of coordination of national social policies (through the OMC). But in the public debate on the ESM, the discussions often refer to harmonization.

The national media have mainly covered the ESM through the debates about EU enlargement and the European constitution, although the EU political authorities did not focus on the ESM on those occasions. Media coverage has thus extended the use of the concept to fundamental European debates while the political authorities had restricted the debates on the ESM to socioeconomic issues. Such a public appropriation of the ESM might be related to the European citizens' feelings that the EU has a lot to do for socioeconomic matters, since a European social welfare system is seen as one of the best ways of strengthening European citizenship. In terms of EU identity, European citizens feel, more or less spontaneously, that the ESM, built on the foundations of cultural and humanistic values, is a unique feature between diverse peoples with common roots. It sets Europe in opposition to the USA, whose collective mentality is broadly perceived as very different (OPTEM 2001: 7). In this way, Europeans tend to check the EU's legitimacy by debating the EU ability to live up to expectations raised by EU institutions about the ESM.

Acknowledgements

The author wishes to thank Furio Cerutti, Sonia Lucarelli and an anonymous referee for their valuable suggestions. I am also grateful to Sandra Kröger for comments on earlier drafts.

Notes

1 These values were not new, they were encapsulated by the *Community Charter of the Fundamental Social Rights of Workers*, but that was the first time they had been linked with the ESM.
2 Such institutions (redistributive social protection, coordinated interest organizations and resolution of social conflicts by consensual means) have been set up by the welfare state's instruments and policies within individual member states (Vaughan-Whitehead 2003).
3 In a recent and highly discussed study for the think-tank Bruegel, the economist André Sapir recapitulates those authors' typologies (i.e. Esping-Andersen 1990) in assessing that 'the notion of a single ESM is largely unhelpful' since four ESMs coexist in the EU: the Nordic model; the Continental model; the Liberal model; and the Mediterranean one (Sapir 2005).
4 The newspapers surveyed are: the *Guardian*, *The Times* (along with *The Sunday Times*) (Great Britain); *La Stampa*, *Il Sole 24 Ore* (Italy); *Le Figaro*, *Libération* (France); *El Mundo*, *El País* (Spain); *Die Welt*, the *Süddeutsche Zeitung* and *Der Spiegel* (Germany).
5 I would like to thank Lisa Tormena for her helpful research on European Press in the Lexis–Nexis database.
6 Spanish newspapers are not going to be the subject of an in-depth analysis because of linguistic incompetence.
7 This concept explains the relative immobility of national social policies by the relevance of inheritance which determines the possible choices and changes in the future. It emerged with Pierson (1994) and is now commonly used in welfare state literature.

References

Commission (1993a) *Green Paper European Social Policy – Options for the Union*, COM (93) 551 final, Brussels, 17 November 1993.
——(1993b) *White Paper on Growth, Competitiveness, Employment – The Challenges and Ways forward into the 21st Century*, COM (93) 700 final, Brussels, 5 December 1993.
——(1994) *European Social Policy – A Way Forward for the Union. A White Paper*, COM (94) 333 final, Brussels, 27 July 1994.
——(2005) *Communication to the Spring European Council 2005 – Working together for growth and jobs*, COM (2005) 24, Brussels, 2 February 2005.
Council of the European Union (2000a) *Lisbon Extraordinary European Council. Presidency Conclusions, 23–24 March 2000*. Online. Available HTTP: < http://europa.eu/european_council/conclusions/index_en.htm > (accessed 29 June 2007).
——(2000b) *Santa Maria da Feira European Council. Presidency Conclusions, 19–20 June 2000*. Online. Available HTTP: < http://europa.eu/european_council/conclusions/index_en.htm > (accessed 29 June 2007).

——(2000c) *Nice European Council. Presidency Conclusions, 7–9 December 2000*. Online. Available HTTP: < http://europa.eu/european_council/conclusions/index_en.htm > (accessed 29 June 2007).

——(2002) *Barcelona European Council. Presidency Conclusions, 15–16 March 2002*. Online. Available HTTP: < http://europa.eu/european_council/conclusions/index_en.htm > (accessed 29 June 2007).

——(2004) *Brussels European Council. Presidency Conclusions, 25–26 March 2004*. Online. Available HTTP: < http://europa.eu/european_council/conclusions/index_en.htm > (accessed 29 June 2007).

——(2005) *Brussels European Council. Presidency Conclusions, 22–23 March 2005*. Online. Available HTTP: < http://europa.eu/european_council/conclusions/index_en.htm > (accessed 29 June 2007).

——(2006) *Brussels European Council. Presidency Conclusions, 23–24 March 2006*. Online. Available HTTP: < http://europa.eu/european_council/conclusions/index_en.htm > (accessed 29 June 2007).

——(2007) *Brussels European Council. Presidency Conclusions, 8–9 March 2007*. Online. Available HTTP: < http://europa.eu/european_council/conclusions/index_en.htm > (accessed 29 June 2007).

Delors, J. (2004) *Mémoires*, Paris: Plon-Pocket.

Ebbinghaus, B. (1999) 'Does a European social model exist and can it survive?', in G. Huemer, M. Mesch and F. Traxler (eds) *The Role of Employer Associations and Labour Unions in the EMU. Institutional requirements for European economic policies*, Aldershot: Ashgate.

Esping-Andersen, G. (1990) *The Three Worlds of the Welfare Capitalism*, Princeton: Princeton University Press.

Eurobarometer (2006) *The Future of Europe. Special Eurobarometer 251. Wave 65.1*, European Commission, Public opinion Analysis, Brussels. Online. Available HTTP: < http://ec.europa.eu/public_opinion/archives/ebs/ebs_251_en.pdf > (accessed 29 June 2007).

European Convention (2002a) *Composition of the Working Groups*, CONV 77/1/02 REV1, 14 June 2002. Online. Available HTTP: < http://register.consilium.eu.int/pdf/en/02/cv00/00077-r1en2.pdf > (accessed 29 June 2007).

——(2002b) *Summary Report of the Plenary Session – Brussels, 5 and 6 December 2002*, CONV 449/02, 13 December 2002. Online. Available HTTP: < http://register.consilium.eu.int/pdf/en/02/cv00/00449en2.pdf > (accessed 29 June 2007).

——(2003) *Final Report of Working Group XI on Social Europe*, CONV 516/1/03, 30 January 2003. Online. Available HTTP: < http://register.consilium.eu.int/pdf/en/03/cv00/cv00516en03.pdf > (accessed 29 June 2007).

Ferrera, M., Hemerijck, A. and Rhodes, M. (2000) *The Future of Social Europe: recasting work and welfare in the new economy*, Report prepared for the Portuguese Presidency of the EU, Oeiras: Celta Editora.

Goetschy, J. (2006) 'Taking stock of social Europe: is there such a thing as a community social model?', in M. Jepsen and A. Serrano Pascual (eds) *Unwrapping of the European Social Model*, Cambridge: Polity Press.

Hay, C., Watson, M. and Wincott, D. (1999) *Globalization, European Integration and the Persistence of European Social Models*, POLSIS Working Paper, no. 3, University of Birmingham.

Hemerijck, A. (2002) 'The self-transformation of the European social model(s)', in G. Esping-Andersen (ed.) *Why We Need a New Welfare State*, Oxford: Oxford University Press.

High Level Group on the mid-term review of the Lisbon strategy (2004) *Facing the Challenge: the Lisbon strategy for growth and employment*, Report for the Commission of the European Communities, November 2004. Online. Available HTTP: < http://ec.europa.eu/growthandjobs/pdf/kok_report_en.pdf > (accessed 29 June 2007).
Hix, S. (1999) *The Political System of the European Union*, New York: Palgrave.
Jepsen, M. and Serrano Pascual, A. (2005) 'The European social model: an exercise in deconstruction', *Journal of European Social Policy*, 15: 231–45.
Majone, G. (1996) *Regulating Europe*, London: Routledge.
OPTEM (2001) *Perceptions of the European Union (General Report). Qualitative study of the public's attitudes to and expectations of the European Union in the 15 member states and in 9 candidate countries*. Online. Available HTTP: < http://ec.europa.eu/governance/areas/studies/optem-report_en.pdf > (accessed 29 June 2007).
——(2006) *The European Citizens and the Future of Europe (Overall Report). Qualitative study among citizens in the 25 member states*. Online. Available HTTP: < http://ec.europa.eu/public_opinion/quali/ql_futur_en.pdf > (accessed 29 June 2007).
Pierson, P. (1994) *Dismantling the Welfare State? Reagan, Thatcher and the politics of retrenchment*, Cambridge: Cambridge University Press.
Radaelli, C. (2003) 'The Open Method of Coordination: a new governance architecture for the European Union?', Report for the Swedish Institute for European Policy Studies, 2003/01. Online. Available HTTP: < http://www.sieps.se/publ/rapporter/bilagor/20031.pdf > (accessed 29 June 2007).
Sapir, A. (2005) 'Globalization and the reform of European social models', *Bruegel Policy Brief*, 2005/01.
Scharpf, F. (2002) 'The European social model: coping with the challenges of diversity', *Journal of Common Market Studies*, 40 (4): 645–69.
Scharpf, F. and Schmidt, V. (eds) (2000) *Welfare and Work in the Open Economy*, Oxford: Oxford University Press.
Stjernø, S. (2005) *Solidarity in Europe*, Cambridge: Cambridge University Press.
Streeck, W. (1999) *Competitive Solidarity: rethinking the European social model*, MPIfG Working Paper, no. 8, Köln: Max-Planck-Institut für Gesellschaftsforschung.
Taggart, P. (1998) 'A touchstone of dissent: euroscepticism in contemporary Western European party systems', *European Journal of Political Research*, 3: 363–88.
Telò, M. (2002) 'Governance and government in the European Union: the Open Method of Coordination', in M. J. Rodriguez (ed.) *The New Knowledge Economy in Europe*, Cheltenham: Edward Elgar.
Telò, M. and Magnette, P. (2001) 'Justice and solidarity', in F. Cerutti and E. Rudolph (eds) *A Soul for Europe*, vol.1, Leuven: Peeters.
Vaughan-Whitehead, D. C. (2003) *EU Enlargement versus Social Europe?* Cheltenham: Edward Elgar.
Wincott, D. (2003) 'The idea of the European social model: limits and paradoxes of Europeanization', in K. Featherstone and C. Radaelli (eds) *The Politics of Europeanization*, Oxford: Oxford University Press.

9 The double face of civil society

Debora Spini

> *La societé civile européenne, dont on a fait un grand usage rhétorique dans ces dernières années, ne rayonne guère au-delà du microcosme bruxellois.*
>
> (Dehousse 2005: 177)

Opposite to the above sceptical view of a Paris-based scholar, European Union (EU) documents and web sites overflow with references to a European civil society, and even the simplest web search with this keyword is bound to meet with an unmanageable amount of responses. The blunt question of whether a European civil society really does, or does not, exist does not help to capture the reality of the European polity.

This chapter will identify two main models of civil society. The first model understands civil society as the system of needs, in the wake of the Hegelian tradition. This kind of civil society has in fact played a very important role – and it still does – in reinforcing performance-based legitimacy. In the second model, civil society is the grounds where public opinion can be born, claiming to be the source of democratic legitimacy. Both models have been present in the European integration process, both continue to strive to gain central stage.

The rest of the chapter will deal with the two models, their application to the European case (sections 2 and 3) and the type of contribution that each of them can provide to the EU's legitimacy and to the Europeans' political identity (section 4).

Civil society: an elusive category

Since the great wave of post-1989 transformations, the expression 'civil society' has become extremely popular in scholarly and political debates, and it expanded from the descriptive to the normative level. Political theory is now confronted with the challenge of conceptualising a civil society capable of acting over and above national boundaries, increasingly perceived as obsolete. The immense literature, developed on the theme of global civil society, tends in general to adopt a Habermasian – or more precisely post-Habermasian – perspective, such as the by-now classic definition by Cohen and Arato (1992), where civil society is mostly conceived as the galaxy of public interest groups, excluding the economic, interest-related dimension. Besides, a growing literature on globalization identifies a civil society as those groups who recognise themselves in the defence of human rights, democracy and human development (Falk 1999). This language does not help to capture the reality of the European polity, as it followed, and still follows, a different pattern; this chapter will follow a different itinerary.

In the history of modern political thought, civil society has traditionally represented the middle ground between private life and an exquisitely political space, more specifically the level of the state and of government. Civil society therefore emerges as a space *in between*, which may be further defined according to two different perspectives. The first one coincides with the genealogy stretching from the Scottish Enlightenment to Hegel and Marx and sees civil society basically as the 'system of needs', a space where collective yet selfish interests are organised and actually compete with each other. Hegel's *bürgerliche Gesellschaft*, however, is not solely the battlefield of selfish drives. In civil society individuals join together to form corporations, social groupings primarily focused on the defence of specific interests that are, therefore, always potentially in conflict with their own peers. Nonetheless, these associations are more than the sum of individual egoisms; they are the space where individuals can – and must – learn to think and behave as a body. Moreover, Hegel highlights how corporations have to 'go public', as they cannot avoid meeting their own peers in the open arena of civil society. This encounter by nature involves conflict, yet it represents an essential step, because every corporation – and the individual members within it – will be exposed to the necessity of finding a reconciliation through the medium of law. Mediating potential and actual conflicts, and leading opposed interests to a general aim is the function of *Recht*; civil society, intrinsically marked by conflict, needs the state in order to 'outgrow' its own essence.

In the second model, civil society appears as a public of 'reasonable' men (mostly!) whose members have learned to think about and judge public affairs, and to perceive themselves as the public opinion. Civil society thus becomes the source and the ultimate *tribunal of legitimacy*, as the space where matters of common relevance may be debated and evaluated through the public use of reason. In the interpretation of authors such as John Stuart Mill this will become the classic liberal view of civil society. Habermas has reinterpreted civil society as the cradle of legitimacy in a more republican perspective. In his *Structural Transformation of the Public Sphere* and even more in *Between Facts and Norms*, Habermas describes civil society as the greenhouse where new issues and demands are formed, picked up and re-elaborated by the public sphere and finally translated into norms by the political system (Habermas 1991, 1996).

In both versions, civil society as a space in between has defined its identity in a kind of dialectic relationship with the state, conceived according to the national–territorial model. If understood as the system of needs, it needed the state to act as a mediator and arbiter, or more specifically, as the producer of those norms which would prevent the space of conflicting interests from imploding. But also, in its version as the point of origin of public opinion and the cradle of legitimacy, civil society had as its reference a constitutional regime of representative democracy, traditionally defined by the borders of a territory. Within these borders, civil society produced new claims and new themes: specifically political actors would then channel and translate such stimuli into policies and law-making. This role may be radically altered in a situation such as that of the post-national constellation, better represented by a model of multitiered or multilevel governance than by the vertical framework of government. Supposedly, the shift towards governance undermines vertical relationships and highlights horizontal relationships, as civil society is often called to directly participate in the function of governance (Rosenau 2003). Ulrich Beck holds that civil society is the third actor in what he defines the metapower game of global governance, acting on equal footing with political institutions and economic power (Beck 2005). In this perspective, civil society is no longer the space where new political themes and issues are first brought to attention nor is it the greenhouse for government legitimacy, and it does not need any more *acteurs généralistes* to articulate discourses that claim to be genuinely public. Although it must not be taken uncritically, this reflection is fascinating, as it opens up a scenario where civil society absorbs the specific quality of political action; it may be relevant for the case of the European Union as a particularly complex example of multilevel governance.

A European civil society? Comparing models

Model one: interests in dialogue

The first model – that of civil society as the field of interest representation populated by actors originating from the world of production and work – has proved to fit quite successfully with the practice and history of the European polity. Since its inception, the EEC (European Economic Community) sought to bring peace and prosperity – or, more precisely, peace *through* prosperity. The founders' generation abandoned the original federalist view in order to embrace a second-hand democratic legitimacy (Warleigh 2003), always in view of Jean Monnet's strategy of 'federalism through functionalism'. A successful performance in the economic field was to provide the EEC with a result-based legitimacy; the understanding of civil society and its consequent role was largely determined by such a perspective. The integration process immediately welcomed and stimulated the birth of pressure groups, in view of reproducing on the Community level the same *neo-corporative dialogue* happening in many national contexts (Magnette 2000: 215). A civil society composed of interest groups harmonised very well with a performance-based conception of legitimacy. At this stage, civil society harboured no ambition to give birth to a European public opinion and thus to reinforce a value-based legitimacy, nor did it claim to contribute to the creation of a European identity – these two effects were, at most, expected to surface as fringe benefits of performance.

In the structure of the EEC, room was made at quite an early stage for what was called 'organised civil society', which meant essentially interest-representing bodies. The Treaty of Rome provided for the European Economic and Social Committee (EESC), which still today defines itself as 'the bridge between Europe and organised civil society' (European Economic and Social Committee 2007). Basically, its function was – and still is – to 'test' policies by running them by the representatives of organised interest groups, and may be defined as a form of *regulated lobbying*. A well-articulated system of interests representation resourced the EEC with expertise and provided a safe space where policies could be tested and negotiated. A structured channel of contacts with civil society made it possible for the EU to anticipate consensus or disagreement. This function was not fulfilled exclusively by the EESC, but took place through formal and informal channels at many levels of the EU.

This relationship has contributed to the shaping of the very structure of the organisations active at the European level. As the competences and fields of action of the Community became more and more complex and specialised, and the practice of comitology gained momentum, pressure groups as well increased in number and became more and more inclined towards specialisation rather than taking up broader agendas. This style of interaction between interest groups and institutions still persists in the life of the EU: Gregor Kreuzhuber, speaker for the Agriculture Commissioner, defined dialogue with professional association as 'a system that works well'. The system, however, does not solely mean friendly consultation, but more aggressive lobbying. Lobbying has boomed within the EU towards both the Commission and the European Parliament. In 2001, *Le Figaro* reported a total figure of 15,000 lobbyists, quite close to the 20,000 present in Washington.[1] The EU database CONECCS features a long, and constantly growing, list of both public and private interest-based organisations active and present at the European level, whereas Justin Greenwood lists 1,450 'formal interests groups' (Greenwood 2005: 19).

The Union has been defined as a governance *for* the people and also *with* the people – hence the role of organised civil society in cooperating in policy-making – but it has not been defined as a governance *of* and *by* the people (Schmidt 2006: 10). The official discourse of the EESC and of the Commission emphasises the dialogue aspects of European governance;

surely the EU has made a major investment in the elaboration of new modes of governance (such as the Open Method of Coordination launched by the Lisbon European Council in 2000), which was meant to open more spaces for participation. Still, the dichotomy 'for/with' versus 'of/by' seems to maintain all its poignancy. This system of consultation reinforces the image of an EU as a body capable of producing 'policies without politics', engaging in procedures of consultation but lacking democratic transparency. Paul Magnette has described European governance as a *technocratie ouverte*; this definition is not contradictory as it may appear, as it points to a scenario where civil society functions as consultant and dialogue-partner on the fringe of a centre of power that remains largely technocratic.

Model two: public opinion

Civil society, understood as the source for public opinion and, consequently, as the source of legitimacy, seems to have a more troubled relationship with European polity. However, this second version is gaining momentum in the debate of the last few years, and this is connected to the dynamics that stretch from the Single European Act to the constitutional process, as can be seen in the Laeken declaration (European Council 2001; Rumford 2002). Civil society – meant as organised interest groups – has been a precious partner in constructing legitimacy through results, by providing knowledge, anticipating feedback, in a word, reinforcing the model of governance *for* and *with* the people. In a context where a specific political quality was required from the EU, a new perspective opened up for civil society in the form of public interest groups, where it could claim to be the breeding ground of value-based legitimacy. These tensions between different models and growing expectations can be found in several documents (European Economic and Social Committee 1999, 2001) and are particularly evident in the *White Paper on European Governance* (Commission 2001), which seems to swing between the two definitions, one closer to a (*grosso modo*) Hegelian vision and one more inclined towards public opinion. Civil society is alternatively described as composed of 'stakeholders' or as coincident with the 'general public' (see Joerges *et al.* 2001; Ruzza 2004). These documents shared the challenge of reconsidering the issues of legitimacy in the perspective of combining representative and 'participative' democracy. Civil society was assigned the role of main partner for the latter, and was reconceptualised as an important breeding ground for European identity based on common values (see European Economic and Social Committee 1999: 27–28).

The constitutional process represented an important stage where public interest groups could claim a new role, as the EU institutions declared their intention to foster a 'Europe of citizens'. Insofar as the Constitution could be expected to give birth to a European *demos* without *ethnos*, transforming 'customers into citizens', a European civil society then had a chance to develop into something more than a meeting ground for different organised interests, a space where conceptions of common good could be discussed and debated (Bellamy *et al.* 2006). The Convention was therefore presented as a forum where civil society organisations had the possibility to make their voices heard, somehow along the lines that conducted the drafting of the Charter of Fundamental Rights of the European Union. Still, defining it as a deliberative arena where the first step was 'listening and hearing' to civil society, in view of realising communicative rationality (Piana 2005; Fossum 2005) is a bit overoptimistic. The Convention was a very important step in stimulating a non-irredeemably ephemeral European public sphere (Loretoni and Henry 2001; Dehousse 2002: 179–226), but it was not alien from shortcomings and weaknesses, as will be discussed below. However, empirical research shows that the workings of the Convention did raise a tolerable level of interest. According to three flash Eurobarometers, European citizens showed a desire to be 'better informed' about the workings of the Constitution (Eurobarometer 2003a,b; 2004). Moreover, one of the Eurobarometers showed that 77 per cent of the respondents 'believed the European Union should adopt a Constitution': current EU member states 78 per cent and new accession states 73 per cent (Eurobarometer 2004: 21). These findings are all the more interesting in light of the negative results of the referenda of spring 2005.

Even the European press registered, at least to a certain extent, the involvement of civil society. Not surprisingly, the French and Italian press were among the first to echo the participation of civil society, as is shown by the articles that appeared from early 2001 to the end of 2002, when the draft of the Constitutional Treaty was presented. On the whole, press coverage was quite good.[2] The great expectations raised by the constitutional process were also reinforced by the February 2003 demonstrations against the Iraq war. The media and relevant observers, in the wake of Habermas and Derrida, saluted the birth of a European public opinion sharing a common identity, even against the cleavages dividing the European governments.[3] Attention to the role of civil society in the constitutional process also revived around 2005, at least in the French press, during the referendum campaign.[4]

However, not all press reports were equally optimistic about the actual role and meaningfulness of civil society as represented in the forum. On the contrary, many voices were extremely critical.[5] More specifically, the galaxy of 'alterglobalism' gathered at the Second European Social Forum meeting in Paris in November 2003 remained extremely critical of the whole constitutional process.[6] These criticisms are particularly relevant, as they come from groups that surely deserve to be considered part of a European civil society, and therefore shed light on some evident weaknesses of the involvement of grassroots groups and militant organisations in the constitutional process. Taking part in the forum were mostly 'domesticated' organisations, well trained in European ways and well nourished by Commission funds, whereas the most radical fringes watched from the outside, sometimes even

148 *Debora Spini*

voicing their loud criticism. Jacques Nikonoff, president of the French branch of Attac, remarked that basically all proposals from NGOs (non-governmental organisations) had been rejected.[7] Therefore, it is evident that civil society in the EU is composed of two souls, often at war with each other; even in its 'civic-minded' version, European civil society is very diverse.

Civil society without a Constitution

The question whether European civil society has succeeded in being something more than a consultative resource on policies appears all the more urgent in the aftermath of the Constitutional referenda. Of course, the usual generic appeal to civil society is present in the official discourse of the Commission, as can be shown in the so-called 'Plan D' launched by the Barroso Commission (Commission 2005)[8]. At any rate, the plan seems to draw a clear division of work: the political actors called to debate about the future of the Union are identified within the member states, whereas on the European level the reference is solely to 'civil society'.

Civil society, understood as the world of stakeholders, continues to function and flourish. The answer to the question posed at the beginning of this section is more hesitant insofar as the second model is concerned, i.e. the galaxy of public interest groups, or non-governmental organisations, that should represent European public opinion *in nuce*. The answer cannot be altogether negative: the presence of civic concern groups is now firmly established. Moreover, since the Convention, European media are beginning to recognise NGOs, and not only lobbies, as part of the EU landscape, although the attention to specifically European civil society does not match that given to 'global' NGOs.[9] Interest groups are now represented in Brussels in large numbers, and, according to Greenwood, they are 'the second largest category of EU interest groups, accounting for around one-fifth of their number'. Greenwood moreover indicates that the Commission's funding for NGO activities is of at least 1 billion euros per year (Greenwood 2005: 179). In 2005, CONECCS listed 700 civil society organisations and over 200 NGOs (Ruzza 2005). It would be very hard to provide a complete list, as these groups are extremely diverse in scope or in constituency. Often the organisations listed are networks of networks, such as the Environmental G8 or the Social Platform, as smaller NGOs find it too demanding, financially and organisationally, to be present on the Brussels scene, and therefore prefer to be represented by larger bodies who have the skills and the expertise to be active.

The performance of public interest groups is uneven; traditionally, consumers and environmentalist associations have the higher impact on policy-making, whereas other groups such as ant-racism groups seem to struggle more (Greenwood 2005; Guiraudon 2001; Ruzza 2006: 174). Sheer numbers do not necessarily mean relevance and capacity to impact policies. Although private interests groups have a well-established pattern of dialogue with the EU the case is less clear with public interest groups. The need to establish a firmer link between public interest groups and the institutional life of the Union had already been the rationale for a proposal to establish a *civil dialogue*, discussed since the 1996–97 Intergovernmental Conference and warmly supported by the EESC (European Economic and Social Committee 1999: 40). The idea was to provide public interest groups with a legal structure to facilitate their participation in policy-making on issues of 'civic' concern, to match the relatively successful social dialogue. The proposal had no success and no legal structure supports a 'civil dialogue'.

The cohabitation between the two souls of European civil society is far from being harmonious. Although an anonymous lobbyist from Brussels complains that chemical industries find it harder to influence the Commission, and that they have been 'replaced' by NGOs, the power balance still seems to be firmly on the side of private interests groups.[10] Civic concern organisations cannot count on the same *mos commune* of negotiation practices that is by now taken for granted by private interest groups. Moreover, they simply have less power then the great lobbies: Erik Wesselius and Olivier Hoedeman from *Alter Europe*, a network grouping 140 NGOs, underline how consultations with NGOs are often purely lip-service.[11] A paradigmatic example is the case of the REACH proposal on the classification of dangerous chemicals. Jorgo Riss, from Greenpeace in Brussels, admits that their 10 members of staff are no match for the at least 140 lobbyists mobilised by the chemical industry on that particular dossier.[12] Following NGOs' accusations against the power of 'lobbycracy', the European Commissioner for Administrative Affairs, Audit and Anti-Fraud, Siim Kallas, has launched a European Transparency Initiative, which is currently undergoing a great deal of criticism, and is being accused of 'watering down' the need to keep lobbying under control (Commission 2006[13]).

In spite of the gap that divides them from interest groups, even NGOs are undergoing a process of professionalisation, transforming grassroots groups to *lobbyistes idealistes*. Requirements of the internal functioning of groups, such as the representation criteria imposed by the Commission to ensure openness and internal democracy (Commission 2002), sometimes backfire on those groups that are supposed to become more democratic for their own constituency. Instead of fostering citizens' participation and closeness to EU life, such standards contribute to the professionalisation of the world of Civil Society Organisations (CSOs) working in close contact with the EU. Grassroots organisations find it very hard to comply with Commission requirements, and therefore only more 'professional' NGOs are likely to remain in the game. Otherwise, grassroots groups are represented in Brussels through large networks of NGOs, which of course maximise efficiency and expertise, but lose contact with their constituency. To keep their status, NGOs and CSOs are implicitly or explicitly forced to take up the functioning model, and, even more so, the style of work, of their counterpart. Following a pattern common to all transnational NGOs (Kaldor 2003) former grass-roots groups become tamed para-bureaucracies, or in this specific case an 'emerging polyglot euro-élite' (Guiraudon 2001: 173). Empirical research has shown that 300 professional consultancy companies had been established in Brussels by 2002; although for the most part they work for business groups, some of them lend their services also to public interest groups. More and more often, activists are replaced by communication professionals, as is in the case of the European Women's Lobby and the European Trade Union Confederation (ETUC) (Saurugger 2006: 279–81). Civil society, at the moment, risks being the battlefield of *lobbyistes–realistes* and *lobbyistes–idealistes*. A comparative analysis of EU official documents and of position papers produced by a selection of large groups or networks from 'Civil Society Organised at the European Level' has shown that the policy discourses of EU institutions and of this kind of public interest group are substantially in agreement. Both parties share the conviction that civil society may be instrumental in policy implementation, in disseminating information, in improving the coordination of vertical governance, functioning as a link between different levels, and in improving horizontal diffusion of policies. CSOs and EU institutions differ on one significant point. The latter emphasise the 'usefulness' of civil society in making EU governance more effective, and, ultimately, in reinforcing performance-based legitimacy, whereas the former voices a claim for clearer rules in the consultation process, and more transparency and accountability on the side of the EU (Ruzza 2006). It would probably be too harsh to say that these data support a vision of civil society at the European level as tamed and 'normalised'; nonetheless, this research shows a basic *entente cordiale* between the two worlds.

The very structure of the Union shapes and moulds the nature and functioning of public interest groups, as it makes it easier to go for lobbying rather than for civic mobilisation (Imig and Tarrow 2001). In the political space of the Union it is hard to recreate the symbolic dimension of politics: why should one shout in the streets of Brussels? But the problem of the delocalisation of decisions has a more complex dynamic. The streets of Brussels remain mostly silent and empty of contentious politics, which continues to be, with few exceptions, the domain of individual states. A peculiar chiasmus is thus created: if the EU is policy-making without politics, just the opposite can be said about member states, i.e. that they are the theatre of politics without policies, where citizens in fact mobilise to an ever-increasing degree, but always in the wrong places (Schmidt 2006). European national elites also bear a degree of responsibility in reverting to the very expedient strategy of blame-shifting, accusing the EU of everything that is going wrong, and failing to alphabetise their constituencies on the working of European governance. This peculiar division of work taking place between the European Union and member states seems again to point towards a governance *with* and *for* the people, and not *by* the people, or at least not by the European people.

European civil society, in all its many souls, has to live and operate in a situation where there is – at least for some substantial time – no constitutional framework to provide European citizens with a definite reference point. This does not imply that the two souls of European civil society do not have any more opportunities, or challenges, to face. Although no Constitution is there to create a *demos*, nonetheless, not everything is lost, and a patrimony of practices and experiences has piled up in recent years. As remarked by Cerutti (2005), 'the European peoples should be given time, but also more concrete ways to *make experience* of the Union'. And in fact, European civil society – in all its many faces, interest groups, NGOs and grassroots movements – can provide the embryo for a European public space. Undoubtedly, a lively galaxy of public interest groups organised at the European level may be an important space for debate and communicative processes that will contribute to the construction of a European identity beyond banal Europeanism. Empirical research shows that European citizens are learning how to juggle their feelings of belonging to national and local communities with a specifically European dimension of identity (Meier and Risse 2003; Euronat 2005). Therefore, it is not sheer wishful thinking which affirms that participating in civic interest groups on the European level represents a learning process where citizens of the Union may practice their 'hyphenated' European identity.

The civic-minded soul of civil society is now facing a temptation, that of presenting itself as 'the' representative of European public opinion. Public interest groups organised at the European level are a precious contribution to the European polity, but cannot voice such a claim. First of all, this is because of their being often domesticated, dependent on Commission funds and Brussels centred. Moreover, NGOs are for their own nature issue oriented, and cannot be automatically expected to replace political actors. In the historical experience of European states, political parties had the role to collect and re-elaborate the stimuli coming from civil society. It has been observed that the EU, because of its internal functioning dynamic, does not seem to favour the development of *acteurs généralistes* (Magnette 2003) such as political parties. This is not solely a European problem: on the contrary, it is evident at the level of many national states. The problem is the generalised crisis experienced by the simple, yet imposing, neo-classic architecture of parliamentarism – 'la majesteuse simplicité formelle des démocraties parlementaires' (Magnette 2000: 203) – which is now being replaced by some kind of extremely post-modern project, or by a composite medieval cathedral (Dehousse 2005). It is almost commonplace to recall that European parties are mostly umbrella organisations; however, some recent examples seem to show a different trend, where national political parties increasingly turn to their European dimension as an important reference point for their identity, as is demonstrated by the recent debates about the *Partito Democratico* in Italy and by the presidential campaign of 2007 in France.

Concluding remarks

What then is the role of European civil society in constructing a political identity and a more solid rooted legitimacy for the European Union? The solution is not in invoking a growing role for a European civil society, in the form of more consultations with Brussels-based networks, be they lobbying for values or for interests. Civil society present at the European level cannot expect to do more than what is in its dual, ambiguous nature. The challenge is how to bring into being a genuine political life for the Union, a challenge made all the more complex by the particular nature of the European polity. The formula stating that the EU is not a state writ large is valid in this case as well: the politicisation of Europe can hardly happen in the terms of a simple repetition of the mechanisms that have worked for national states, which anyway are, as mentioned above, experiencing a phase of crisis. A European public space has come to light, in spite of the many disillusions and drawbacks. It may be partially sustained by more transnational associations, but its primary nourishment will be provided by the compenetration of national and European political issues in the debates in individual states. The public space of the EU may be conceived as composed of many intersecting levels. The challenge before the European polity is to involve and transform the national polities (Schmidt 2006) and in this perspective a very important role may be played by European civil society. In fact, supernational organisations and networks have proved to cause what has been called a boomerang effect, or, in other words a sort of virtuous circle between the national and the super- and transnational level (Kaldor 2003: 96). The first model of European civil society – the more 'Hegel-inspired' one – is not excluded from this perspective; after all, doing business together may prove conducive to closer bonds among European citizens. Of course, the most important role in this process of creation of a European public arena is to be played by the second model of civil society, that conceived as a space where Europeans may engage in debates about matters of common concern, political projects and shared values. Civil society is contiguous, but not altogether coincident, with politics; so, the development of a lively civil society cannot be invoked as a panacea to legitimise the Union and to reinforce a value-based identity. In this sense, the capacity of CSOs present at the European level to interact creatively with political and social actors present at the level of individual polities will be an essential step in the process of politicisation of the Union, which means, ultimately, in the creation of a genuine European public space. Without such a dynamic, civil society, even in its more public-minded form, will be confined – as the European case shows very clearly – to a competition for influence that remains limited to a 'lobbying for values'.

Acknowledgements

I wish to thank Dario Castiglione, from Exeter University, for reading this chapter and providing precious insights. I also wish to thank all the members of our Florence Group for the comments they made to earlier versions of this chapter.

Notes

1 'L'influence grandissantes des lobbies', *Le Figaro*, 19 March 2001. For this chapter I have used the result of the research on Lexis–Nexis using as keywords 'civil society' and 'NGOs'. I have identified as crucial moments the most important phases of the works of the Convention and of the constitutional process, from the opening in 2001, through the presentation of the Constitution's draft in 2002 and the referenda in 2005. I have also selected as particularly relevant the weeks immediately surrounding the various European Social Fora, and the wave of anti-war demonstrations in February 2003. Moreover, I have screened the results using as an additional reference the word 'lobby'.
2 'Le débat sur "l'après-Nice" relancé par le président de la Commission Européenne; Prodi appelle à la refondation', *Le Figaro*, 14 February 2001; 'L'après-Nice et l'architecture future de l'Union', *Le Figaro*, 26 February 2001; 'M. Prodi, l'intelligence et l'autorité', *Le Figaro*, 28 October 2002; 'The Future of Europe: A pivotal moment in history', the *Guardian*, 28 February 2002; 'Brüssel mit Herz; Mit einem Bekenntnis zur Sozialpolitik grenzt sich der Jugendkonvent der Europäischen Union von den Erwachsenen ab', *Süddeutsche Zeitung*, 13 July 2002; 'Europas letzte Chance; Die Union muss einfacher und wirksamer werden, um vor ihren Bürgern auch künftig zu bestehen', *Süddeutsche Zeitung*, 23 July 2002; 'Lettere dall'Europa; ecco i pilastri della nuova Carta', *Il Sole 24 Ore*, 27 October 2002; 'Prove di governo per l'economia', *La Stampa*, 29 October 2002; 'El Futuro de Europa', *El País*, 24 November 2002.
3 'Une Europe divisée mais des Européens unis. Au-delà des gouvernements, une véritable opinion européenne est en train de naître', *Le Figaro*, 11 February 2003; 'Zapatero dice que toda Europa sabe ahora que la voz de Aznar no es la de Espagna', *El País*, 17 February 2003; 'Die neue Friedensbewegung', *Süddeutsche Zeitung*, 17 February 2003.
4 'La societé civile obtiendra-t-elle plus de droits?', *Libération*, 20 April 2005; 'L'horreur démocratique; "Quelle Europe voulons-nous?"; Quand le président d'Attac France remet en question la Constitution', *Le Figaro*, 25 May 2005.
5 'La société civile est invitée à présenter ses suggestions sous la Toile; Un forum virtuel sur l'avenir de l'Europe', *Le Figaro*, 15 April 2002; 'La Convention à l'écoute de la société civile', *Le Figaro*, 26 June 2002.
6 'Vers une "alterpolitique"? Des dirigeants de la CFDT, d'Attac et du PS débattent des débouchés du mouvement 2003', *Libération*, 10 November 2003; 'ONG et syndicats appellent à manifester contre la future Constitution. Une manif contre la constitution L'Europe en ligne de mire', *Libération*, 17 November 2003.
7 'L'horreur démocratique; "Quelle Europe voulons-nous?". Quand le président d'Attac France remet en question la Constitution', *Le Figaro*, 25 May 2005; see also 'La Convention à l'écoute de la société civile', *Le Figaro*, 26 June 2002.
8 Cf. 'El Futuro de Europa', *El País*, 16 June 2005; 'Idées en Berne au Parlement de Strasbourg', *Libération*, 10 June 2005.
9 Although of course the attitude of the press is very different. The coverage is very good in the French newspapers *Le Figaro* and *Libération* and in the German *Süddeutsche Zeitung*. In the UK, a progressive newspaper such as the *Guardian* follows European issues with great attention; the point of view of European NGOs also receives some space. Little or no mention in *The Times*, which instead monitors quite closely NGOs active on the global level. These comments are evidently very sketchy, but on the whole seem to fit quite well with the results

154 *Debora Spini*

of the *Europub* research project on European Media; see http://europub.wz-berlin.de.
10 'Que prepare Bruxelles?', *Le Figaro*, 29 October 2001.
11 '"On ne lutte pas à armes égales"; Erik Wesselius, chercheur et activiste, dénonce le poids des lobbies et relativise la transparence que veut mettre en place la Commission', *Libération*, 4 May 2006; 'Au paradis des lobbies. Visite guidée avec une ONG des coulisses bruxelloises des groupes de pressions industriels', *Libération*, 31 May 2004.
12 'Bruxelles sensible aux arguments toxiques; Intense lobbying des industriels contre le projet d'évaluation des produits chimiques', *Libération*, 30 October 2003.
13 'Quand Bruxelles met ses lobbyistes sous pression', *Libération*, 29 May 2006; 'EU lobbyists under attack: campaigners angry that curbs on special interest groups have been watered down', the *Guardian*, 30 May 2006.

References

Beck, U. (2005) *Power in the Global Age. A new global political economy*, Cambridge: Polity Press.
Bellamy, R., Castiglione, D. and Shaw, J. (2006) (eds) *Making European Citizens: civic inclusion in a transnational context*, Houndmills, New York: Palgrave.
Cerutti, F (2005) 'Europe's deep crisis', *European Review*, 13: 525–40.
Cohen, J. and Arato, A. (1992) *Civil Society and Political Theory*, Cambridge, MA: MIT Press.
Commission (2001) *A White Paper on European Governance*, COM (2001) 428 final, Brussels, 25 July 2001. Online. Available HTTP: < http://europa.eu.int/eur-lex/en/com/cnc/2001/com2001_0428en01.pdf > (accessed 20 June 2007).
—— (2002) *Communication: Towards a reinforced culture of consultation and dialogue – General principles and minimum standards for consultation of interested parties by the Commission*, COM (2002) 704 final, Brussels, 11 December 2002.
—— (2005) *The Commission's Contribution to the Period of Reflection and Beyond: Plan D for democracy, dialogue and debate*, COM (2005) 494 final, Brussels, 13 October 2005. Online. Available HTTP: < http://ec.europa.eu/commission_barroso/wallstrom/pdf/communication_planD_en.pdf > (accessed 20 June 2007).
—— (2006) *Green Paper on European Transparency Initiative*, COM (2006) 194 final, Brussels, 3 May 2006. Online. Available HTTP: < http://ec.europa.eu/transparency/eti/docs/gp_en.pdf > (accessed 20 June 2007).
Dehousse, R. (2002) (ed.) *Une constitution pour l'Europe?* Paris: Presses de Sciences Politiques.
—— (2005) *La fin de l'Europe*, Paris: Flammarion.
Eurobarometer (2003a) *Convention on the Future of Europe – Wave 1. Flash Eurobarometer 142/1*, June 2003, European Commission, Public opinion Analysis, Brussels. Online. Available HTTP: < http://ec.europa.eu/public_opinion/flash/fl142_1_convention_en.pdf > (accessed 20 June 2007).
—— (2003b) *Convention on the Future of Europe – Wave 2. Flash Eurobarometer 142/2*, September-October 2003, European Commission, Public opinion Analysis, Brussels. Online. Available HTTP: < http://ec.europa.eu/public_opinion/flash/fl142_2_convention_en.pdf > (accessed 20 June 2007).
—— (2004) *The future European Constitution. Flash Eurobarometer 159*, January–February 2004, European Commission, Public opinion Analysis, Brussels. Online.

Available HTTP: < http://ec.europa.eu/public_opinion/flash/fl159_fut_const.pdf > (accessed 20 June 2007).
Euronat (2005) *Representation of Europe and the Nation in Current and Perspective Member States: Media Elites and Civil society, Final Report*. Online. Available HTTP: < http://www.iue.it/RSCAS/Research/EURONAT/200505Rep.EURONAT-Final.pdf > (accessed 20 June 2007).
European Council (2001) *Laeken Declaration on the Future of Europe, Attachment to the Presidency Conclusions*, European Council Meeting in Laeken, 14–15 December 2001 (SN300/01 ADD1). Online. Available HTTP: < http://www.euconvention.be/static/LaekenDeclaration.asp > (accessed 20 June 2007).
European Social and Economic Committee (EESC) (1999) *The Civil Society Organised at European Level*, Proceedings of the First Convention, Brussels, 15–16 October 1999. Online. Available HTTP: < http://backupcese.qwentes.be/sco/events/actes_sco_en.pdf > (accessed 20 June 2007).
——(2001) *Opinion of the Economic and Social Committee on Organised Civil Society and European Governance: the Committee's contribution to the drafting of the White Paper*. Online. Available HTTP: < http://eescopinions.eesc.europa.eu/EESC opinionDocument > (accessed 20 June 2007).
——(2007) *The EESC: a bridge between Europe and organised civil society*, Brussels, EESC. Online. Available HTTP: < http://www.eesc.europa.eu/documents/publications/pdf/booklets/EESC-2007-002-EN.pdf > (accessed 20 June 2007).
Falk, R.A. (1999) *Predatory Globalization: a critique*, Cambridge: Polity Press.
Fossum, J. E. (2005) 'Contemporary European constitution-making: constrained or reflexive?', in E. O. Erikssen (ed.) *Making the European Polity. Reflexive integration in Europe*, London: Routledge.
Greenwood, J. (2005) *Interest Representation in the European Union*, Houndmills, New York: Palgrave.
Guiraudon, V. (2001) 'Weak weapons of the weak', in D. Imig and S. Tarrow (eds) *Contentious Europeans: protest and politics in an emerging polity*, Lanham: Rowman & Littlefield.
Habermas, J. (1991) *The Structural Transformation of the Public Sphere: an inquiry into a category of bourgeois society*, trans. Thomas Burger with Frederick Lawrence, Cambridge, MA: MIT Press.
——(1996) *Between Facts and Norms: contributions to a discourse theory of law and democracy*, trans. William Rehg, Cambridge, MA: MIT Press.
Imig, D. and Tarrow, S. (eds) (2001) *Contentious Europeans: protest and politics in an emerging polity*, Lanham: Rowman & Littlefield.
Joerges, C., Mény, Y. and Weiler, J. H. (2001) (eds) *Mountain or Molehill? A critical appraisal of the Commission White Paper on governance*, Jean Monnet Working Papers, 6. Online. Available HTTP: < http://www.jeanmonnetprogram.org/papers/01/010601.html > (accessed 20 June 2007).
Kaldor, M. (2003) *Global Civil Society: an answer to war?* Cambridge: Polity Press.
Loretoni, A. and Henry, B. (2001) (eds) *La Carta dei diritti fondamentali: verso una Costituzione europea?*, *Quaderni Forum*, 15 (2), Florence: Forum per i Problemi della Pace e della Guerra.
Magnette, P. (2000) *L'Europe, l'État et la démocratie: le souverain apprivoisé*, Bruxelles: Editions Complexe.
——(2003) *Le régime politique de l'Union européenne*, Paris: Presses de la Fondation Nationale des Sciences Politiques.

Maier, M. and Risse, T. (2003) (eds) *Europeanization, Collective Identities and Public Discourses. IDNET Thematic Network Final Report*. Online. Available HTTP: < www.iue.it/RSCAS/Research/Tools/IDNET/200303IDNET_FinRep.pdf > (accessed 20 June 20007).

Piana, D. (2005) 'Constructing the European constitutional discourse. Arguments and common values in the European Convention', in S. Lucarelli and C. Radaelli (eds) *Mobilizing Politics and Society? The EU Convention's impact on southern Europe*, London: Routledge.

Rosenau, J. (2003) *Distant Proximities: dynamics beyond globalization*, Princeton, NJ: Princeton University Press.

Rumford, C. (2002) *The European Union: a political sociology*, Oxford: Blackwell.

Ruzza, C. (2004) *Europe and Civil Society. Movement coalitions and European governance*, Manchester: Manchester University Press.

——(2005) *EU Public Policies and the Participation of Organized Civil Society*, Working Papers del Dipartimento di Studi Sociali e Politici, Università di Milano. Online. Available HTTP: < http://www.sociol.unimi.it/papers/2005-11-23_Carlo%20Ruzza.pdf > (accessed 20 June 2007).

——(2006) 'European institutions and the policy discourse of organised civil society', in S. Smismans (ed.) *Civil Society and Legitimate European Governance*, Cheltenham: Edward Elgar Publisher.

Saurugger, S. (2006) 'The professionalisation of public interest groups: a legitimacy problem for civil society in the EU?', in S. Smismans (ed.) *Civil Society and Legitimate European Governance*, Cheltenham: Edward Elgar Publisher.

Schmidt, V. (2006) *Democracy in Europe: the EU and national polities*, Oxford: Oxford University Press.

Warleigh, A. (2003) *Democracy and the European Union: theory, practice and reform*, London: Sage.

Part V
Outside the EU
Policies and images

10 Human rights promotion

Rosa Balfour

Introduction

European Union (EU) promotion of human rights has recently become a fertile avenue for research and interpretation. Some have located the development of such a policy in the 'ontological' attributes of the EU, arguing that the principles that guided the development and enlargement of the European project (peace, reconciliation, democratisation, multilateralism, human rights, etc.) are the 'constitutive' features (Manners 2006) that make the EU a distinctive and unique polity, or 'normative power' (Manners 2002). Others locate the origins of such a policy in the structural attributes of the EU foreign policy system, which aims at influencing through a range of pacific and civilian means, structural and long-term changes (Keukeleire 2002).

More empirically based studies highlight that with the exception of the enlargement process, where the EU has acted as a 'transformative' power (Grabbe 2006), human rights often clash with other foreign policy objectives related to security, economic interests, or with the broader aim of maintaining good relations with certain states, with divergences between the member states, with inefficiencies of the EU foreign policy system and differential treatments of partners (Smith 2001; Olsen 2000; Youngs 2004; Balfour 2006, 2007). Studies in democracy promotion assistance have also emphasised many problems within the policies themselves, from misplaced priorities, conservative approaches to human rights issues and tensions between contrasting foreign policy priorities (Youngs 2001).

One area that has so far drawn little attention, as far as EU studies are concerned, is the degree to which human rights in EU foreign policy constitute a principle shared by the member states and citizens of the EU and reflected and promoted by EU institutions in such a way that they can be considered a defining element of their political identity. This chapter aims to explore this different perspective and ask whether the EU's choice of pursuing human rights promotion in its foreign policy reflects in any way a core piece of its political identity, whereby identity is intended as both the perceptions of Europeans as EU citizens as well as the self-definition of the institutions; whether such political identity contributes to conferring legitimacy

160 *Rosa Balfour*

upon the EU (according to its citizens); and whether the gap between rhetoric and performance can hurt EU legitimacy.

It will do so by analysing survey data as well as debates in the press to ascertain the degree to which the self-representation of the EU as a human rights champion is shared, reflected or criticised in the perceptions of citizens. But it will also search for diversity between member states behind the broad consensus over an external human rights policy through debates in the press over handling certain foreign policy issues, namely the use of sanctions in three different countries: Belarus, Zimbabwe and China. It will attempt to illustrate this first by looking at the origins and reasons of the EU external human rights policy, then it will move on to identifying its distinctive features and its legitimacy in terms of its formal dimension and of public opinion support before discussing the ways in which these issues become debated in the context of difficult policy choices, such as sanctions.

Explaining the emergence of human rights in European foreign policy

The controversies that regularly emerge when attempting to conduct foreign policy based on human rights are at odds with the apparent relative ease with which the EU member states espoused the principles. Progress was made especially with the end of the Cold War, with the European Council Declaration on Human Rights, the Resolution on Human Rights in Development Policy and the Treaty on European Union that introduced the Common Foreign and Security Policy (CFSP), all in 1991. The Treaty explicitly stated that one of the aims of foreign policy was 'to develop and consolidate democracy and the rule of law, and respect for human rights and fundamental freedoms' (Treaty on European Union, Title V, Art. J.1; Treaty of Amsterdam, Title V, Art. 11).

On the one hand, it can be argued that there 'could be no disagreement about such anodyne "motherhood and apple pie" aims' (Cameron 1999: 25). The trouble was that at that time, the Franco-German decision in 1990 to put 'political union' on the agenda of the intergovernmental conferences alongside economic and monetary union did not solve the fundamental differences over pursuing a more common foreign policy. In an attempt to break the deadlock on negotiations, the Italian Presidency informally gathered the foreign ministers to discuss a list of principles that could be applied to the nascent CFSP, which included human rights, to foster consensus between the member states (Nuttall 2000). In other words, human rights were part of that *minimum common denominator* guiding the CFSP.

Twelve years later, the debates that took place in the context of the Convention on the Future of Europe reflected a similar approach. In the working group on external action chaired by Jean Luc Dehaene, it was established that prior to discussing the reforms necessary to make EU foreign policy more consistent, cohesive, efficient and capable, it was necessary to identify the principles guiding the policy, and a very broad consensus emerged early in the proceedings on what the guiding principles of EU external action should be (European Convention 2002a,b). Their formulation found a word-by-word application in the Constitutional Treaty and in the Lisbon Treaty:

> The Union's action on the international scene shall be guided by the principles which have inspired its own creation, development and enlargement, and which it seeks to advance in the wider world: democracy, the rule of law, the universality and indivisibility of human rights and fundamental freedoms, respect for human dignity, the principles of equality and solidarity, and respect for the principles of the United Nations Charter and international law.
> (Treaty of Lisbon, Art. 10A)

A closer analysis, however, shows that the development of the EU's external human rights policy was not simply an emanation of internal values. There were a number of motivations determined by a *mixture of principled and instrumental arguments*, backed by assessments of the changing international context and by external demands, diversely espoused by the member states, which can be summarised in three categories: normative–idealist grounds, rational or efficiency-based arguments, reaction to the changing international context and the ideological vacuum left by the end of East–West confrontation, which favoured human rights advocacy and public opinion support.

In the very early 1990s the constituency in favour of a 'principled foreign policy' was, by and large, limited to some northern European countries, though it did find justification in the experience of the Helsinki Process.[1] Alongside Sweden's long-standing tradition, the Netherlands had put human rights promotion as an essential element of its foreign policy since 1979 (Baehr 1996) and Denmark's development policy was strongly rooted in ethical considerations rather than in security and economics (Olsen 2000). Even if Britain's experience in the second half of the 1990s with 'ethical foreign policy' had become controversial, the 2004 enlargement strengthened this constituency with many new member states espousing the promotion of human rights not only to justify their critical positions towards Russia, but also globally. But still today not all countries fully share this approach. In the Italian Ministry of Foreign Affairs, for instance, human rights are relegated to the multilateral office.

Rather than with ethics, other countries were more concerned with the efficiency of aid spending and the accountability of tax payers' money. Attaching strings to aid policies had become an increasingly used trend by international and individual donors, and by the end of the 1980s the World

Bank included political criteria in the conditionality tied to market reform (Crawford 1996). This logic can also be found in most of the EU's assistance programmes, where concern for efficient and targeted spending has been tackled not only by management procedures (which has been repeatedly questioned by the European Parliament and the Court of Auditors), but also by clarifying the conditions attached to accessing and using funds and by introducing increasingly specific lists of objectives to be achieved through EU assistance. The inclusion of the 'human rights clause' in agreements with third countries, whereby the EU can suspend assistance or even the agreement itself in case fundamental principles are breached, could also be seen as a way to justify cutting or suspending aid.

Alongside internal dynamics, contextual factors also need to be taken into account. In the late 1980s, there were demands from Latin American states, which were hoping that the 'human rights clauses' would ensure that the EU would revise its trade and cooperation agreements should there occur an internal reversal of the democratisation process (Crawford 1998). At the time of Maastricht, the EEC/EU was to a large extent responding to rapidly changing events in the world, from the fall of the Berlin Wall, the dissolution of the Soviet Union, and the break up of Yugoslavia. One of the responses with regard to Central and Eastern Europe was to prepare a path for their integration into the EU. By clarifying the conditions for belonging to the club, a process of self-definition in terms of values and principles started within the EU too, and human rights played their part as well, with the introduction of Arts 6 and 6.2 in the Treaty of European Union and Art. 7 in the Amsterdam Treaty that respectively make human rights a fundamental principle common to all member states, make the European Convention for the Protection of Human Rights and Fundamental Freedoms part of the *acquis*, and introduce negative measures in case of breach of such principles.

The inspiring principles for international action derive from the Universal Declaration of Human Rights ratified by the United Nations in 1948 and its following Covenants of Rights of 1966, which established that the rights of individuals can be above those set by their national authorities (Held 1995), and from some key CSCE documents such as the Helsinki Final Act (1975) and the Charter of Paris for a New Europe (1990). This is supposed to clear the path against accusations that an external human rights policy might infringe on state sovereignty, or that it reflects an imposition of Western or European-based values at the expense of cultural diversity. Furthermore, the EU member states have ratified themselves those conventions, and their submission to international law and to the jurisdiction of the International Criminal Court represent both a distinctive and legitimising feature.

The demise of the USSR was thus a key process that enabled the EC/EU to interpret human rights norms created through the Helsinki process and apply them to the new states in Eastern Europe as well as to the international community (Thomas 2001). This process would have also helped define EC/EU identity (Risse *et al.* 1999). From a more critical position, some authors see the success of normative values, public opinion pressure and advocacy groups as having constrained Western governments to take up the human rights mantra (Chandler 2002b), but that such apparently non-ideological consensus has legitimised foreign intervention and provided the powerful with a tool to control the less powerful (Chandler 2002a). From this point of view, the rise of human rights policies can be seen as a function of hegemony where power is exercised through right rather than might (Evans 1998).

In short, ideational, contextual, instrumental reasons and external demands *together* led the member states to introduce an external human rights policy, and interaction with the outside world, especially through enlargement, led them to strengthen internal provisions for human rights protection. This mixture of idealism and pragmatism can also be found in the justifications for pursuing human rights policies. The European Security Strategy reads, for instance, that

> the best protection for our security is a world of well-governed democratic states. Spreading good governance, supporting social and political reform, dealing with corruption and abuse of power, establishing the rule of law and protecting human rights are the best means of strengthening the international order.
>
> (European Council 2003: 11)

The EU's external human rights policy: what institutional distinctiveness and legitimacy?

Since these developments in the early 1990s, the EU has set up institutions and policies to promote human rights abroad. The question regards whether such features make it an actor 'with a difference' compared with other states and organisations, and whether such a role confers the EU with public opinion support and legitimacy. Both these issues will feed into an understanding of the role external human rights might play in the EU's political identity. Indeed, many states and citizens of the world will claim to support human rights principles, but an analysis of the institutional structures and policies, of the degree to which the member states have submitted their sovereignty to international law, and of the ways in which the EU pursues human rights principles abroad do highlight a number of features that the EU does not share with any other large state-based actor.

Because of both the nature of human rights issues and of EU foreign policy, the policy domain of human rights promotion is best understood as a *cross-pillar activity*. The post-Cold War conceptualisation of human rights invests areas related to human security, conflict prevention, socioeconomic development, as well as political and civil rights. At the EU level, the range of activities that are pertinent to human rights promotion cut across the first and second pillars (EC and Common and Foreign Security Policy), as they involve aid, trade and economic assistance (EC), political and diplomatic relations (CFSP), and they constitute one of the principles of the institutionalised agreements that the EU develops with third countries, which are governed by both first- and second-pillar decision-making mechanisms. Also, the consequences of 9/11 have given new salience to the relationship between personal liberties and security, as well as to the third Justice and Home Affairs pillar, which deals with many aspects related to the fight against terrorism.

In order to bridge this broad spectrum of concerns governed by both supranational and intergovernmental decision-making mechanisms, the Commission has established that 'respect for human rights and democracy should be an integral, or "mainstream", consideration in all EU external policies' (Commission 2001). The institutions have all set up committees and working groups to ensure that human rights are included in all foreign policy activities, and in 2005 the High Representative for CFSP appointed a Personal Representative for human rights to liaise with the Commission and bridge the pillar divide. Under pressure from the EP, all external assistance includes human rights and democracy as one of its objectives, be it through specific budget lines (the European Initiative for Democracy and Human Rights) or by earmarking a percentage of aid to human rights promotion, making the EU together with its member states the most generous human rights and democracy donor.

Most general foreign policy strategies include a human rights component, from the 2001 Conflict Prevention Strategy to the 2003 European Security Strategy. The EU has also developed guidelines on fighting the death penalty, torture, human rights dialogues, children in armed conflict and human rights defenders. Finally, such principles are formalised not only through treaties and international law, but also through the strong preference that take the form of institutionalised agreements with third countries that govern the EU's external relations (Smith 2003), all of which contain a clause in which human rights are established as an 'essential element' of the agreement, whereby a country can be sanctioned should the principles be breached. As far as public scrutiny of EU activities is concerned, since 1998 the Council of the EU has to produce two yearly reports on the EU internal and external human rights policies, which are evaluated by the EP and compared with its own yearly report, which dates back to the early 1980s.

The legalisation of the principles through treaty reform and through contractual agreements with third countries, the creation of institutional structures, however imperfect, dealing with the policies and ensure 'mainstreaming', the aid programmes and the submission of the member states to international law are all distinctive elements that put the EU in a different position compared, for instance, with the USA, which has resisted binding multilateral instruments such as ratifying the International Criminal Court.

However, the formal legitimacy of the EU in pursuing human rights remains incomplete: internal and external human rights policies are accountable to the member states rather than to the EU. The Lisbon Treaty, if ratified, will introduce two key innovations strengthening the EU's claim as a global human rights promoter. First, incorporating the Charter of Fundamental Freedoms (albeit as a Protocol) will give the European Court of Justice (ECJ) jurisdiction over human rights within Europe. Second, giving the EU a legal personality will enable it to accede to those international covenants to which the member states belong. It was in 1996 that the ECJ put a stop to the EU's bid to accede to the European Convention on Human Rights on the grounds that it did not have a legal personality.

The other legitimacy deficit regards the nature of EU foreign policy: given the intergovernmental nature of the CFSP, the member states rather than the EU *per se* are the main vehicles of formal legitimacy of the external human rights policy. It has been a prerogative of the European Parliament to scrutinise closely EU action for human rights and foreign policy, and it has gained some stronger decision-making powers over the use of the external relations budget. However, so long as the CFSP remains inter-governmental and outside the jurisdiction of the ECJ, it is the member states that ensure the legitimacy of their foreign policies by acting collectively rather than as a single polity; it is through them that resources for Common Foreign and Security Policy CFSP action have been mobilised (though the budget has been considerably increased); it is through them that political and diplomatic decisions are made, including sanctions; and it is through them that humanitarian interventions, be they of military or civilian nature, are legitimised. In other words, it is not the EU as such that enjoys legitimacy when pursuing human rights abroad but its member states, accountable to national parliaments rather than to the European Parliament. This is more than a technicality: governments often resort to international and European norms and institutions to justify certain actions with national public opinion.

Nevertheless, there is *broad public support* for the EU as a human rights promoter. A large proportion of EU citizens believe that human rights, peace and democracy are 'the three values that best represent' the EU (Eurobarometer 2006b). The concept of human rights itself is deeply embedded in two originating features that characterise the political identity of the integration project, tied as they are to new practices of sovereignty (the degree to which it is legitimate to interfere in affairs internal to a state), and to war and peace (the degree to which integration through democratisation and the establishment of fundamental rights in Europe was also a conflict prevention project).

Also, there is a demand and expectation for the EU as a whole to address global human rights problems. In 2006 various public opinion surveys found strong support of human rights and/or democracy promotion policies, with 77 per cent of Union citizens[2] believing that the EU rather than national governments should promote democracy and peace in the world

(Eurobarometer 2006a). Similar results according to Transatlantic Trends (2006) (71 per cent), and to the University of Siena's Elite Survey which reports 69 per cent support for democracy promotion in public opinion and 90 per cent at the level of Commission officials and Members of the European Parliament (Centre for the Study of Political Change 2006). This should be read in conjunction with strong support for the creation of an EU Foreign Minister (69 per cent of public opinion, 79 per cent of MEPs and 96 per cent of Commission officials according to Centre for the Study of Political Change Elite Survey 2006),[3] and a continuous support for a common foreign policy and common security and defence policy, although this does not apply to strengthening the EU militarily.[4]

Furthermore, surveys conducted on specific EU policy areas also reveal a growing consensus towards supporting democracy abroad, on the use of conditionality (Eurobarometer 2005) and seeing democracy as an important objective of policies towards neighbours, after fighting terrorism and crime (Eurobarometer 2006b).

These results suggest that the EU is seen as a more appropriate organisation for the global promotion of human rights than its member states. In short, despite important limits on the EU's formal legitimacy as a foreign policy actor, it can be reasonably claimed that there is widespread support for a stronger EU role in world affairs and that the pursuit of human rights should be one of its priorities, giving Weberian legitimacy to such a pursuit (Cerutti, Chapter 1).

Debating human rights sanctions

If the picture were so simple, whereby human rights are a defining principle of the EU that translates into its political identity and are backed by a degree of legitimacy (limited by the national legitimacy path of foreign policy), one would expect a far less uneven performance. This section does not aim to explain the performance problems but evaluate whether, beneath the surface of consensus, different views of the ways in which human rights should be translated into foreign policy can help understand the role of human rights as a contested domain.

Sanctions have been an area in which the EU was reluctant to engage unless acting under the UN umbrella. However, over the past few years the EU has increasingly been using the tool of targeted sanctions as well as debating their use and effectiveness. In 2004 the Council defined the principles for an autonomous sanctions policy, although reiterating its commitment to use them only for specific objectives (fight against terrorism, proliferation of weapons of mass destruction and 'as a restrictive measure to uphold respect for human rights, democracy, the rule of law and good governance'), and 'as part of an integrated, comprehensive policy approach which should include political dialogue, incentives, conditionality and could even involve, as a last resort, the use of coercive measures in accordance with the UN Charter' (Council of the European Union 2004). After the widespread criticisms over the impact on the Iraqi population of the sanctions imposed throughout the 1990s, the EU has overwhelmingly favoured 'targeted sanctions' against individuals or over specific types of exports.[5]

Three cases have been selected here: the debates over targeted sanctions against Belarus and Zimbabwe, and over lifting the arms embargo against China. It must be clarified that this chapter does not analyse the political issues surrounding the cases; it merely aims to gauge the debate in the press and in political circles over the arguments in favour and against the use of sanctions justified by human rights-based arguments, over the best means to support human rights and over the legitimacy of such political choices. The sources are based on all relevant EU documents and a survey of eight European newspapers between 2001 and 2006.[6] Owing to space limits, they will be quoted only in an exemplary fashion.

Considered by the USA one of the 'outposts of tyranny', Belarus is the only country in Europe towards which the EU has been applying a policy of near isolation on principled grounds for the past 10 years. The freezing of the Partnership and Cooperation Agreement in 1997 and the severe reduction in aid have not led to any change in Minsk's impermeability to Brussels. Enlargement changed EU perceptions of Belarus thanks to the new member states, which not only have a more 'principled' position with regard to human rights and democracy promotion, by virtue of their own experience of domination and democratisation, but also because of geographical proximity. This has contributed to raising the issue in the press, albeit marginally.[7] Since the inception of the European Neighbourhood Policy (ENP), the debate in Brussels has revolved around finding new means to support some change in the country.

Attempts to develop positive engagement strategies with sectors of civil society have managed to get broad support between the member states, stimulating the Commission to develop assistance programmes that bypass national governments and try to engage directly with society (see Commission 2006). But the contentious issues have been over the negative measures against the government. After the flawed presidential elections in March 2006 that gave Lukashenko his fourth term in office, the Council approved the introduction of a visa ban and the freezing of financial assets of key officials. This broad consensus was reached with the inclusion of those countries that traditionally avoid stepping on Moscow's toes.[8] But the Commission proposal of suspending Belarus from the Generalised System of Preferences justified by non-conformity to International Labour Organisation standards was approved only with great difficulty, thanks to the opposition of a few countries, including those keen to develop a more 'muscular' human rights policy in the former Soviet space, on the grounds that economic sanctions were likely to lead to loss of jobs and to an anti-European backlash in Belarus. The issue had to be raised twice at the General Affairs and External Relations Council before eventually being approved at the end of December 2006. The opposing countries, Poland, Lithuania, Latvia, Greece and Cyprus, became a minority once Italy joined the UK and Sweden in supporting the sanctions (which it had opposed for reasons entirely separate from the Belarus case). It is also interesting to note that the sanctions hit wood and textile exports, but not energy ones (as a transit country of Russian gas to Europe): by leaving *key European interests untouched*, the targeted sanctions did not hit the interests of energy-importing member states.[9]

With regard to Zimbabwe, the debate revolved around whether to apply sanctions to punish the brutal crushing of political opposition groups conducted by the dictatorial President Mugabe (fraudulently re-elected in March 2002), land seizures (mostly of white settlers), and the expulsion of the EU's electoral monitoring mission. Under pressure from public opinion, the UK was instrumental in introducing in February 2002 the CFSP restrictive measures (visa ban and freezing of assets against the government and ruling elite) and the suspension of development assistance except for those projects that supported the population directly, sanctions that were renewed a year later in the midst of an even hotter debate. But their use was highly contested between the member states, revealing deep divisions, especially between France and Britain.[10] While Britain – belatedly according to Blair's critics[11] – supported the use of sanctions but only in conjuncture with the EU and the Commonwealth, France and Belgium preferred maintaining a dialogue with Mugabe because of his support of the peace proposal to end war in the Democratic Republic of Congo.[12] The 'compromise' between these two positions was patchy and contradictory: as the EU agreed to renew the targeted sanctions (including the visa ban), Mugabe travelled to Paris to attend the Franco-African summit backed by the other African states which would not have attended without Zimbabwe's presence.[13] The EU–African summit scheduled for the following April, however, was indefinitely postponed because of the inability to reach an agreement on Zimbabwe's participation.

EU human rights policy on this occasion revealed itself to be hostage to Franco-British rivalries over influence in Africa, and caught in the dilemma between engaging or sanctioning a country which could play an important part in regional stability. This dilemma divides public opinion too. The Eurobarometer survey on development aid, for example, showed that according to the interviewees the reduction of conflict and war should be the main priority of development aid. At the same time two-thirds of the respondents agreed with attaching democratic conditions to aid (Eurobarometer 2005). The Zimbabwe case exemplifies the ways in which these two objectives were in conflict with one another.

With regard to China, the debate revolved around whether it was appropriate to lift the arms embargo put in place after the Tien'anmen events in 1989. In a 'U-turn' from its previous policy that pledged to strengthen human rights,[14] Germany, keen to strengthen economic ties with China and backed by France, started to raise the issue in 2003 and 2004, and by the end of the year seemed to have convinced most of its European partners to move from the embargo to a code of conduct on arms sales.[15] Justifications for lifting the embargo ranged from it being 'anachronistic' as well as 'inefficient', but even more explicit reasons were used. Solana himself questioned whether an emerging superpower and expanding market 'deserved the same treatment as Zimbabwe or Myanmar',[16] supporting the critique that the EU uses negative measures primarily against small countries of little consequence to European countries in terms of economics or security (Smith 2001).

However, once China's parliament voted an anti-secessionist law that justified military intervention to halt Taiwan's bid for independence, Schröder's position succumbed to pressure from his own coalition (the Green Party led by the Foreign Minister),[17] from the USA, whose position was shared by Britain and the Netherlands, from the Scandinavian countries and the EP, acting on principled grounds. Public opinion counted too: according to Javier Solana, Britain argued that it was not possible to explain to the public that the reasons for raising the embargo were no longer valid.[18] In the event the decision to suspend the arms embargo was indefinitely delayed. The Chinese case captured many EU contradictions in a nutshell: while it 'closes its eyes on Beijing's human rights, it challenges the US ally on the arms sales (and then backtracks), all in order to conquer large chunks of the immense Chinese market'.[19]

The cases briefly examined here show that applying human rights in the EU's foreign policy is a *divisive endeavour* between the member states. In all cases it was hard to reach an agreement between the member states, and in all cases there was a split, even if in the case of Zimbabwe it was overcome by temporarily breaching the visa ban to allow Mugabe to visit Paris, the condition that Chirac had set to approve the renewal of the sanctions.[20] All cases highlight divisions over competing priorities – struggle for influence in Africa, competition over access to the Chinese market – and over means – sanctions versus engagement, both justified on human rights grounds. Human rights-based arguments regarded the impact of trade-related sanctions on the population and on the EU's image in the society of the target country (Belarus); whether engagement or sanctions were the best means to exercise pressure on the government to improve labour standards (China); and Zimbabwe's role in regional conflict and relations with the other African states that opposed sanctions.

The analysis of the press gives a somewhat different picture. Diversity between the member states regards the attention given to the EU and to its external human rights policies. Of all the countries surveyed, Britain was the one in which human rights and foreign policy were most debated, whereas France and Italy showed very little coverage of the theme. But whereas in France the few articles revealed a debate on the issues, the Italian press did not convey any sense of awareness on the problems of EU human rights policies. With regard to the cases, Belarus (but only marginally) and China attracted the attention of all newspapers, whereas Zimbabwe was ignored in Spain. Conversely, in Britain Zimbabwe was amply debated in Parliament and in the press, where it even reached the sports pages,[21] and the opposition Conservative Party rode the tide to criticise the government and the EU. On the whole the three cases deserved very little coverage and interest in Italy; not much in France; in Spain coverage was by and large limited to *El Pais*. The only country in which the three cases attracted the attention of all the newspapers surveyed was Britain.

Despite this different attention, common threads emerge in all countries. One regards accusations of hypocrisy and differential treatment of countries depending on their importance to the EU or to some of its member states. According to the *Guardian*, one of the most vocal and critical newspapers on human rights issues, 'the democratic failings of the former Soviet republic [Belarus] pale into insignificance compared with those of other governments that the west, far from penalising, has rewarded generously'.[22] Indeed, alongside the cases where a debate over sanctions was raised at the EU level, most newspapers highlight the many countries towards which sanctions or strong condemnation of human rights abuses were not acted upon, from Russia to Egypt, not to speak of the accusations of hypocrisy and of instrumental use of human rights arguments to justify the war in Iraq and the fight against terrorism.

Another theme found in all countries regards a degree of awareness in the press on the other interests that play against human rights promotion. Much of the coverage of Belarus, while reporting on its human rights deficits, focused on the Russian–Belarusian energy problems and on the EU problems of reconciling human rights with energy interests in Russia. Britain's asylum policy came into the spotlight because of the impact of travel bans on asylum seekers from Zimbabwe. And commercial interests in China were amply covered by the press.

A final aspect relates more directly to the definition of human rights: a question raised by some political elites and the press regards the ways in which negative measures can have an impact on the basic rights of the population concerned. In the cases treated here, trade sanctions against Belarus raised the problem of their impact on those whose livelihood depended on commerce, while sanctions against Zimbabwe would result in food shortages and mass starvation.

Double standards and the tools to promote human rights are thus the subject of debate and criticism in the press. Public opinion surveys show that when asked about the tools to promote democracy, a broad consensus was found on monitoring elections and supporting groups independent of government (between 80 and over 90 per cent of citizens, MEPs and Commission officials), whereas the options of political and economic sanctions attracted greater uncertainty especially in public opinion (respectively 55 per cent and 58 per cent in favour), whereas military intervention is seen as an appropriate means to promote democracy only by one in four European citizens and by even fewer MEPs and officials (Centre for the Study of Political Change 2006).

Conclusions

Although it would be hard to deny that human rights play an important role in the definition of the EU's political identity, the consensus over this masks important divergences between the member states. Within the public the debates revolve not so much on the values *per se*, but on the means and opportunity of promoting them through foreign policy and the ways in which they might compete with other priorities. Nonetheless, having raised expectations in public opinion, set the standards, built the institutions, included human rights in the policies and projected a specific image, the EU has limited its freedom of manoeuvre on human rights issues, as the above quotations of Solana demonstrate. As the *Guardian* observes regarding Robin Cook, British Foreign Minister between 1997 and 2001,

> the emphasis [he] has placed on human rights may have a more lasting impact. No future British government will be able to ignore the much derided ethical dimension. Nor, as foreign policy is increasingly collectivised, will any other EU member state. In effect, Mr Cook has attempted that most difficult thing to change: attitudes.[23]

A similar argument could be applied to the EU. However, the ways in which human rights manifest themselves in policy as well as in European debates suggest a dynamic relationship among political identity, legitimacy and politics. Human rights concerns can be expressed in foreign policy as a consequence of public opinion pressure, but human rights-based arguments can also be used to justify different policy choices. In the case of Belarus, human rights arguments were used for and against the suspension of the Generalised System of Preferences. Similarly, France and Germany justified engaging with rather than sanctioning human rights-abusing governments (Zimbabwe and China respectively) not only as a means to achieve other priorities which might be considered more important, but also as a way to persuade these governments to improve their human rights standards. Notwithstanding the credibility of such justifications, one can hypothesise that if human rights are used as a justification, it is because acting upon that principle is seen as a legitimate endeavour of the EU. And if the Eurobarometer is reliable, such justifications meet compliance, as European citizens seem fairly satisfied with the EU's external human rights policy by giving it, on average, a 5.6 satisfaction rate on a 0–10 scale, a better grading than most of the areas surveyed (Eurobarometer 2006a), despite press criticism.

Nonetheless, the double standards employed by the EU undermine its moral standing in applying sanctions.[24] But the critique is not limited to the

EU. Individual governments are also held responsible. French policy towards Africa was particularly criticised in the French press, arguing that working in partnership with the EU was not sufficient to legitimise Paris's political choices.[25]

Finally, many commentators consider the EU less guilty than the USA in applying double standards. There is a high frequency of newspaper articles that see the USA as not in a position to take the moral high ground on human rights. *El Pais* greeted the decision to keep the arms embargo against China, but considered the US role in pressurising the EU as 'lo unico malo': 'Europeans believe in our moral superiority over Bush's United States because we are always in favour of peaceful resolutions of conflicts and of respecting human rights'.[26]

Acknowledgements

The author would like to thank her fellow colleagues in the research project that led to this publication for their challenging comments, interdisciplinary insights, and continuous encouragement and support. Special gratitude goes to Sonia Lucarelli and Furio Cerutti. The ideas expressed in this chapter are the responsibility of the author alone and not those of any organisation.

Notes

1 The resort to the Conference on Security and Cooperation in Europe (CSCE) and the Helsinki process developed from 1975 onwards satisfied major players, from the USA and the EC member states, to the Soviet Union and the emerging democracies in Eastern Europe. See Keohane *et al*. (1993).
2 National differences range from 93 per cent support in Cyprus to 63 per cent in the UK (Eurobarometer 2006a).
3 Transatlantic Trends (2006) reports a maximum 74 per cent support in Spain down to a 48 per cent support in Slovakia.
4 Fifty-eight per cent of EU citizens are against this possibility (Centre for the Study of Political Change 2006).
5 See the list of sanctions or restrictive measures in force (measures adopted in the framework of the CFSP, latest update: December 2006) at http://ec.europa.eu/comm/external_relations/cfsp/sanctions/measures.htm (accessed 3 July 2007).
6 The newspapers analysed are: *El Mundo*, *El Pais*, *Il Sole 24 Ore*, *La Stampa*, *Le Figaro*, *Libération*, the *Guardian*, *The Times* (including *The Sunday Times*).
7 See, for instance, 'Solidarity anniversary turns focus on Belarus: call for peaceful revolution in Europe's last dictatorship', the *Guardian*, 1 September 2005; 'Con Varsovia frente a Minsk', *El Pais*, 2 August 2005.
8 'L'Union fait front contre la dernière dictature d'Europe', *Libération*, 21 Mars 2006.
9 'EU decides to impose mini-trade sanctions on Belarus', *EU Observer*, 20 December 2006.
10 'Mugabe divise Paris et Londres', *Libération*, 24 January 2003. *Le Figaro* published articles with similar arguments.
11 'Too little too late', according to Conservative MP Michael Ancram in, 'Blair must take a stand on Mugabe: next week's earth summit will have to call Zimbabwe to account', the *Guardian*, 23 August 2002.

12 'A cynical dialogue', *The Times*, 7 March 2001.
13 'Europe fudges deal on Mugabe sanctions', the *Guardian*, 13 February 2003; 'Chefs d'Etat en toute impunité', *Libération*, 20 February 2003.
14 'Schröder vies for title of Europe's top arms salesman', *The Times*, 13 October 2004.
15 'All'Aja espressa la volontà politica di continuare a lavorare per la revoca delle sanzioni', *La Stampa*, 9 December 2004.
16 'Chine-Union européenne: les ventes d'armes attendront', *Libération*, 20 April 2005.
17 'Cina, Schröder è solo: le armi a Pechino', *Il Sole 24 Ore*, 15 April 2005.
18 Interviewed in 'China no necesita dinero, sino nuestra experiencia', *El Pais*, 9 November 2003.
19 'Duro monito cinese all'Europa', *Il Sole 24 Ore*, 17 April 2005.
20 Without examining the complications of the decision-making system, in the Belarus case a qualified majority vote was necessary to suspend the country's participation in the GSP (Generalized System of Preferences), whereas in the cases of Zimbabwe and China a unanimous vote was necessary.
21 This was due to the English cricket team's participation in the World Cup, held in Zimbabwe, while the British press was not allowed in the country. The fact that this issue caused much debate at the time of deciding the war against Iraq was also criticised. See 'Who's the real villain?', the *Guardian*, 24 January 2003.
22 'You cannot be serious: the Belarus saga exposes the hollowness of the west's support for human rights and democracy', the *Guardian*, 27 March 2006.
23 'Putting ethics on the map: Robin Cook's achievement deserves support', the *Guardian*, 9 April 2001.
24 See, among many, 'Who observes the observers? The west's condemnation of Zimbabwe's election process is a breathtaking case of double standards', the *Guardian*, 18 March 2002.
25 'En dépit des déclarations du chef de l'Etat français en ouverture du 22e sommet franco-africain', *Le Figaro*, 22 February 2003.
26 'El embargo europeo de armas a China. A la caza del dragon', *El Pais*, 27 March 2005.

References

Baehr, P. R. (1996) *The Role of Human Rights in Foreign Policy*, London and Basingstoke: MacMillan Press.
Balfour, R. (2006) 'Principles of democracy and human rights. A review of the European Union's strategies towards its neighbours', in S. Lucarelli and I. Manners (eds) *Values and Principles in European Union Foreign Policy*, London: Routledge.
——(2007) 'Promoting human rights and democracy in the EU's neighbourhood: tools, strategies and dilemmas', in R. Balfour and A. Missiroli (eds) *Reassessing the European Neighbourhood Policy*, EPC Issue Paper, no. 54, June 2007, European Policy Centre. Online. Available HTTP: < http://se1.isn.ch/serviceengine/File Content?serviceID=PublishingHouse&fileid=5D3331BC-CE56–1C4F-9347-A9E93 B3BA5BC&lng=en > (accessed 3 July 2007).
Cameron, F. (1999) *The Foreign and Security Policy of the European Union. Past, present and future*, Sheffield: Sheffield Academic Press.
Centre for the Study of Political Change (2006) *European Elites Survey 2006*, Centre for the Study of Political Change at Università degli Studi di Siena, project supported by Compagnia di San Paolo. Online. Available HTTP: < http://www.gips.unisi.it/circap/ees_overview > (accessed 3 July 2007).

Chandler, D. (2002a) *From Kosovo to Kabul*, London: Pluto Press.
—— (2002b) 'Introduction: rethinking human rights', in D. Chandler (ed.) *Rethinking Human Rights. Critical approaches to international politics*, Basingstoke: Palgrave.
Commission (2001) *The European Union's Role in promoting Human Rights and Democratisation in Third Countries*, COM (2001) 252 final, Brussels, 8 May 2001. Online. Available HTTP: < http://ec.europa.eu/external_relations/human_rights/doc/com01_252_en.pdf > (accessed 3 July 2007).
—— (2006) *Non Paper. 'What the European Union could bring to Belarus'*, document released by Ferrero-Waldner, European Commissioner for External Relations and European Neighbourhood Policy, Brussels, 21 November 2006. Online. Available HTTP: < http://ec.europa.eu/comm/external_relations/belarus/intro/non_paper_1106.pdf > (accessed 3 July 2007).
Council of the European Union (2004) *Basic Principles on the Use of Restrictive Measures (Sanctions)*, 10198/1/04 PESC 450 REV 1, Brussels, 7 June 2004.
Crawford, G. (1996) *Promoting Democracy, Human Rights and Good Governance Through Development Aid. A comparative study of the policies of four Northern donors*, Leeds: Centre for Democratisation, University of Leeds.
—— (1998) 'Human rights and democracy in EU development co-operation: towards fair and equal treatment', in M. Lister (ed.) *European Union Development Policy*, Basingstoke and London: MacMillan.
Eurobarometer (2005) *Attitudes towards Development Aid. Special Eurobarometer 222*, European Commission, Public opinion Analysis, Brussels. Online. Available HTTP: < http://ec.europa.eu/public_opinion/archives/ebs/ebs_222_en.pdf > (accessed 3 July 2007).
—— (2006a) *The Future of Europe. Special Eurobarometer 251*, European Commission, Public opinion Analysis, Brussels. Online. Available HTTP: < http://ec.europa.eu/public_opinion/archives/ebs/ebs_251_en.pdf > (accessed 3 July 2007).
—— (2006b) *The European Union and its Neighbours. Special Eurobarometer 259*, European Commission, Public opinion Analysis, Brussels. Online. Available HTTP: < http://ec.europa.eu/public_opinion/archives/ebs/ebs_259_en.pdf > (accessed 3 July 2007).
European Convention (2002a) *Note from the Praesidium to the Convention on 'EU External Action'*, CONV 161/02, Brussels, 3 July 2002. Online. Available HTTP: < http://register.consilium.eu.int/pdf/en/02/cv00/00161en2.pdf > (accessed 3 July 2007).
—— (2002b) *Report from Working Group VII 'External Action' to the Members of the Convention. Final report of the Working Group VII on External Action*, CONV 459/02, Brussels, 16 December 2002. Online. Available HTTP: < http://register.consilium.eu.int/pdf/en/02/cv00/00459en2.pdf > (accessed 3 July 2007).
European Council (2003) *A Secure Europe in a Better World. European Security Strategy*, Brussels, 12 December 2003.
Evans, T. (1998) 'Introduction: power, hegemony and the universalization of human rights', in T. Evans (ed.) *Human Rights Fifty Years On. A reappraisal*, Manchester and New York: Manchester University Press.
Grabbe, H. (2006) *The EU's Transformative Power. Europeanization through conditionality in Central and Eastern Europe*, Basingstoke: Palgrave MacMillan.
Held, D. (1995) *Democracy and the Global Order. From the modern state to cosmopolitan governance*, Cambridge: Polity Press.
Keohane, R. O., Nye, J. S. and Hoffmann, S. (1993) (eds) *After the Cold War. International institutions and state strategies in Europe, 1989–1991*, Cambridge, MA and London: Harvard University Press.

Keukeleire, S. (2002) 'Reconceptualizing (European) foreign policy: structural foreign policy', paper presented at the first Pan-European Conference on European Union Politics, Bordeaux, 26–28 September 2002. Online. Available HTTP: < http://soc.kuleuven.be/iieb/docs/0209-SK-ECPR.pdf > (accessed 3 July 2007)

Manners, Ian (2002) 'Normative power Europe: a contradiction in terms?', *Journal of Common Market Studies*, 40 (2): 235–58.

——(2006) 'The constitutive nature of values, images and principles in the European Union', in S. Lucarelli and I. Manners (eds) *Values and Principles in European Union Foreign Policy*, London: Routledge.

Nuttall, S. J. (2000) *European Foreign Policy*, Oxford: Oxford University Press.

Olsen, G. R. (2000) 'Promotion of democracy as a foreign policy instrument of "Europe": limits to international idealism', *Democratization*, 7 (2): 142–67.

Risse, T., Ropp, S. C. and Sikkink, K. (1999) (eds) *The Power of Human Rights: International Norms and Domestic Change*, Cambridge: Cambridge University Press.

Smith, K. E. (2001) 'The EU, human rights and relations with third countries: "foreign policy" with an ethical dimension?', in M. Light and K. E. Smith (eds) *Ethics and Foreign Policy*, Cambridge: Cambridge University Press.

——(2003) *European Union Foreign Policy in a Changing World*, Cambridge: Polity Press.

Thomas, D. C. (2001) *The Helsinki Effect: international norms, human rights, and the demise of communism*, Princeton, NJ: Princeton University Press.

Transatlantic Trends (2006) *Key Findings 2006*. A project of the German Marshall Fund of the United States and the Compagnia di San Paolo, with additional support from the Fundação Luso-American, Fundación BBVA, and the Tipping Point Foundation. Online. Available HTTP: < http://www.transatlantictrends.org/trends/doc/2006_TT_Key%20Findings%20FINAL.pdf > (accessed 3 July 2007).

Youngs, R. (2001) 'European Union democracy promotion policies: ten years on', *European Foreign Affairs Review*, 6 (3): 355–73.

——(2004) 'Normative dynamics and strategic interests in the EU's external identity', *Journal of Common Market Studies*, 42 (2): 415–35.

11 Judicial policies and European enlargement
Building the image of a rule of law promoter

Daniela Piana

For the EU, the enlargement towards the Central and Eastern European Countries (hereinafter CEECs) was a strategic opportunity to define, formalize and to some extent reshape its image. Indeed, candidates were expected to reform their institutions and policies in order to adapt to the model of democracy adopted by EU officials and political representatives as the 'European' model of democracy.

In that model, judicial function[1] worked in two ways: on one hand, candidates were expected to guarantee judicial independence, because judicial function should apply the law *erga omnes*; on the other hand, they were expected to improve judicial capacities, since judicial function should be able to handle, in an efficient and effective way, conflicts emerging among private actors and among citizens and public institutions (Shapiro 1981). Moreover, judicial capacities were required because candidate states were expected to enable judicial actors to enter a pattern of judicial cooperation (de Kerchove 2004).

Even though there is nothing new in promoting judicial independence and judicial capacity in the context of democracy promotion (Kleinfeld Belton 2005), the European policy of enlargement somehow looks peculiar (Kubicek 2003). In countries that had experienced a totalitarian or post-totalitarian regime (Linz 1976), the enforcement of individual rights came out as a key point of EU membership, which works in a twofold way. In official statements, a formal view of the rule of law was indeed preferred, and legal norms were expected to fully account for the pattern of judicial administration. Put differently, the EU considered justice to be the result of a correct, fair and predictable process of law enforcement, in which substantial issues – i.e. moral, political and cultural issues in general – do not play any significant role. This view also justifies the idea – endorsed by the EU at the beginning of enlargement – that the legitimacy of the EU model for the promotion of the rule of law would be revealed by the EU's capacity to dismantle the communist legacy. On the other hand, the enforcement of rights, which occurs through the case law of the European

Court of Justice and of domestic constitutional courts, relies upon an encompassing view of the rule of law, a view which is linked to moral values and a way of seeing the relationship between politics and law (Tamanaha 2004). This was something totally new for CEEC citizens, and hence put forward to CEEC citizens as the true advantage coming from EU membership.

The emphasis put on judicial independence and judicial capacity increased the weight of judicial issues in the overall image of the EU promoted in the CEECs. Owing to that weight, the impact of the enlargement policy in terms of identity-building for judges and CEEC citizens is of extreme importance for the legitimacy of the EU. In the candidate countries, indeed, the EU has not only promoted a democratic model of governance, but also membership of the European legal and political space as a prerequisite to achieving a better governance, a more effective democracy and the guarantee to protect citizens' fundamental rights. Therefore, the European *policy of promoting democracy* intentionally addressed the demand and supply sides of law making and law enforcement. Hence, a fruitful way to assess the effectiveness of the enlargement policy as an identity-building policy is to look at the extent the 'European' dimension has shaped the legal culture in the new member countries. This analysis does not claim in any way to give an overall and comprehensive account of this issue. It will start by focusing on the European policy of promoting the rule of law, paying particular attention to the norms and values underlying the judicial function of political systems. Then, it will address the impact on legal elites and on citizens, relying on three indicators: references to the EU model in CEEC judicial policies, references to EU standards in the transnational legal networks created during enlargement, and the weighting of EU norms in the self-representation of judges after the enlargement. Finally, I give some hints concerning the role played by the judicial function in shaping the identity of CEEC citizens as EU citizens. The analysis concludes with some remarks regarding the consequences that promoting the rule of law in post-communist countries has on the self-image of Europeans and on the image that the EU has promoted eastwards as a *sui generis* model of good governance (Jacoby 2004).

Normative and cognitive input of the European policy to promote the rule of law

Generally speaking, the image of the judicial function promoted by the EU in the CEECs is composed of several aspects, partially linked to the principle of the rule of law and partially because future members should be enabled to take part in an effective way in the European judicial cooperation process. In particular, the European policy of democracy promotion in the CEECs relied on a set of principles and values defining a model of democratic governance where judicial function plays on two levels, domestic and supranational, applying domestic legal norms and interacting with the European Court of Justice and the European Court of Human Rights.

The first set of norms and principles used to shape the rule of law promotion policy relied on the Council of Europe legacy, which is based on the European Convention of Human Rights and on the principles of the so-called 'European constitutionalism' (Mancini 2000). The latter deems democracy a result of the implementation of the rule of law. It considers it possible to create democracy through the law (Council of Europe 2005b) and thus it recognizes judicial functions as pivots in creating and maintaining well-functioning and legitimate democracies. Accordingly, judicial function is also expected to answer to policy needs coming from minorities which do not have any voice in different arenas, such as representative arenas for instance. Even if this entails a questionable view of representative democracy, which is far from being the simple outcome of constitutionalism, a legitimate and effective judiciary nevertheless proved to be the architrave of a legitimate democracy.

The model shaped by the Council of Europe and promoted in the CEECs included the drafting of a fixed constitution, whose norms should be ensured by a specialized body, vested with the power of judicial review: the constitutional courts (Bartole 2000). All these mechanisms reveal a kind of constitutionalism deeply linked to the interpretation of legal provisions, instead of being reduced to the application of law *erga omnes*. In that sense, a substantial view of what should be the relationship between law and society, law and politics, politics and society or, put simply, of power and freedom, necessarily becomes part of the process of rights enforcement. The legitimacy of the interpretation and of the adjudication is very sensitive to the legitimacy of judges themselves.

In 1993 the EU decided to embark upon enlargement towards the CEECs. It relied on the political discourse and on the legal legacy of the Council of Europe, whose legitimacy (input legitimacy) in the field of judicial cooperation and international security provided sound ground upon which to move and justify the EU policy of rule of law promotion (Piana 2006b).

In order to ensure that the enlargement would not undermine the process of European integration, in 1993 the European Council set up the Copenhagen criteria. They state that 'human rights' and the 'rule of law' should be implemented for candidate countries which want to achieve EU membership (Kochenov 2004).[2]

EU discourse refers to some key elements, considered to be pillars of the EU model of judicial administration: the right to due process,[3] the efficiency of the judiciary (Juncker 2006), the independence of the judiciary guaranteed by the High Judicial Council and the competence of judicial staff, as guaranteed by public training offered by a centralized judicial school (Piana 2006a, 2007).[4]

In 1995 the European Council of Madrid also included judicial capacity among the prerequisites to membership, which was phrased as being part of the overall institutional and administrative capacity of the state. The EU was moving towards a political discourse more sensitive to the issue of judicial cooperation, since judicial actors coming from the CEECs were expected not only to impartially apply the law, but also to enter into an effective pattern of cooperation with their colleagues. In particular, ordinary courts and constitutional courts were expected to enter into a dialogue across domestic borders, aiming to harmonize the domestic legal systems and to enforce the EU law in a truly integrated European legal space.

In 1999 the European Council held in Helsinki gave new emphasis to that process and set up the obligations of the states with regard to the Third Pillar policy fields – Justice and Home Affairs (Avel 2001). Old and new member states were obliged to reform their judicial systems, to modernize the organization of judicial offices and to provide judges and prosecutors with a stronger competence in comparative law and EU law as well.[5] First, judicial actors are obliged to interact in order to implement the principle of mutual recognition of judicial decisions – a judicial decision taken in one country also applies in any other EU country (Jimeno-Bulnes 2003). Then, judicial actors should know EU law and the legal systems of the other EU countries better than they did before, since this know-how facilitates their cooperation. Finally, judicial offices should be provided with ICT (information, communication, technology) tools and management tools in order to enable them to collect data, stock dossiers and exchange information (Piana 2007).

Judicial systems were faced with a very extensive and complex set of input measures. In that sense, European leverage was not only merely legal, but also cognitive and normative (Schimmelfennig 2002: 12). It turned out that the EU was not only influential in providing a set of legal norms and a blueprint for building formal institutions suitable for a truly constitutional democracy, but was also able to provide new members, their citizens and their legal elite with a cognitive framework for thinking about justice and for defining what might be considered a 'good model of judicial administration'.

In that sense, the EU set standards for shaping domestic judiciaries, admitting the CEECs legal elite to the EU legal community and providing citizens with a benchmark for evaluating the pattern of justice obtained through EU membership.

This feature also facilitated policy enactment by EU institutions after 1999, which was aimed at reshaping judicial policy at a European level. Policy networks and epistemic communities (Haas 1992) composed of judges, legal experts and lawyers were created in order to deepen the process of judicial cooperation (Commission 2006a; European Union 2006). This process increased the weight of 'justice' in the issues that the EU expects to shape the core of the European model of governance.

In that sense, the enlargement of the EU, the promotion of the rule of law and judicial cooperation in the European legal space has reshaped the European image, stressing the judicial function as one of the key pillars of the EU political project. Notwithstanding the importance of the EU's leverage in the effectiveness of judicial reforms in CEECs, it could be argued that the image of the 'European' model of judicial administration promoted through enlargement seems to suffer from a fundamental shortcoming. According to *official* EU discourse, judges should behave independently from any non-judicial power and should perceive themselves as actors held accountable only to the law. Therefore, no discretionary power, no arbitrariness, no interpretative function can exist in judicial procedures (see Commission 2006c). However, this does not hold in reality. Judges are involved in a complex process of legal interpretation and legal adaptation which is required in order to suit the domestic legal systems to the EU set of norms and values.

As a matter of fact, *enlargement* has gone far beyond these objectives: it has also created institutional spaces in which the judicial function works through interpretative and discretionary actions (Favoreu 1990; Sadurski 2005), and these have turned out to be a dramatically important aspect in the administration of justice today. This holds true in particular with regard to the implementation of constitutional provisions in CEECs. During the pre-accession period, judges in these countries increasingly referred to non-statutory norms when interpreting human rights clauses. In that way, they participated in the process of *identity-building* in the CEECs (Schwartz 2000) and indirectly in the process of identity-building within EU constitutionalism (Sadurski 2005; Piana 2006a). Furthermore, the sense of tradition exhibited by constitutional courts has consolidated the process of image-building with regard to the European legal tradition. They have created an internal legal culture considered to be truly 'European', a common culture that has then justified the 'dialogue' among domestic judiciaries and the references to EU jurisprudence. Thus, constitutional justice has bridged the gap between European legal tradition and domestic legal culture and it has enhanced the CEECs' perception of themselves as true constitutional democracies (Sadurski 2003; Wyrzikowski 2000).

Some sparse but important case law can be mentioned to confirm this trend. In 1992 the Bulgarian constitutional court delivered its final comment[6] with regard to the constitutionality of the Movement for Rights and Freedoms, a party created in 1990 with the support of the Turkish minority. The court deemed the party legitimate, arguing that in the past the Bulgarian regime had discriminated against the Turkish minority. To come to terms with the past, the Article of the Constitution that states that 'no party can be created on ethnic basis' was interpreted in the favour of the Movement for Rights and Freedoms (Ganev 2002). In 1994 the Czech constitutional court delivered a sentence accepting the international conventions on human rights, arguing that European Convention for Human Rights'

(ECHR) jurisprudence directly applies in the Czech Republic. The argument relied upon the coherence between the EU legal tradition and the Czech legal tradition, which dates back to the period before the communist regime (Priban 2002).[7] In 1999 the Hungarian court interpreted and expanded the provisions which defend the social rights of Hungarian citizens through jurisprudence. It allowed policy-makers to adopt a policy of positive discrimination in order to enforce social rights (Halmai 2002). The argument provided by the court was 'morally oriented', i.e. based on the moral character of social rights, instead of on the basis of their procedural legitimacy (Boulanger 2003).

Nevertheless, this empirical evidence should not be overstated. The absorption of the 'European' norms within the constitutional dialogue between constitutional and ordinary courts does not entail the full and indiscriminate adoption of the EU legal norms within the CEECs' legal systems. Some scholars, indeed, have correctly pointed out that for these countries, instead of fully integrating EU legal norms, judges have maintained the primacy of domestic legal norms. This is the case particularly for constitutional justice, which is at the forefront of the process of legal integration between domestic and international systems (Kuhn 2003).[8]

This notwithstanding, it is correct to remember the reasons advocated to not integrate or to partially integrate EU legal norms. Judges often advocated on the base of the primacy of domestic sovereignty (Kuhn 2003: 569). They do not oppose EU legal norms because of their 'European' dimension, but because of their 'international' or 'exogenous' dimension.

I will come back to that point later on in the conclusions, to assess their effective importance for the purpose of the present analysis.

Identity-building and the self-perception of the legal elite

As stressed above, starting from enlargement, rule of law and justice in particular have emerged as a pillar of the EU model of governance. One of the main consequences of that process can be detected in the increasing importance given to the Europeanization of the legal elite. Indeed, once the post-communist tradition was dismantled, the legal elite was socialized within EU constitutional culture.

Legal norms partially influence the image of the European model of governance promoted in the candidate countries, although they are not the only factors that should be taken into account in how it is shaped. Indeed, beyond legal norms, enlargement has spread through the moral principles accepted and used by judges to interpret legal provisions, especially when they are called on to enforce fundamental rights.

It could be claimed that enlargement has set the conditions for developing an *idem sentire* among the legal elites of the CEECs and in the old members. In order to assess the empirical reliability of this statement, one could rely on three different indicators: arguments exploited by CEEC policy-makers in promoting judicial reforms at home; ethical principles defined for European judges; and the self-perception of judges as a 'Europeanized' legal elite.

Once the pre-accession negotiations started, the Romanian Ministry of Justice strongly advocated European-oriented judicial reforms. The EU model – in particular a public and centralized judicial school and a strong Judicial Council – was used to reshape the political agenda and to drive judicial reforms towards EU standards: 'EU standards reshaped our judiciary' and 'being trained and independent are part of our "being Europeans"'.[9] In 2001, when the General Prosecutor and the Ministry of Justice were in conflict over the reshaping of the Bulgarian judiciary, the General Prosecutor argued for a model where the instruction and the investigation are both under the supervision of the General Prosecutor's Office, and are both accountable to the Ministry of the Interior. The EU model, which argues in favour of the independence of instruction and investigation from the executive, was used to strike down the Prosecutor's arguments. In the electoral campaign an EU-oriented judicial reform was exploited as a primary argument in order to win the political match (East European Constitutional Review 1999).

The promotion of the rule of law was also called for by older European judges. In 1998, during a meeting held in Geneva, judges representing the founding countries of the EU claimed the judicial space to be the 'most important European project after the Euro'.[10]

With regard to the second indicator, we can say that the normative input addressed to judicial staff has been successful in influencing the standards used in monitoring, advising and driving judicial reforms, and in regulating judicial behaviour. The documents issued by judicial organizations outline a set of normative statements coherent with this general view. The European Judges Association, in particular, has in recent years strongly stressed the fact that judicial independence should be at the core of judicial policies, at the domestic and at the European level (Oberto 2003).[11] Moreover, judges have taken a strong position within the Consultative Council of European Judges (CCJE) and the Consultative Council of European Prosecutors (CCPE) advocating reforms aimed at creating institutional guarantees of independence, for instance the High Judicial Council and the Judicial School, both independent from the interference of the executive. Furthermore, legal epistemic communities refer to a common core of European constitutionalism. This core of common legal values is recalled within the case law of the Constitutional Courts. In particular references to the European Convention for Human Rights, which is considered the heart of European constitutionalism, the courts are allowed to go beyond the strict application of national law and to anchor their judicial decisions to values and principles which are 'European', rather than 'Polish' or 'Czech'.[12] It is not by chance that the more judges' associations in CEECs have participated in setting judicial standards, the more they are inclined to use EU arguments at home (see Sadurski 2002). Czech, Hungarian and Romanian judges are the

Judicial policies and European enlargement 183

most active promoters of the process of standard setting at the European level. They attend European meetings *en masse* and animate the agenda of the epistemic communities created by the EU and the Council of Europe. They also bridge EU standard and domestic judicial policies (Piana 2007).

Aware of the existence of common values driving judicial behaviour in adjudication, judges also agree upon the primacy of those values when they handle cases where interpretative action is required. In other words, the 'European dimension' of principles and norms in adjudication is conceived as an added value, something that should be in a certain sense considered as a constraint or a regulative principle. The composite effects of that process of communication and argumentation among legal experts work in a complex way. This notwithstanding the role played by judicial network communication and judicial training sessions in shaping and fostering the EU identity of judges should not be neglected.

At the transnational level, in the arenas created or encouraged by the European Commission (European Network for Judicial Training)[13] and by the Council of Europe (Venice Commission,[14] European Commission for the Efficiency of Justice – CEPEJ,[15] Consultative Council of European Judges,[16] Lisbon Network[17]) the responsibility of judges is addressed more explicitly. Although at the beginning of enlargement great attention was paid to the executive function of adjudication, in recent years emphasis has been on the responsibility for dealing with case flow and on the interpretation of cases which may be socially sensitive, among other things.[18]

Although a full account here of the role played by European norms in adjudication is not yet possible, it is still possible to grasp the trend in the mentality of judges, at least for those who have increasingly taken part in the meetings, conferences, or seminars held in the arenas listed above. In a survey conducted in Strasbourg in 2005 with a sample of the judges who are members of the epistemic communities, the 'European dimension of behavioural norms' comes out as a value worth being taken into consideration.[19] This value ranks higher for issues directly addressed by the European epistemic communities.[20]

Table 11.1 shows the assessment of the influence of EU normative and cognitive input for some policy sectors which were all addressed by the European policy of rule of law promotion in CEECs. Judges were asked to set a value for the influence of EU input in policies addressing the organization, education, ethics and discipline of judicial actors. The perceived influence was asked with regard to domestic policies and with regard to supranational policies, since the EU is committed to a process of harmonizing domestic judicial policies in all these policy fields. Table 11.1 shows that the EU normative and cognitive influence is perceived in a stronger way in the policy sectors that are more involved in the Europeanization process, and more focused on and affected by the EU policy of rule of law promotion.

The question they were asked to answer was 'To what extent do you think that the European dimension is relevant for the following issue in judicial

Table 11.1 Assessment on Europeanization by legal experts in EU epistemic communities

Issue	Domestic level	European level
General	7.2	8.2
Organization of judicial system	9.5	8.7
Judicial education	6.5	9.2
Judicial ethics	4.25	4
Training in non-legal matters (management, ICT, etc.)	2	2
Judges evaluation	2	2

Source: Piana 2005.
Note: The survey measures the perceived importance of the European input for the issues listed in the first column. The survey was in a question and answer form, with responses that could range from insufficient (2/10), to sufficient (6/10), to very much (10/10). Multiple choice implies that only one answer is correct.

policies?', distinguishing between the domestic and the European levels. For instance, the survey wanted to detect whether they perceived the existence of truly European judicial policies – at least in some fields – and if they also perceived a difference between the impact of European norms and standards at the transnational level and at the national level. If they did, one could argue that Europeanization has spread to norms and values insofar as to supersede domestic policies.

Issues related to the organization of the judiciary – for instance the creation of a High Judicial Council and of a Judicial School[21] – and those related to programmes of judicial education, which are mostly addressed by European epistemic communities – seem to have been ranked highest by judges.

As Table 11.1 shows, the issues most perceived as 'Europeanized' are the ones addressed by the European process of standard setting, which started with enlargement and which is at the basis of the promotion of the rule of law in the expanding EU. Empirical evidence suggests that among legal experts the promotion of the rule of law has worked as a mechanism of identity-building. One could also go ahead with the argument and point out that the inclusive effect of transnational communication and socialization created a supranational arena, composed of Western and Eastern judges, involved in the definition of quality standards for the judicial policy field (Vauchez 2005). As a matter of fact, not all judges are involved in this supranational activity, and neither do they want to be. This phenomenon only touches the highest levels of judicial systems, i.e. judges of the Court of Cassation, of the Supreme Courts, of the High Judicial Council. Nonetheless, it is a way for external normative input to penetrate domestic judicial systems.

Although one cannot draw any conclusion about the overall impact of EU promotion of the rule of law with regard to the legal culture of domestic judges and prosecutors, we can at least say that the 'European' dimension of their social image has become a part of the reservoir of meanings of post-enlargement identity (Madsen and Vauchez 2005).

Substantial legitimacy and citizens' trust: a perverse effect?

This section shall explore the legitimacy–identity relationship with regard to EU citizens in general and CEEC citizens in particular. There is an important reason for exploring the trust of CEEC citizens in our analysis. The EU's promotion of the rule of law in the enlargement process was politically related to the capacity of the EU to promote itself as a system of governance oriented towards enforcing human rights and fundamental freedoms. European constitutionalism is strongly entrenched in these two values: enforcement of human rights at the transnational level and an independent judiciary to act as a check on domestic legislatures within national systems and at the European level (Stone Sweet 2000). The promise addressed by the EU to the future citizens strongly emphasizes the capacity of the European Court of Justice (ECJ) to enforce rights, especially where and when domestic courts may fail to do so. Therefore, the trust of citizens in EU adjudication to enforce their rights is significant in detecting whether citizens of the CEECs perceive the European dimension of their identity as rights holders in the European legal space. It would therefore be interesting to see whether, and to what extent, EU pressure has made the judiciary more trusted by CEEC citizens.

Table 11.2 shows the trends in trust accorded to the judiciaries by CEEC citizens. The table relies upon two different sets of data. The first three columns show the trend of trust as revealed through the World Value Surveys. The last two columns show the trend of trust which emerged from the

Table 11.2 Trust of citizens in the judicial system in Central and Eastern European countries

Country	Trust of citizens in the judiciary 1990–2004				
	WVS 1989 (%)	WVS 1991 (%)	WVS 1999 (%)	CCEB 2001 (%)	CCEB 2004 (%)
Bulgaria	45.4	36.6	27.9	23	18
Estonia	45.5	32.7	–	46	41
Lithuania	47.2	38.6	22.2	30	27
Latvia	32.4	35.2	38.3	37	29
Poland	31.4	28.4	21.3	24	21
Czech Republic	44.1	–	29.0	30	29
Romania	–	–	–	35	29
Slovenia	–	–	–	31	30
Slovak Republic	–	–	–	19	16
Hungary	87.5	59.6	51.0	48	47

Source: World Values Survey (1991–2000) and Candidate Countries Eurobarometer (Eurobarometer 2001, 2004).
Note: For some of these countries (Czech Republic, Hungary, Poland, Slovak Republic) we can also compare data from CEORG (see Central European Opinion Research Group Foundation 2004: Czech Republic 50.6 per cent; Hungary 31.7 per cent; Poland 58.6 per cent; Slovak Republic 63.4 per cent). This data reveals quite a similar pattern of distrust in the judiciary.

Eurobarometer surveys. The table should be analysed taking into account the time span of enlargement, which started in 1993, to then pass through the pre-accession phase before finishing in 2004 (for 10 countries), and in 2006 (for Romania and Bulgaria). Table 11.2 provides a view of the trend in trust from 1989, when the communists fell, to 2001, when the majority of judicial reforms were undertaken by CEEC governments. Since surveys refer to different years for each country – for instance in Poland the survey was realized in 1989, 1991 and 1999 and in Czech Republic the survey was performed in 1989 and 1999 – the World Values Survey can provide us with aggregate data to figure out a general trend, although it is not possible to draw comparisons between countries for each year.

Although the two surveys showed slightly different rankings, a common result is evident and that is the decrease in trust in almost all of the countries.

In that sense, it seems that the judicial policies adopted after the breakdown of the communist regimes did not succeed in fostering the trust of citizens in judicial decisions. At the domestic level, the function has not succeeded in entering the common images that citizens have of a truly constitutional democracy. In other words, the CEECs' judiciaries do not foster the *substantial legitimacy* of the European model of governance, at least judging by the perceptions of CEEC citizens.

This general trend, which shows the existence of an increasing distrust on the part of citizens towards the judiciaries, should be analysed bearing in mind the level of trust recognized by citizens in the European judicial actors, for instance the European Court of Justice and the European Court of Human Rights. In 2001 the Eurobarometer survey revealed that only 37 per cent of CEEC citizens trust the judiciary (52 per cent distrust it) (Eurobarometer 2001: Ch. 6.1). In 2004, the Eurobarometer revealed a fall in trust in social and political institutions in candidate countries. For instance, in CEECs the judiciary was trusted by 27 per cent of citizens, compared with the 62 per cent of citizens who did not trust it. This outcome is even more telling when compared with the average for EU citizens (both old and prospective members): only 45 per cent accorded total trust to the judiciary (Eurobarometer 2004: 10).

With regard to the image of the EU, 47 per cent of people believe that it does entail a better way of protecting rights (Eurobarometer 2001: Ch. 6.1), whereas 53 per cent trust the European Court of Human Rights. In 2003, 50 per cent of Romanian, Czech and Bulgarian citizens declared that they trusted the European Court for Human Rights. This fact seems to suggest a trade-off between trust in the domestic judiciary and trust in the supranational judiciary. This is confirmed by the level of awareness that people in CEECs have regarding the European Court of Justice (up to 73 per cent), a level which is well over the average ranking for other EU institutions (only the EU Parliament is known about by 75 per cent of CEECs citizens) (Eurobarometer 2003: 170–73).

These data shed new light on the impact that the enlargement of the European space of Freedom, Security and Justice has had upon the substantial legitimacy of the EU. First, with regard to the judicial function exercised 'at home', we have seen that CEEC judiciaries have not gained from the promotion of judicial reforms. These reforms have been a pillar of European enlargement: the judicial function has played a crucial role in the legitimation of the model of governance offered to the new citizens by the EU. But in fact, we can say that nowadays the EU is not seen by CEEC citizens as a political project, the core function of which is the administration of justice *at home*. On the contrary, the tables above indicate a trade-off between national and supranational judicial administrations. Indeed, the defence of human rights, which is expected of the European Courts in Luxemburg and in Strasbourg, comes out as a key point in the *identity of CEEC citizens*. The EU is a political project whose benefits can be assessed in the field of human rights enforcement.

Even if a definitive assessment cannot be drawn from the evidence provided here, we could claim that enlargement has created the conditions for including the 'judicial function' among the key elements of substantial European legitimacy. Since the promotion of the rule of law addressed towards the candidates has entailed the enhancement of judicial cooperation among old and new members and among European judiciaries, a number of spill-over effects might be expected in the near future. Indeed, while EU citizens seem to ask for the protection of fundamental rights, EU magistrates focus much more upon the enhancement of EU judicial politics aimed at fighting crime and at coordinating judicial action across national borders. The promotion of the rule of law realized in the candidate countries has entailed two different but interacting consequences: CEEC citizens consider the EU a truly *super partes* institution, defending human rights and struggling against any political power, but expect their national judiciaries to be unable to handle their demands for justice.

A tentative assessment and a research proposal

As part of the enlargement process, the EU has also defined a model of judicial function which has been labelled as properly and typically 'European' (European Council 1999). Therefore, the judicial function deeply influences the legitimacy of public policy and has a role to play in consolidating national and supranational political institutions (Weiler and Wind 2003). Despite the official view of enlargement, the European policy of rule of law promotion seems to involve a process of legitimation for the EU itself, at least in the sense of a jurisdiction where rights can be effectively enforced. This effect went above and beyond the image of the judicial function promoted by the EU in official documents, which stressed the role that judicial actors should play at the domestic level.

The analysis sketched above gives some hints about the effectiveness of the European strategy of rule of law promotion in shaping the identity of actors playing a role within the judicial organizations, both on the demand (citizens) and on the supply (judges) sides. First the evidence shows that, even though the procedural dimension of the judicial function is in actual fact the one most emphasized by the EU institutions, citizens and judges are exposed to the influence of a much broader set of norms. Legal norms – i.e. the *acquis communautaire* – are only a part, and a small one at that, of a much bigger and deeper set of norms, which are actually moral or social in nature. These norms are the most effective ones in influencing the feeling of 'being European' in the actors involved in the process of law enforcement. This is the reason why obstacles to legal integration, often faced by EU legal norms penetrating domestic legal systems, do not undermine the thesis of this analysis. They only give evidence about the difficulty of integrating 'external' norms, undermining or constraining the formal cohesion of domestic legal systems. Resistance to integration is indeed much due to the mismatch between the EU legal approach to law enforcement – based on the argumentative mode – and the CEECs' approach – based on a deductive and formalistic mode. It would be the same for any external source of legal norms.

The legitimacy arises from the fact that the issue of 'judicial function' has entered the EU's semantic 'reservoir of meanings, arguments and symbols' (Cerutti in the Introduction to this volume). The substantial legitimacy of the EU results from a composite of collective trust in the judiciaries, both national and supranational, the performance of EU policies in dismantling the communist legacy (such as unfair and discretionary patterns of justice) and the self-image of the legal elite, whom we expect to share a common legal culture.

In terms of political identity and legitimacy, the Europeanization of the judicial system, as pursued by the EU in the 10 countries that joined the Union in 2004, has produced diverging results: a strong sense of 'being European' among judges and legal experts while among the wider public, whose trust remains low, the attempt at Europeanization has so far failed to boost the legitimacy of the national judicial systems; far higher, but only just above 50 per cent, is the credibility of the European–EU legal institutions (European Court of Human Rights, European Court of Justice).

On the whole, the issue of the judiciary seems to play a role in the areas regarded by the citizens, and more particularly by professionals, as characterizing Europe's political space. But while the European Courts enjoy the citizens' trust, probably because of the simple fact of being European, the efforts made at Europeanizing the national judiciaries have not in themselves enhanced their credibility.

It can be assumed that citizens want first to see a better performance by their own judicial systems in delivering justice before they acknowledge the legitimacy of this essential component of the polity, especially in post-communist times. The European perspective has become part of the political identity of Eastern Europeans, but more as a hope (when looking at European Courts) and a criticism (when looking at national ones) than as an awareness of some still-to-come European quality in their judiciaries.

Acknowledgements

I am very grateful to Sonia Lucarelli and Furio Cerutti, who read and commented on a previous version of this chapter, for their remarks, comments and criticisms, and to the editorial reviewers.

Notes

1. I will use the terms 'judicial function', 'judicial administration', 'judicial dimension' to refer to the same phenomenon.
2. These criteria were adopted by the European Council in 1993. They set the conditions – institutional, legal and political – for obtaining membership. The European policy of promoting the rule of law is analysed in Kubicek (2003).
3. See Arts. 6 and 7 of the Convention for the Protection of Human Rights and Fundamental Freedoms.
4. See Commission (2006b); this model conforms to the civil law tradition (Merryman 1969).
5. Indeed, in order to implement the principle of mutual recognition, judges and prosecutors should be aware of the legal mechanisms of other EU countries.
6. Constitutional Court of Bulgaria, Sentence 14/1992.
7. Constitutional Court of the Czech Republic, Sentence 12/1994.
8. This negative attitude towards European legal norms appeared in the pre-accession strategy. Indeed, since the end of the pre-accession strategy the integration of the EU *acquis communautaire* has become mandatory. This notwithstanding, the use of EU case law depends on the legal culture of domestic legal elites, since it directly enters into the process of the legal interpretation of domestic norms. For a comparative view of the process of legal adaptation, see Kellermann (2001).
9. 'Politique. Roumanie', *La Croix*, 16 May 2006.
10. 'Les juges européens veulent enquêter par-dessus les frontières', *La Croix*, 26 November 1998.
11. See also Council of Europe (2005a), where judicial training is explicitly addressed.
12. Interview with a member of the Venice Commission, Venice, 14 October 2006; see also Bartole (2000).
13. This network was created in 2000 by the French Presidency of the EU to coordinate programmes of judicial training. See http://www.ejtn.net/www/en/html/index.htm. This network was not actually created intentionally by the European Commission. The EU Commission has instead encouraged the initiative taken by the European French Presidency.
14. The Venice Commission was created in 1990 by Antonio La Pergola on behalf of the Council of Europe. Its mission is to promote democracy through the law. It works by giving advice in the field of constitutional justice. Countries which are members of the Council of Europe can ask for its recommendations, studies or opinions. See http://www.venice.coe.int/site/dynamics/N_calendar_ef.asp?L=.
15. Created by the Council of Europe, with the strong advocacy of Dutch and German legal experts. See www.coe.int/cepej.
16. A consultative body, which delivers opinions and recommendations to the Council of Ministries of Justice.
17. The network was created in 1995 by the DG of Legal Affairs in the Council of Europe. See http://www.coe.int/T/E/Legal_Affairs/Legal_co-operation/Legal_professionals/Judges/Lisbon_network/.
18. The Council of Europe has organized seminars and conferences dealing with 'Justice and Society' and 'Justice and the Media'.

19 The impact of the European integration upon the self-perception of judges is stronger for judges working in the High Courts. Indeed, they are directly exposed to the input – training, social learning, communication of information – coming from Brussels.
20 Epistemic communities are groups, networks or committees of experts. They share a specialized competence in a policy field. The communities I am considering in this context are composed of legal experts, jurists, judges and prosecutors. They were asked for an evaluation of between 2 and 10. The survey was conducted in two stages on my behalf by the secretary of the Lisbon Network and of the CEPEJ, in Strasbourg, in November 2005 (Piana 2005).
21 This indicator suggests that judges have acknowledged the European dimension of judicial education, which reflects what is advocated by the European Commission; see Commission (2006b).

References

Avel, D. (2001) 'Le développement de la coopération judiciaire européenne', *Revue du marché commun et de l'Union Européenne*, 445: 112–42.

Bartole, S. (2000) 'Final remarks. The role of the Venice Commission', *Review of Central and East European Law*, 26 (3): 351–63.

Boulanger, C. (2003) *Beyond Significative Relationships, Tolerance Intervals and Triadic Dispute Resolution: constructing a comparative theory of judicial review in post-communist countries*, paper presented to the Law & Society Association, Annual Conference, Pittsburgh, 5–8 June 2003.

Central European Opinion Research Group Foundation (CEORG) (2004) *Survey on Trust in Social Institutions*, September 2004. Online. Available HTTP: < http://www.ceorg-europe.org/research/2004–9.pdf > (accessed 20 June 2007).

Commission (2006a) *Communication on 'A Citizen's Agenda: delivering results for Europe'*, COM (2006) 211 final, Brussels, 10 May 2006.

—— (2006b) *Communication on Judicial Education in the European Union*, COM (2006) 356 final, Brussels, 29 June 2006.

—— (2006c) *PHARE Interim Evaluation. From Pre-Accession to Accession. Thematic Reports issued in 2006*. Online. Available HTTP: < http://ec.europa.eu/enlargement/financial_assistance/phare/evaluation/interim_en.htm#thematic_reports > (accessed 20 June 2007).

Council of Europe (2005a) *Action Plan, Warsaw Summit, 16–17 May 2005*, CM (2005) 80 final, 17 May 2005.

—— (2005b) *Building Democracy through the Law*, Strasbourg, Office of Official Publications.

East European Constitutional Review (1999) 'Constitutional Watch. A country-by-country update on constitutional politics in Eastern Europe and the ex-USSR', *East European Constitutional Review*, 8 (1–2), New York: New York University Law School and Central European University. Online. Available HTTP: < http://www.law.nyu.edu/eecr/vol8num1–2/constitutionwatch/index.html > (accessed 20 June 2007).

Eurobarometer (2001) *Complete Report. Candidate Countries Eurobarometer 51.1, Spring 2001*, European Commission, Public opinion Analysis, Brussels, Online. Available HTTP: < http://ec.europa.eu/public_opinion/cceb_en.htm > (accessed 20 June 2007).

—— (2003) *Complete Report. Candidate Countries Eurobarometer 60.0, Autumn 2003*, European Commission, Public opinion Analysis, Brussels, Online. Available HTTP: < http://ec.europa.eu/public_opinion/cceb_en.htm > (accessed 20 June 2007).

—— (2004) *Comparative Highlights. Candidate Countries Eurobarometer 61.0, Spring 2004*, European Commission, Public opinion Analysis, Brussels, Online. Available HTTP: < http://ec.europa.eu/public_opinion/cceb_en.htm > (accessed 20 June 2007).
European Council (1999) *Presidency Conclusions, Helsinki European Council, 10 and 11 December 1999*. Online. Available HTTP: < http://www.europarl.europa.eu/summits/hel1_en.htm > (accessed 20 June 2007).
European Union (2006) *Press release. Implementing The Hague Programme: the way forward*, MEMO/06/254, Brussels, 28 June 2006. Online. Available HTTP: < http://europa.eu/rapid/pressReleasesAction.do?reference=MEMO/06/254&format=HTML&aged=1&language=EN&guiLanguage=en > (accessed 20 June 2007).
Favoreu, L. (1990) 'Constitutional review in Europe , in L. Henkin and A. Rosenthal (eds) *Constitutionalism and Rights. The influence of the United States constitution abroad*, New York: Columbia University Press.
Ganev, V. (2002) 'The rise of constitutional adjudication in Bulgaria', in W. Sadurski (ed.) *Constitutional Justice, East and West*, Dordrecht: Kluwer Publishers.
Haas, P. (1992) 'Introduction: epistemic communities and international policy coordination', *International Organization*, 46 (1): 1–35.
Halmai, G. (2002) 'The Hungarian approach to constitutional review: the end of activism? The first decade of the Hungarian Constitutional Court', in W. Sadurski (ed.) *Constitutional Justice, East and West*, Dordrecht: Kluwer Publishers.
Jacoby, W. (2004) *The Enlargement of the European Union and NATO: ordering from the menu in Central Europe*, Cambridge: Cambridge University Press.
Jimeno-Bulnes, M. (2003) 'European judicial cooperation in criminal matters', *European Law Journal*, 9 (3): 614–30.
Juncker, J.-C. (2006) *A sole ambition for the European Continent*. Report by Jean-Claude Juncker, the Luxembourg Prime Minister, presented to the Parliamentary Assembly, Strasbourg, 11 April 2006. Online. Available HTTP: < https://wcd.coe.int/ViewBlob.jsp?id=1015193&SourceFile=1 > (accessed 20 June 2007).
Kellermann, A., De Zwann J., Czuczai J. (2001) (eds) *EU Enlargement. The constitutional impact at the EU and national level*, the Hague: TMC, Asser Press.
de Kerchove, G. (2003) *Quelles reformes pour l'espace judiciaire européen*, Brussels: ULB Press.
Kleinfeld Belton, R. (2005) 'Competing definition of rule of law. Implications for practitioners', *Carnegie Papers*, no. 55, January.
Kochenov, D. (2004) 'Behind the Copenhagen façade: the meaning and structure of the Copenhagen political criterion of democracy and the rule of law', *European Integration On-line Papers*, 8 (10). Online. Available HTTP: < http://eiop.or.at/eiop/texte/2004–10a.htm > (accessed 20 June 2007).
Kubicek, P. (2003) (ed.) *The European Union and Democratization*, London: Routledge.
Kuhn, Z. (2003) 'The application of the European law in the new member states: several (early) predictions', *German Law Journal*, 6: 563–82.
Linz, J. (1976) 'Totalitarian and authoritarian regimes', in F. Greenstein and N. Polsby (eds) *Handbook of Political Science*, vol. 3, Reading, MA: Addison-Wesley.
Madsen, M. R. and Vauchez, A. (2005) 'European constitutionalism at the cradle: law and lawyers in the construction of the European political orders (1920–60)', in *Lawyers' Circles: lawyers and European legal integration*, special issue of *Recht der Werkelikheid*, edited by A. Jettinghoff and H. Schepel, The Hague, Elsevier Reed: 15–36.
Mancini, G. F. (2005) *Democrazia e costituzionalismo nell'Unione europea*, Bologna: Il Mulino.

Merryman, J. (1969) *The Civil Law Tradition*, Stanford: Stanford University Press.
Oberto, G. (2003) *Recrutement et formation des magistrats en Europe. Etude comparative*, Editions du Conseil de l'Europe.
Piana, D. (2005) *Survey on Europeanization by legal experts in EU epistemic communities*, unpublished survey conducted in Strasbourg, November 2005.
——(2006a) 'Constitutional cultures in new member states. Between tradition and Europeanization', in J. Ziller and W. Sadurski (eds) *After Enlargement*, Dordrecht: Kluwer Publishers.
——(2006b) *Reforms and judicial cooperation in the European promotion of the rule of law: a comparative analysis of new members*, Open Society Institute. Online. Available HTTP: < http://www.eumap.org/journal/submitted/piana.pdf > (accessed 20 June 2007).
——(2007) 'Unpacking transfer, discovering actor', *French Politics*, 5 (1): 33–65.
Priban, J. (2002) 'Judicial power vs. democratic representation: the culture of constitutionalism and human rights in the Czech legal system', in W. Sadurski (ed.) *Constitutional Justice, East and West*, Dordrecht: Kluwer Publishers.
Sadurski W. (2002) (ed.) *Constitutional Justice, East and West: democratic legitimacy and constitutional courts in post-communist Europe, in a comparative perspective*, Dordrecht: Kluwer Publishers.
——(2003) 'EU enlargement and human rights', in N. Neuwahl (ed.) *European Union Enlargement: law and socioeconomic changes*, Montréal: Les Editions Thémis.
——(2005) *Rights Before Courts: a study of constitutional courts in post-communist states of Central and Eastern Europe*, Dordrecht: Springer.
Schimmelfennig, F. (2002) 'Introduction: the impact of international organizations on the Central and Eastern European states – Conceptual and theoretical issues', in R. H. Linden (ed.) *Norms and Nannies. The impact of international organizations on the Central and East European states*, Lanhan: Rowman.
Schwartz, H. (2000) *The Struggle for Constitutional Justice in Post-Communist Europe*, Chicago: University of Chicago Press.
Shapiro, M. (1981) *Courts: a comparative and political analysis*, Chicago: University of Chicago Press.
Stone Sweet, A. (2000) *Governing with Judges: constitutional politics in Europe*, Oxford: Oxford University Press.
Tamanaha, B. (2004) *On the Rule of Law: history, politics, and theory*, Cambridge: Cambridge University Press.
Vauchez, A. (2005) 'Les juristes et la construction d'un ordre juridique européen', *Critique Internationale*, no. 26, Mars 2005.
Weiler, J. H. H. and Wind, M. (2003) *European Constitutionalism Beyond the State*, Cambridge: Cambridge University Press.
World Values Surveys, European and World Values Survey four-wave integrated data file (1981–2004) v.20060423, 2006. The European Values Study Foundation and World Values Survey Association. Aggregate File Producers: ASEP/JDS, Madrid, Spain/Tilburg University, Tilburg, the Netherlands. Aggregate File Distributors: ASEP/JDS and ZA, Cologne, Germany. Online. Available HTTP: < http://www.worldvaluessurvey.org > (accessed 20 June 2007).
Wyrzikowsky, M. (2000) *Constitutional Cultures*, Warsaw: Institute for Public Affairs.

12 How do the others see us? European political identity and the external image of the EU

Lorenzo Fioramonti and Sonia Lucarelli

A significant branch of literature nowadays claims that the European Union (EU) is a 'distinctive' world power. The argument is that the EU behaves differently in world politics as it is differently constituted: its initial *telos* (peace through integration), its historical developments and its current institutional and normative framework (a post-Westphalian entity with a set of core norms) are believed to make it act as a 'qualitatively' different global actor.

Based on these premises, recent research has started testing whether the EU is an intrinsically different (i.e. better) international actor, by focusing on gaps between the EU's rhetoric and deeds (e.g. Panebianco 2006; Smith 2006). However, this literature has looked mainly at inconsistencies and, at times, inefficiencies (in terms of the capability–expectations gap) and has neglected a fundamental aspect in the relationship between the EU and the rest of the world; that is, how non-European societies view the EU and the potential feedback that this has on the European political identity. As it was noticed in Chapter 2, the self-identification and legitimization processes can be affected not only by the EU's overall performance (policy) but also by the reception of the *others'* views of the EU (which is inevitably influenced by the policy performance, but also decoded through the observers' cognitive frames).

But, what is this view? Despite the importance of the issue, there are few studies on the external image of the EU[1] and there is virtually no research on how the external image affects the EU's political identity and legitimacy. Hence, the purpose of this chapter is to illustrate the main images of the EU in a sample of non-European countries and analyse the issues presented by some key European newspapers in order to tentatively assess how such external images can feed back into the European public debate and, potentially, influence the citizens' self-identification process. Each section begins with a short methodological note.

Viewed from the outside: the external perceptions of the EU

How is the EU perceived in the rest of the world and how can we go about studying it? As we have seen, both questions have been underexplored in the literature. In order to collect some initial data on this topic, we conducted an international survey on the external image of the EU, which was implemented by a group of researchers in 2006–7 (see note 1). The survey investigated how a set of domestic constituencies (public opinion, political elites, civil society organizations and the media) view the EU in a sample of countries: Australia (Stats 2007), Brazil (Poletti 2007), Canada (Croci and Tossutti 2007), China (Poletti *et al.* 2007), Egypt (Bayoumi 2007), Japan (Chaban and Kaufman 2007), India (Fioramonti 2007a) and South Africa (Fioramonti 2007b). The rationale underlying the selection of countries was to gain an exhaustive picture of how the EU is viewed in a set of industrialized and emerging societies as well. Three industrialized nations (Australia, Canada and Japan) were selected according to a principle of continental representation. The remaining emerging societies (Brazil, China, Egypt, India and South Africa) were identified on the basis of their leading role within their own regions.[2]

In this chapter, we report some of the findings of the country case studies and borrow some additional insights from a study on transnational non-governmental organizations (NGOs) and social movements (Andretta and Doerr 2007), which was also part of the overall survey. For each country, researchers used a set of sources: mass media (generally newspapers but also TV), opinion polls, websites and, occasionally, face-to-face interviews (see Lucarelli 2007a). Moreover, the multiplicity of constituencies and sources allowed for a broad range of views in each country. Clearly, the findings needed to be interpreted in light of the national sociopolitical culture.

Our analysis highlights several different and, at times, opposing images of the EU. Table 12.1 summarizes some of the most common images in the countries and among transnational NGOs.

Less known and less debated actor for public opinion

Despite the fact that the EU flag is regularly displayed in all EU delegations and is printed on thousands of booklets and brochures, very few people have an idea of what the EU is and, even less, of what its policies, motives and goals are. The degree of knowledge of the EU seems to be very much dependent on the individuals' level of education, socioeconomic background and profession. Furthermore, the perception of the European continent is frequently filtered through relationships with individual European countries (i.e. UK, France, Germany), particularly in the case of former colonies (e.g. India and South Africa).

A particularly low degree of knowledge of the EU is registered among citizens in emerging societies. In China, South Africa and Brazil, only a minority of citizens know enough to have an opinion about the EU: respectively 23 per cent of Chinese in 2001 (World Values Survey 2001), compared with 45 per cent in South Africa (Afrobarometer 2002) and 43 per cent in Brazil (Lagos 2004, 2005). However, although in South Africa

Table 12.1 Main external images of the EU

Public opinion	Political elites	Civil society organizations	The media
Australia			
• Significant knowledge of the EU • Mainly positive image • Economic power • Protectionist power	• Elites' perception influenced by pre-eminent bilateral relation with individual EU member states (Britain) • Important, but not most important partner • Negative images prevail (trade barriers). Positive images refer to EU unity, human rights policy	• Little attention • Important role in human rights but more coherence is deemed necessary • Leading environmental agent	• EU virtually invisible • Frame: mainly *political*, second economic, last social. Most prominent sub-frame: international conflict management, anti-terrorism, constitution, enlargement, environment
Brazil			
• Limited knowledge • Appreciation varies according to level of education	• Strategic opportunity • Both economic partner and rival • Sizeable impact on the international system	• Promoter of environmental sustainability • Neo-liberal actor	• Economic power (trade) • Political attention is mainly devoted to internal EU transformation
Canada			
• Scarce sources • Positive image • Call for more EU 'presence' to counterbalance USA	• Positive views linked to environment, social policy (education and research), political–diplomatic initiatives • Negative images linked to Common Agricultural Policy • No attention from political parties	• Promoter of environmental sustainability	• Little attention to EU • Most focus on institutional dimension • Internationally, economic dimension prevails • Political dimension focuses on human rights, EU in the Middle East

(*continued*)

Table 12.1 continued

Public opinion	Political elites	Civil society organizations	The media
China			
• Positive view not correlated with age/education	• Strategic opportunity • Development-friendly • Supporter of multilateralism/multipolarism • Appreciation of soft security • Negative appreciation of EU's human rights policy • EU–China 'complementarity'	• Not available	• Little coverage • Essentially *political* and *economic* actor • Appreciation: neutral to positive
Egypt			
• Few sources available • Important partnership, yet regional partnerships are preferred • Higher expectations	• Possible counterbalance to the USA • Economic opportunity but also constraint • EU policy is security driven • Criticism of EU's human rights and democracy conditionality	• Potential human rights and democracy promoter (yet not for Muslim Brothers)	• Security seeker • EU's economic 'protectionism' (Common Agricultural Policy) is criticized • Counterbalance to the USA • Appreciation of the integration experience • Lack of EU–Egypt mutual understanding denounced • Criticism of EU's human rights and democracy conditionality
India			
• Little-known actor	• Supporter of multipolarism • Security seeker • Strategic opportunity • A protectionist market • EU–India shared values	• Promoter of environmental sustainability • Neo-liberal and protectionist (Common Agricultural Policy) actor	• Little-known actor and unclear entity • Economic and political power, but by far second to the USA • Various references to EU's human rights policy, aid policy, soft security (largely positive images) • Security seeker

(continued)

Table 12.1 continued

Public opinion	Political elites	Civil society organizations	The media
Japan			
• Random surveys • Ambivalent and controversial findings	• Similar security priorities, democratic values and Japan–EU economic visions • EU model of environmental protection • EU 'object of study'	• Invisible partner for NGOs • More appreciated by business community	• EU mainly economic actor, but political focus in crucial years (enlargement, Iraq war, etc.)
South Africa			
• Less known actor and viewed as ineffective	• Model of regional integration • Strategic opportunity • A protectionist market	• Neo-liberal actor in foreign policy • A social model internally	• Little-known actor
Social movements and NGOs			
• Similar framing of the EU among European and non-European civil society. Similar attempt at creating 'another', more democratic, peaceful, ecological and social Europe. • Ambivalent picture of a powerful political community with both hegemonic but also socially transformative and democratic aspirations. • Overall criticism of the EU as a neo-liberal economic power. • Non-European NGOs dealing with non-economic issues, such as human rights, women's rights and peace, regard the EU as a potential ally to bring transformation for the better (human rights and democratization). • Non-Europeans criticize European NGOs for their lack of democratic credentials.			

(Afrobarometer 2002), citizens are more familiar with international institutions such as the UN and the World Bank or regional institutions such as the African Union, in Brazil the EU is more widely known than other institutions such as the World Trade Organization (WTO) and the North American Free Trade Agreement (Lagos 2004). India remains a country deeply influenced by American culture and, in spite of new prospects generated by a common Erasmus programme with the EU, the bulk of Indian students look to the USA to further their studies and professional careers (Lisbonne de Vergeron 2006: 25). In Japan public opinion surveys show that although knowledge of 'Europe' is rather widespread among the population (although only a slim majority, 51 per cent, felt some degree of affinity with their Western European counterparts), knowledge of 'the EU' is low (Chaban and Kauffmann 2007).

In Egypt, levels of public awareness of the EU are moderate and largely confined to intellectual, political and economic elites (Ebeid 2004: 5). In the 2004 Youth Aspiration Survey, 97 per cent of those who had an opinion about the EU considered it to be a foreign policy priority for Egypt (whereas a more limited 38 per cent replied 'Gulf countries', 62 per cent 'Palestine' and 79 per cent 'the US'). However, to the question 'What is *the best orientation* for Egypt in its relations with neighbouring areas?', only 18 per cent replied 'Europe and the Mediterranean countries', whereas 34 per cent replied 'the Middle East' and 93 per cent 'the Arab region' (Bayoumi 2007).

All in all, only a minority of those citizens who have an opinion about the EU perceive the latter to be effective or credible. For instance, in South Africa only 15 per cent of citizens believe that the EU is an effective actor (Afrobarometer 2002). Similarly, when asked to assess the contribution of global actors towards democracy, development, peace and free trade, only a small minority of Brazilian citizens consider the EU to be the most effective actor in supporting development (12 per cent) and democracy (22 per cent), whereas the USA is believed to be slightly more effective (with peace promotion being the only exception, for which the EU is seen as the best promoter by 22 per cent of citizens compared with 17 per cent for the USA) (Lagos 2005). Interestingly, Brazilian opinion polls reveal that better educated people consider the EU to be a much more effective contributor to global peace, free trade, democracy and development than the USA, with percentages ranging between 29 per cent and 53 per cent for the EU, and dropping to 7 per cent and 21 per cent for the USA (Lagos 2004). In China, only 30 per cent of citizens had some confidence in the EU in 1990, but this figure had grown to 40 per cent in 2001 (World Values Survey 1990, 2001) and, in 2004, 77 per cent of Chinese who had an opinion about the EU believed that the EU's role in world affairs was mainly positive (PIPA-GlobeScan 2005).

According to the World Powers Survey, in 2006 only a small portion of citizens around the globe perceived the EU to be a significant world power compared with those who chose the USA or China. The picture does not

Table 12.2 World powers today (and in 2020)

Country of respondents (below)	European Union (%)	China (%)	USA (%)
Brazil	15 (14)	26 (32)	71 (39)
China	17 (14)	44 (71)	84 (42)
India	7 (7)	34 (43)	85 (51)
Japan	25 (17)	31 (40)	63 (40)
Total	32 (30)	45 (55)	81 (57)

Source: Bertelsmann Stiftung 2006.

change a great deal when analysing people's opinions regarding what will be key world powers in the future (see Table 12.2).

A strategic opportunity and a trade giant

By and large, the most recurrent image of the EU is somewhat linked to its economic might. For Indian, Chinese, South African and Brazilian elites, the EU is a strategic opportunity for development and economic growth and is mainly described as a trade partner and the biggest market in the world. Likewise, economic linkages between these countries and the EU are by far the most common issues presented by the media (this is particularly the case in Brazil and South Africa). As far as the Japanese media is concerned, the EU is mainly described as a commercial actor and the two waves of EU enlargement are presented as an important trade opportunity for Japan (Chaban and Kauffmann 2007). In the words of Brazil's former Secretary General for External Relations, De Seixas Correa, 'the partnership with the EU is of primary importance. Its fifteen members, together, represent the largest market for Brazilian exports and the main source of foreign direct investment in Brazil' (quoted in Poletti *et al.* 2007). For the Indian Prime Minister, Manmohan Singh, the EU is 'not only India's largest trading partner, but also our largest source of foreign direct investment'.[3] Chinese officials also see the EU and European countries through the lens of 'economic complementarity' (Zhang Yesui 2005).

A security seeker

The EU is often associated with peacemaking processes and security concerns. For instance, according to a 2005 Internet opinion poll focusing on the main expectations of Egyptians from the Euro-Mediterranean partnership, the majority of respondents believed that the partnership would positively affect the Arab–Israeli conflict in the Middle East. In *Al Ahram*, op-eds are generally concerned with the political role of the EU in the Middle East as a whole, with a specific focus on the Israeli–Palestinian conflict, rather than on the partnership framework (Ebeid 2004: 6). Some analysts maintain that the role played by the EU in the Palestinian conflict is also crucial for how the strongest banned political movement in the country, the Muslim Brotherhood, understands the EU's global role (Bayoumi 2007). At the same time, it must be noted that the EU's efforts to cooperate with its southern Mediterranean neighbours are often interpreted as a security measure to avoid such problems reverberating into Europe rather than a genuine attempt to help Middle Eastern countries solve their problems (Gad 2001).

In the Indian press, the EU is mentioned as an important actor in the peace processes in Jammu-Kashmir and Sri Lanka. Indian newspapers also praise the pro-democracy role played by the EU during the Nepalese crisis in early 2006 and feature various news items describing the EU's diplomatic initiatives to avoid direct confrontation in Iran and North Korea. This 'image' of the EU is also shared by Indian political elites who, in their official speeches, often refer to the EU as an ally in the fight against terrorism and a promoter of global security (Fioramonti 2007a).

Similarly, the EU was regularly mentioned by the South African media in relation to the Zimbabwean crisis in 2001–2. As mentioned above, Brazilian public opinion views the EU as one of the global actors that contributes most to international peace (after the UN, but before the USA) (Lagos 2004, 2005).

A supporter of multilateralism (or, at least, multipolarism)

Political elites frequently view the EU as a key player in a future 'multipolar' world and, at times, as a champion of 'multilateralism'.

In China, references to multilateralism as a goal shared by both the EU and China are rather common. On different occasions, Premier Wen Jiabao has expressed this synergy very clearly by defining 'China and the EU as important forces for world peace and stability committed to multilateralism and to the promotion of democracy and the rule of law in international relations' (quoted in Poletti *et al.* 2007).

On a similar note, Shyam Saran, former Indian Foreign Secretary, believes that the 'EU represents a very important pole in a multipolar world'.[4]

The same discourse is recurrent among Brazilian political elites, although more emphasis is put on the notion of 'multipolarism'. In this context, emphasis on multipolarism should be read in light of the quest for a counterbalance to the US leadership and a world order in which Brazil could gain its place among the great powers (Poletti 2007).

It must be noted that the whole issue of 'multipolarism' and 'multilateralism' is intertwined with the official discourse around common values and is often presented in response to the current international system dominated by the USA. Such a discourse (which is particularly recurrent in public statements regarding the strategic partnerships with China, India and Japan) is definitely permeated by rhetoric, which makes it rather difficult to gauge to what extent the multipolar/multilateral role of the EU is genuinely appreciated. Moreover, what is understood as 'multilalteralism' is also affected by political culture and rhetoric. For instance, in China multilateralism is viewed as a way to safeguard the UN system and state sovereignty against unilateral policies, whereas in the EU's case multilateralism is seen as a practice of coordination that goes beyond state power and has largely changed the very concept of sovereignty.

Model of regional integration

There exists a significant amount of political speeches and official documents that describe the EU as a key example of successful regional integration. It is likely that, at least in the case of Brazil and South Africa, such an emphasis is also due to these countries' specific ambitions in supporting regional integration processes within their own geographic spheres of influence.

In the case of Egypt, the experience of the EU is often presented by the press 'as an exemplary experience of integration and as the most reasonable and realistic alternative to the failing pan-Arab projects' (Bayoumi 2007; see also Nafie 2004), although intra-Arab economic cooperation continues being the best option for the wider public as well as for the elites (Soltan 2001).

In Japan, leading newspapers such as *The Daily Yomiuri*, *The ASAHI Shimbun* and *The Nikkei Weekly* devote a number of articles to European internal affairs and most of them highlight the EU's enlargement as a positive example of the peaceful benefits of regional cooperation and, perhaps, as an example to follow in Asia (Chaban and Kauffmann 2007).

A protectionist actor

The image of the EU as a protectionist market is very common among politicians, trade unionists and business organizations in developing economies (particularly in Brazil, India and South Africa) and in the civil society sector across all countries. In this regard, the main critical target is the EU common agricultural policy and the various non-tariff trade barriers that, in the eyes of many non-European countries, distort international trade and bring about negative consequences for emerging markets. Political elites and business groups alike criticize the EU for promoting free trade abroad when implementing protectionist policies back home. For instance, Brazilian President Lula da Silva described the EU as a 'great protectionist agricultural power' (Lula da Silva 2003). Similar observations are shared by business organizations in South Africa and India. Even in the case of Japan, the press reported criticism of the unfair European protection of agriculture and fishing, perceived as detrimental to the Japanese economy (Chaban and Kauffmann 2007).

Trade unions and local NGOs see the EU's agricultural policy as another component of the long-standing unfair practices imposed on Africa, Asia and Latin America by the former colonizers and advocate for a system of *fair* trade (rather than free trade), in which protectionist policies are admissible only when applied to developing economies in order to bridge the development gap with Europe. Criticism of the EU's agricultural policy reinforces the portrait of the EU as a global actor characterized by double standards and inconsistencies.

The EU as a (possible) counterbalance to US hegemony

Contrary to expectations, our analysis did not highlight a significant difference in the external perceptions of the EU in comparison to the USA (particularly as far as trade is concerned). However, in some instances the EU is seen as a possible counterbalance to the US's hegemony.

A 2004 Globescan survey of more than 23,000 people in 23 countries found that citizens in 20 states would see it as 'mainly positive' if Europe were to become more influential than the USA in world affairs. Table 12.3 reports the results for Australia, Brazil, Canada, China, India, Japan and South Africa.

Although India shows the lowest percentage of positive responses, the view of the EU as a counterbalance to the USA is nevertheless present in public discourse and in the media. In the Egyptian press, 'the EU ranks second in volume of coverage after the US, but the tone is definitely more positive in the opposition press' (Ebeid 2004: 6). Similar views can also be found in political parties' documents in both Egypt and China. Finally, it is interesting that the Japanese media highlights similarities between the EU and Japan's approaches to conflict prevention and democracy promotion in Iraq, by somehow making a distinction with the US strategy in the area (Chaban and Kauffmann 2007).

Table 12.3 Europe vs. USA influence in world

How would you see it if Europe were to become more influential than the USA in world affairs

	Mainly positive (%)	*Mainly negative (%)*
Australia	62	23
Brazil	53	28
Canada	63	26
China	66	16
India	35	38
Japan	35	13
South Africa	63	25

Source: PIPA-GlobeScan 2005.
Note: Remaining percentages indicate responses such as 'neither', 'no difference', 'don't know' or 'depends'.

A protector of the environment

Particularly in the press, the EU tends to be presented as a model of (global) environmental protection. This image, which is less widespread than those described thus far, seems to be growing rapidly, especially as a consequence of the EU's activism in pursuing the Kyoto Protocol on climate change. Such an initiative seems to have created rising expectations of the EU playing a leading role in the fight against global warming. Among the countries included in this analysis, emphasis on global environmental concerns was rather common in Australia, Canada, India and Japan.

Is there feedback on the Europeans' political identity?

The external images of the EU are relevant for the self-identification process of the Europeans only insofar as they influence the public debate within Europe. By and large, the media is a promising source of information about public debates. As noticed in Chapter 2, if an issue does not enter the public debate steered by the media, it hardly becomes a concern around which identities can be shaped and reinterpreted.

The media can be regarded at the same time as a reflection of a wider public debate (proxies of public debate) and as an instrument shaping public debate. In a social constructivist framework, this double role of the media is part of the social construction of societies and political groups. Thus, we can claim that a media analysis invariably contributes to our understanding of a fundamental element of the self-identification process. At the same time, though, it must be stressed that the mere appearance in the media does not guarantee that a given issue becomes relevant for the processes of identity formation.

Owing to methodological constraints, we exclusively used the press as a proxy of the overall European public debate given that an analysis of both the TV and the Internet would have required a much higher level of resources. Operationally, we selected a sample of newspapers[5] from Britain, France, Italy and Spain according to specific timelines, so as to cover certain crucial international events during which the EU's global images were more likely to surface.[6] The specific events include: the WTO talks in Doha (time span analysed 6–20 November 2001); the World Summit on Sustainable Development in Johannesburg (time span analysed 23 August to 11 September 2002); the World Social Forum 2001 in Porto Alegre (time span analysed 22 January to 6 February 2001); the World Social Forum 2002 in Porto Alegre (time span analysed 28 January to 12 February 2002); the run-up to the war in Iraq and the bombing of Baghdad (time span analysed 1 January to 1 May 2003); the Global Summit of Women in Cairo (time span analysed 7–19 June 2006); and the UN Climate Change Conference in Nairobi (time span analysed 3–24 November 2006). The purpose of this media review was to analyse how the various 'images' described so far were represented and discussed in the European press. Although we do not assume that the European press is simply and directly influenced by external views, we are nevertheless confident that the selection of these key international events helps narrow down the range of issues that are more likely to be influenced by external, non-European voices.

In general, we found that the European press paid limited attention to the role of the EU/Europe in connections with the various events covered. Within our sample, the number of articles dealing with the EU/Europe is rather low overall. This is particularly true as regards the Cairo Global Summit of Women, which went virtually unnoticed in the European press. On the occasion of the World Social Forums (WSFs) in Porto Alegre in 2001 and 2002, some newspapers paid only marginal attention to the role of the EU/Europe: in the 2001 WSF, the EU/European role did not occupy centre stage in any of the (only) nine articles mentioning the EU/Europe. During the second WSF, despite a larger number of articles (34), the level of emphasis remained roughly the same. The only case in which coverage of the EU/Europe was more substantial was during the World Summit on Sustainable Development (WSSD) held in Johannesburg in 2002.

Of particular relevance were the analyses of the EU's role in the Doha round negotiations made by *The Times* and the *Guardian*, by far the most critical newspapers among our sample. The EU is reported as being 'under fire from developing nations for its agricultural subsidies, which they say are barring open trade'[7] and is also directly accused of protectionism and an inward-looking attitude: 'But it does not take much imagination – or scientific knowledge – to appreciate why poor countries see this [European attitude] as protectionism, almost undisguised'.[8] Much attention is also paid by the *Guardian* to the critical inconsistency between EU's agricultural protectionism and its declared interest to contribute towards free trade and development for poor nations. According to the British newspaper: 'The EU is isolated over agriculture, with the US, the Cairns group of agricultural free traders and poor countries, many of which depend on agriculture for export revenue, all backing the call for eliminating subsidies.'[9] Such a critical view of the EU's protectionism and its effects on developing countries is revived in the British press during the WSSD, when, however, another image of the EU also appears: that of a global actor sensitive to environmental issues and a counterbalance to the US.[10] However, such appreciation already seems to have waned four years later, on the occasion of the Nairobi UN Climate Change Conference, when the two British newspapers take a substantially negative stance on the EU, which not only 'created [the] carbon problem in the first place', but who also 'create[d] a complex, flawed emissions trading scheme that achieves nothing'[11] and 'is falling woefully short of its targets for cutting greenhouse gas emissions'.[12]

In contrast, *Le Figaro* assumes a largely positive stance towards the EU/Europe and partly defends it from the external criticism of selfishness: 'Europe wants to protect its agriculture against the most neo-liberal countries and expects that environmental protection as well as the respect of certain social norms are taken into account in the negotiations'.[13] The newspaper also presents a rather positive assessment of the EU in the aftermath of the WSSD and reports the views of the EU as a 'different' power *vis-à-vis* the USA by depicting it as an actor open to dialogue and a promoter of multilateralism and international legality. On the basis of these strengths, *Le Figaro* believes that 'it is essential that Europe, with the support of France, becomes the champion of the new North–South dialogue'.[14]

The other French newspaper analysed here, *Libération,* reports some slightly more negative views on the EU. Its overall position remains ambiguous: if the EU is accused of protectionism and hypocrisy, it recognizes that the EU, contrary to the USA, is multilateral and attentive to the environment. This view by non-European representatives is reported during the WSSD and in the five articles regarding the Nairobi conference, where criticisms from southern NGOs are also featured.

The Italian newspapers *La Stampa* and *Il Sole 24 Ore* report external views that depict the EU as being weakened by its internal lack of cohesion, although providing a counterpart to the USA (since the EU is seen as an international actor with a 'different' understanding of world politics). The views of developing societies and poor countries are also reported while covering the WSSD, particularly with reference to the injustices caused by the EU agricultural policy: 'a European cow gets in subsidies one and a half as much as the salary of a peasant in the Third World. According to the African and Asian delegates, this is the main cause of their poverty.'[15]

In order to assess how these various 'images' are represented in the internal European debate in crucial areas of 'high politics' such as diplomacy and the use of force, we also analysed the coverage of the EU made by the above-mentioned newspapers before and during the first phase of the Iraqi campaign (1 January to 1 May 2003). However, because of the significant amount of articles mentioning the EU (about 15,000 in the time span analysed), it is not possible to analyse them in detail here. We will therefore discuss only the main similarities found across the sample.

In general, it is possible to identify at least one important common theme: the EU is commended for adopting a diplomatic strategy towards Saddam Hussein's regime, while being criticized for not having been able to unite its member states behind this position.

The Spanish *El País* goes even further by describing the EU as a power with shared values, such as the promotion of enduring peace and multilateralism:

> The great responsibility of Europeans is that Europe is today the main, if not the only, promoter of this goal [a peaceful, multilateral and diverse world]. Thus, the quest for peace in Iraq must be pursued along with the European battle for a new international legal system.[16]

The French newspaper *Libération* is quite critical of the European divisions concerning the Iraq campaign and heavily criticizes the EU for not having taken a stronger stance against the US-led war. Similarly, but less emphatically, *Le Figaro* supports the decision of the 'old Europe' not to intervene in Iraq, but also highlights the fracture that this caused among the member states. According to *Le Figaro,* the Iraqi campaign undermined the EU's ambition to speak with one voice in world affairs while underlining the need for Europe to strengthen its military capacity: 'the appeal for a European military force and a unified foreign policy is aimed at acquiring a collective power, [...] which is the only way to preserve international influence.'[17]

A similar view is echoed by *La Stampa* and *Il Sole 24 Ore*, which focus on the internal divisions of the EU when it comes to 'second pillar' policies and reveal slightly more pessimistic views with regard to the global role of the EU in issues concerning war and peace and international security. Nevertheless, as argued by *Il Sole 24 Ore*: 'If Europe acts unitarily and avoids haphazard moves, it will be able to make a significant contribution to the post-war period.'[18]

For *The Times*, which is often critical of the EU's global aspirations, Europe will be the loser 'if it tries to challenge the US, because other countries will inevitably gravitate towards America's great military might'.[19] In contrast, the *Guardian* supports the EU's emphasis on diplomatic pressure and features an article in which Jeremy Rifkin argues that 'the Iraq crisis has united Europeans and armed them with a clear sense of shared values and future vision'.[20]

In conclusion, it could be said that except for a few cases, the image of a global actor promoting multilateralism and rules-based international politics is not very common among the newspapers analysed in this section. Moreover, it must be underscored that the traditional criticisms directed at EU protectionism and its hollow development rhetoric are more frequently reported as critiques by international NGOs, rather than as direct complaints of developing nations. Overall, the EU's role is evaluated more positively in terms of its contribution to global environmental issues rather than with regard to its promotion of democracy and development in emerging markets. The preliminary findings of our analysis also make us believe that these external images enter the European public mainly as a result of the channelling role played by European civil society forces (especially NGOs but also some journalists and intellectuals), rather than through the actions and speeches of European policy-makers and political parties, who appear to be still too focused on the domestic agenda.

Concluding remarks

This analysis was meant to spark debate about the external image of the EU and its impact on the European public debate and, thereby, the self-identification process of European citizens. Obviously, the analysis would need to be further improved by a stronger methodological design and a comprehensive study of additional sources, including the bulletins and declarations of European NGOs, social movements and political parties, as well as a systematic analysis of TV programmes. Needless to say, this is the ambition of our next research plan. Yet, through a preliminary analysis of the external image of the EU and the public debate within Europe, we can already identify some important findings.

First of all, the EU does not seem to be widely regarded as a 'normative power'. Besides the recognition of the EU as a model of regional integration, the EU tends to be regarded as a (neo-)liberal power, not too dissimilar from the USA. Surprisingly, the EU's multilateral virtues are appreciated particularly by China, but clearly with a different understanding of what multilateralism is. Equally surprising is the substantial lack of acknowledgement of the EU's international 'solidarity policy' *par excellence*: development cooperation. By contrast, developing countries seem to be much more concerned about the damage brought about by the EU's agricultural policy than the amount of EU development assistance they receive.

Most of these external images are channelled through civil society groups and then reported by the European press, which plays an important role in filtering critical views of the EU. The press also underlines the progressive role played by the EU in areas such as environmental protection and it seems to be very attentive to the EU's performances in this field.

We believe that some of these external perceptions have gained currency in the European public debate and are very likely to influence the Europeans' self-identification process. What is crucial in order for this to take place is the degree of *importance* attached by domestic (European, national) institutions and individuals to the specific issues at stake, as some other contributions in this volume also underline (cf. D'Andrea, Chapter 5, and Badii, Chapter 7). In this respect, recent developments seem to point to an ever-growing attention from both external actors and the European media to the EU's efforts in confronting global warning. A failure to match widespread expectations in this field could have a damaging effect on the EU's international credibility and well as its internal legitimacy.

Acknowledgements

This chapter draws part of its data from a survey on *The External Image of the European Union,* coordinated by Sonia Lucarelli at the Forum on the Problems of Peace and War (Florence), in the framework of the Network of Excellence GARNET (Lucarelli 2007a,b). We are grateful to GARNET and the Italian Ministry of Foreign Affairs for their financial contribution, to our fellow contributors to the survey, and to the large number of people who provided comments and support.

Notes

1 Indeed, there are very few systematic studies on the others' image of the EU. The largest project on the EU's external image is *The EU through the Eyes of Asia* coordinated by Martin Holland (http://www.europe.canterbury.ac.nz/appp/project_description/).
2 More countries, including key actors such as the USA and Russia, will be part of the second wave of this survey planned for 2008–9.
3 See '"Strategic partnership" likely to be formalised with EU', *The Hindu*, 8 November 2004.
4 'India–EU Partnership will set the Stage for Closer Ties', *The Hindu*, 6 November 2004.
5 The *Guardian; The Times* (along with *The Sunday Times*); *Le Figaro; Libération; La Stampa; Il Sole 24 Ore; El Mundo; El País*. All newspapers were accessed though the Lexis–Nexis database.
6 We are aware of the fact that an analysis of the TV would have strengthened our study enormously. However, because of data availability, we were not able to undertake a comprehensive review of TV programmes and news bulletins.
7 'Hopes Rise for Progress in New Round of Trade Talks', *The Times*, 12 November 2001.
8 'Tricky Questions Loom for Bush', *The Times*, 9 November 2001.
9 'Europe Isolated by WTO', the *Guardian*, 14 November 2001.
10 'Earth Summit 2002', the *Guardian*, 24 August 2002.
11 'France's Carbon War is a Strike Against Brussels', *The Times*, 15 November 2006.
12 The *Guardian Weekly*, 3 November 2006.
13 'Réunion à Doha de la Conférence de l'OMC', *Le Figaro*, 9 November 2001 (authors' translation).
14 'Les petits pas de Johannesburg', *Le Figaro*, 4 September 2002 (authors' translation).
15 'Sui sussidi resta lo scontro tra primo e terzo mondo', *La* Stampa, 28 August 2002 (authors' translation).
16 'La batalla europea', *El País*, 29 March 2003 (authors' translation).
17 'Un an après le choc du premier tour de l'élection présidentielle; L'engagement républicain: défi ou repli?', *Le Figaro*, 23 April 2003 (authors' translation).
18 'Europa a piccoli passi', *Il Sole 24 Ore*, 19 April 2003 (authors' translation).
19 'Straw Admits Job was on the Line over Iraq', *The Times*, 26 April 2003.
20 J. Rifkin, 'Thanks, Mr President: Bush's Actions are Helping Europe to Fashion a New Sense of Identity,' the *Guardian*, 26 April 2003.

References

Afrobarometer (2002) *Afrobarometer 2002. A comparative series of national public attitude surveys on democracy, markets and civil society in Africa*. Online. Available HTTP: < http://www.afrobarometer.org > (accessed 18 November 2007).

Andretta, M. and Doerr, N. (2007) 'Report on trade unions, social movements and NGOs: European and non European perspectives', in S. Lucarelli (ed.) *Research Report: the external image of the European Union*, GARNET Working Paper no. 17/7. Online. Available HTTP: < http://www.garnet-eu.org/fileadmin/documents/working_papers/1707/13%20Trade%20Unions,%20Social%20movements%20and%20NGOs.pdf > (accessed 18 November 2007).

Bayoumi, S. (2007) 'Country report: Egypt', in S. Lucarelli (ed.) *Research Report: the external image of the European Union*, GARNET Working Paper no. 17/7. Online. Available HTTP: < http://www.garnet-eu.org/fileadmin/documents/working_papers/1707/9%20Egypt.pdf > (accessed 18 November 2007).

Bertelsmann Stiftung (2006) *World Powers in the 21st Century. The results of a representative survey in Brazil, China, France, Germany, India, Japan, Russia, the United Kingdom, and the United States*, Berlin, 2 June 2006. Online. Available HTTP: < http://www.cap.lmu.de/download/2006/2006_GPC_Survey_Results.pdf > (accessed 18 November 2007).

Chaban, N., Elgström, O. and Holland, M. (2006) 'The European Union as Others see it', *European Foreign Affairs Review*, 11 (2): 245–62.

Chaban, N. and Kauffmann, M. (2007) 'Country report: Japan', in S. Lucarelli (ed.) *Research Report: the external image of the European Union*, GARNET Working Paper no. 17/7. Online. Available HTTP: < http://www.garnet-eu.org/fileadmin/documents/working_papers/1707/11%20Japan.pdf > (accessed 18 November 2007).

Croci, O. and Tossutti, L. (2007) 'Country report: Canada', in S. Lucarelli (ed.) *Research Report: the external image of the European Union*, GARNET Working Paper no. 17/7. Online. Available HTTP: < http://www.garnet-eu.org/fileadmin/documents/working_papers/1707/7%20Canada.pdf > (accessed 18 November 2007).

Ebeid, H. (2004) 'The partnership in Southern eyes: reflections on the discourse in the Egyptian press', *Euromesco Papers*, no. 37. Online. Available HTTP: < http://euromesco.com.pt/media/euromescopaper37_hebeid.pdf > (accessed 18 November 2007).

Fioramonti, L. (2007a) 'Country report: India', in S. Lucarelli (ed.) *Research Report: the external image of the European Union*, GARNET Working Paper no. 17/7. Online. Available HTTP: < http://www.garnet-eu.org/fileadmin/documents/working_papers/1707/10%20India.pdf > (accessed 18 November 2007).

—— (2007b) 'Country report: South Africa', in S. Lucarelli (ed.) *Research Report: the external image of the European Union*, GARNET Working Paper no. 17/7. Online. Available HTTP: < http://www.garnet-eu.org/fileadmin/documents/working_papers/1707/12%20South%20Africa.pdf > (accessed 18 November 2007).

Fioramonti, L. and Lucarelli, S. (2007) 'The EU viewed by the Others: drawing some conclusions', in S. Lucarelli (ed.) *Research Report: the external image of the ? European Union*, GARNET Working Paper no. 17/7. Online. Available HTTP: < http://www.garnet-eu.org/fileadmin/documents/working_papers/1707/15%20Conclusions.pdf > (accessed 18 November 2007).

Gad, E. (2001) *The EU and the Middle East: past experiences and future horizons*, Cairo: Al-Ahram Center for Political and Strategic Studies.

Lagos, M. (2004) (ed.) *América Latina & Unión Europea, percepción ciudadana*, Latinobarómetro 2004, Santiago de Chile: Focus Eurolatino.

—— (2005) (ed.) *La Unión Europea y su posicionamiento entre las potencias mundiales*, Santiago de Chile: Focus Eurolatino.

Lisbonne de Vergeron, K. (2006) *Contemporary Indian views of the European Union*, London: Chatam House.

Lucarelli, S. (2007a) (ed.) *Research Report: The External Image Of The European Union*, GARNET Working Paper no. 17/7. Online. Available HTTP: < http://www.garnet-eu.org/fileadmin/documents/working_papers/1707/1%20Survey%20Front%20Page-Content-Authors-Acknowledgments.pdf > (accessed 18 November 2007).

—— (2007b) (ed.) *Beyond Self Perception: the Others' view of the European Union*, special issue of *European Foreign Affairs Review*, 12 (3).

Lula da Silva, L. I. (2003) 'Encerramento da IV Reunião Plenária do Fórum Empresarial Mercosul União Européia', Hotel Blue Tree – Brasília – DF, 29 October 2003. Online. Available HTTP: < http://www.mre.gov.br > (accessed 18 November 2007).

Nafie, I. (2004) 'Between us', *Al-Ahram Weekly*, Issue no. 681, 11–17 March 2004. Online. Available HTTP: < http://weekly.ahram.org.eg/2004/681/op1.htm > (accessed 18 November 2007).

Ortega, M. (2004) (ed.) *Global Views of the European Union*, Chaillot Paper no. 72, Paris: EU Institute for Security Studies.

Panebianco, S. (2006) 'Promoting human rights and democracy in European Union relations with Russia and China', in S. Lucarelli and I. Manners (eds) *Values and Principles in European Union Foreign Policy*, London: Routledge.

Poletti, A. (2007) 'Country report: Brazil', in S. Lucarelli (ed.) *Research Report: the external image of the European Union*, GARNET Working Paper no. 17/7. Online. Available HTTP: < http://www.garnet-eu.org/fileadmin/documents/working_papers/1707/6%20Brazil.pdf > (accessed 18 November 2007).

Poletti, A., Peruzzi, R. and Zhang, S. (2007) 'Country report: China', in S. Lucarelli (ed.) *Research Report: the external image of the European Union*, GARNET Working Paper no. 17/7. Online. Available HTTP: < http://www.garnet-eu.org/fileadmin/documents/working_papers/1707/8%20China.pdf > (accessed 18 November 2007).

PIPA-GlobeScan (2005) *23-Nation Poll: 'Who Will Lead the World?'*, On-line Report, Program on International Policy Attitudes, April 2005. Online. Available HTTP: < http://www.pipa.org/OnlineReports/EvalWorldPowers/LeadWorld_Apr05/LeadWorld_Apr05_rpt.pdf > (accessed 18 November 2007).

Smith, K. E. (2006) 'The limits of proactive cosmopolitanism: the EU and Burma, Cuba and Zimbabwe', in O. Elgström and M. Smith (eds) *The European Union's Roles in International Politics. Concepts and analysis*, London: Routledge.

Soltan, G. (2001) 'The Arab polls: Egyptian public opinion towards economic conditions and regional integration', *Al Ahram*, 18 June 2001.

Stats, K. (2007) 'Country report: Australia', in S. Lucarelli (ed.) *Research Report: the external image of the European Union*, GARNET Working Paper no. 17/7. Online. Available HTTP: < http://www.garnet-eu.org/fileadmin/documents/working_papers/1707/5%20Australia.pdf > (accessed 18 November 2007).

World Values Surveys, European and World Values Survey four-wave integrated data file, (1981–2004) v.20060423, 2006. The European Values Study Foundation and World Values Survey Association. Aggregate File Producers: ASEP/JDS, Madrid, Spain/Tilburg University, Tilburg, the Netherlands. Aggregate File Distributors: ASEP/JDS and ZA, Cologne, Germany. Online. Available HTTP: < http://www.worldvaluessurvey.org > (accessed 18 November 2007).

Zhang Yesui (2005) *Forging ahead into the Future and Furthering the Development of China-EU All-round Strategic Partnership*, article written by Vice Foreign Minister Zhang Yesui on the 30th Anniversary of the Establishment of Diplomatic Ties between China and EU, 1 May 2005. Online. Available HTTP: < http://www.mfa.gov.cn/eng/zxxx/t194651.htm > (accessed 18 November 2007).

13 Conclusion

Furio Cerutti and Sonia Lucarelli

In this conclusion we will discuss political identity and legitimacy in the EU by looking at some, but not all, of the aspects highlighted in the chapters, and we also intend to offer further food for thought, some of which is in a policy-oriented sense.

Epistemological remarks

Let us preliminarily raise *epistemological* and related methodological questions. This book has three epistemological pillars. First of all, it gives a conceptual clarification by attempting to sketch a theory of the meaning of EU political identity and legitimacy (Cerutti's introduction), as well as the role of foreign policy and external image in internal identity formation (Lucarelli in Chapter 2). A larger chunk of the volume is dedicated to policy analysis of the particular type that we deem significant for understanding the self-identification and legitimation processes. Finally, we have paid attention to the elements that specifically signal the production of meaning: memory/remembrance (Bottici) and spatial representation of the polity (Therborn).

We are not going to comment on our own chapters but wish however to stress that we regard the multidisciplinary, and in the most felicitous cases, interdisciplinary attitude put to work in this volume as the only one fitting for matters as 'soft' and elusive as identity and legitimacy. Philosophical speculations over what the Europeans should think of themselves as well as statistical calculations based on Eurobarometer or other surveys are both a poor and sometimes misleading approach. In the light of the theoretical framework we have tried to sketch, it is also crucial to look jointly at the two central topics in all their many facets. Among these for example the symbolical contents of space shaping or collective remembrance are no less important than the EU policies.

Let us start with the policy analysis chapters. Has the approach pioneered in this volume proved to be fruitful for peering into the European process of self-identification? We believe it has, regardless of the fact that some of the policies examined (e.g. on global warming or biotechnology) do not yet have a primary influence on the feeling of being European. Whatever the results in terms of the actual effect on identity-building, it has proved productive to study ethically relevant policies (on medical biotechnology, biosafety, global warming and human rights) with a view to working out the values as well as the conflicts that they imply. In particular, these policies have been studied from two different perspectives.

In the first place, the authors analysed the ethical and political positions that the policies contain in their legal and political formulation. This goes beyond customary policy analysis, as it looks for the philosophical, ethical or religious roots of certain policy choices (it is not by chance that three of those chapters are written by political philosophers – Acuti, Badii and D'Andrea). In a broader research project those roots would be better uncovered by working on internal Commission and Council documents and interviewing the policy-makers involved.

In the second place, authors analysed the reception given to such policies in the public space as the proper venue of identity formation. This was done by looking at both the press (mainly indicating the opinion leaders' position) and mass opinion polls, such as the Eurobarometer (indicative of the common citizens' stance). Despite the limits of these sources (we would like to see this inquiry extended to TV channels, to include in-depth interviews and to be undertaken in more member states – particularly those of new accession), we believe they constituted an important source of information for our analysis.

If the first perspective on the potential contribution of policies to identity-building (the analysis of the ethical and political positions underlying public policies) already gives an original contribution to the topic, a further one is provided in the chapters, by Lucarelli (Chapter 2), and by Fioramonti and Lucarelli (Chapter 12), which, by getting rid of the preposterous concept of an 'international identity'[1] of the Union, have opened the way to an innovative research path: they address not just the *external image* of the Union, the near negligence of which is nevertheless a curious phenomenon in European studies, but also the feedback link between this image and the influence that it may have on identity formation in Europe. However great or slight that this influence may be at the present time, it remains a topic for attention in future studies.

Lastly, in Chapter 3 by Bottici, memory or remembrance of the Second World War represent a significant symbolical element in European identity formation, as does Brussels in Therborn's chapter. Why do we deem these inquiries to be relevant to our epistemological stance? The reason is rather ontological and lies in what we think to be the structure of politics in general and European integration in particular: even if European identity is to be *thin* and strictly political, it cannot distil from the experience, the needs and the wishes of the Europeans if it is not mediated, communicated or reproduced by symbols. For example, Therborn's picture of Brussels or rather of the *Quartier européen* shows an EU uncertain of whether to represent its power as a single market or an upcoming polity in more immediate architectural terms.

Political results

Drawing on the analytical and historical chapters we see signs indicating that a core of European political identity exists, but with severe limits, which are then mirrored in the role it plays for the legitimacy of the Union. Moreover, we acknowledge *spillover effects* from the regulatory, policy-making role of the Union into identity-building processes. Finally, the chapters underline the relevant role played in identity-building by symbols of several types.

In particular, the studies undertaken have pointed to three main types of spillover from policy-making into identity. First of all, the *EU's regulatory role* ignites an identity-building debate (regardless of whether it leads to new substantial legislation or not). This is the case with medical biotechnology and biosafety issues, and to an extent also with EU policy on climate change (car industry regulations, emissions trading) (see Chapters 6, 7 and 8). Positions divided by different national cultures or different ideologies are bound to speak out in a common space, to take note of the others' attitudes and reasons, to negotiate in order to come to a shared position, even if this may consist of recognizing a persistent diversity beyond a thin layer of commonality.

Second, a spillover effect is at work when *failures in regulation*, such as in the case of BSE, explode, and the unfolding crisis involves the *legitimacy* of the Union as a whole, an institution that while regulating the market is also supposed to provide an elementary *public good* such as (bio)safety. As Acuti shows (Chapter 6), a deep-seated cultural factor such as a shared trust in science seems to bind Europeans together and to define the backdrop of policy decisions.[2] Similar problems of legitimacy due to ineffectiveness are underlined by Rosa Balfour (Chapter 10) in relation to the human rights policy of the EU. Such a policy is characterized by problems of effective engagement and performance (as a substantive condition of legitimacy, cf. Cerutti's Introduction), particularly, though not exclusively, due to rivalries between member states (the UK and France, for example). For this reason, despite the fact that human rights remain the paramount value shared by Europeans – along with democracy and peace – not even this value can be considered stable and unquestionable. For this to be the case, the EU needs to reassert human rights protection in a forcible, coherent and *effective* way as something essential to the European *polity*. Moreover, as in the minds of the Europeans (and even more in those of the people watching us from outside) human rights are not disjointed from social rights, and the EU does not have much legitimacy to make claims to on this terrain. For the EU to enhance its legitimacy, it needs to modify its trade (tariffs) and agricultural policies (subsidies) along with their devastating impact on imports from developing countries (again cf. Fioramonti and Lucarelli's Chapter 12).

A third type of spillover regards debate on the relationship between current regulation and the consequences for *future generations*. This type of link emerges neatly in D'Andrea's chapter on global warming. Even though not at the top of the Europeans' list of preoccupations, climate change already constitutes a widely felt issue and the Kyoto strategy a widely shared position among EU citizens, also with regard to the different American stance. Moreover, an enhanced role for it with regard to common values, goals and concerns for future generations is expected after Kyoto, when the EU will have to decide whether or not to take upon itself an economic burden in terms of forced innovation and possibly much higher losses in gross domestic product than the costs of implementing Kyoto. Such a debate does not (and will not) fail to bring self-identification issues to the fore: What kind of future do we want to design? What comes first, the self-interest of contemporaries or a feeling of obligation towards posterity? These issues are a tough challenge for the EU: if it fails to reach a single position, thereafter it will be more difficult for anybody 'to feel European'; if it consents to a low-level compromise with other world powers and fails to take the lead towards an effective reduction in emissions its legitimacy as a norm-setting, future-oriented power will be shattered inside and outside the continent – outside it is already now far from sparkling (see Chapter 12).

It should be underlined that feedback from EU policy to European identity might be highly uneven in its effects depending not only on different European countries (differences among Western European countries are visible in all chapters), but also on different referents within the countries. Daniela Piana's Chapter 11 is a case of both. Piana's analysis of the Europeanization of the judiciary in the new member states of Central and Eastern Europe underlines the existence a strong feeling of finally belonging to Europe among members of the judiciary, while in the same countries citizens, although strongly appreciating the European courts, do not feel to be in Europe in their own home countries, because they do not think their national legal systems have really been transformed and brought to a European level. The Europeanization of identities may also create, perhaps only temporarily, such a divide between an elite or professional group and a citizenry which, while aspiring to become European, effectively still feels far from it. In future studies on political identity and legitimacy in the EU a large amount of research should address the *état de conscience* of the Eastern Europeans, who are living a phase of regained national identity and therefore seem to have a different approach, not to mention more resistance, to 'feeling European' than the countries that pooled their sovereignty with all the others more than 50 years ago.

Next to policies, a second fundamental access to identity comprises of *symbols* of several types: like icons that evoke ideal policies, like keywords left behind by historical experiences, like geographical and social spaces. Far from being policies in themselves, the 'European social model' (ESM) and 'European civil society' are rather keywords or icons created to symbolize a set of effective or ideal policies and, what is more, the meaning that should be attributed to them. The ESM was introduced as a formula aimed at signalling that the EU (then the EC) is a matter not just of economic but also social improvement. Although it is undeniable that the several social models existing in the whole of Europe have more similarities among themselves than each of them with the American or other models of industrial and social relationships, thus giving some reality to the ESM formula, it is also true that this formula has not provided any scope for the harmonization of social policies across Europe; indeed, more recently the EU leadership has rather restricted its usage and significance. Vaïa Demertzis, however, argues that at the same time the ESM has been taken more seriously by the European public, or at least the parts of it that want to give a strong social imprint to the European construction – notwithstanding the fact that, like any other value, in principle social values can be acknowledged by all while almost everybody may then interpret them in a different way. Furthermore, the wish to give the EU a more precise content, for example in the sense of greater social protection against the vagaries of the labour market, may overtake the choice to have the EU (as a polity) at all, and lead to results such as in the French referendum of 2005, in which some of the *nonistes* on the left proclaimed their 'non au Traité constitutionnel, oui à l'Europe' provided it is a 'social' Europe – the overall political result of which is known. This raises a broader question: it has often been said that more political conflict and more partisanship in the EU would bring about more participation of the citizens and enhance their feeling of being European citizens. The suggestion remains on the drawing board of research and experiment, but cannot be seen as a panacea, because, as we have just learnt from France, politicized conflicts can also be disrupting for a union of states and only secondarily of citizens which remains in any case a market authority before all else. Furthermore, it is our guess that for identity formation in Europe the ability to put new challenges such as climate change or the revolution in biotechnology on the agenda of public debate will be more important than a EU-wide extension of the traditional party divide in the national parliaments.

It is advisable to take the same caution with the ESM as with 'European civil society', another iconic keyword of many a debate on the EU. This is why we are commenting on it at this point, although Debora Spini's chapter also contains elements of conceptual clarification that bring it close to the first pillar of our epistemology; however, the conceptual clarification she brings about may feel somewhat cold for supporters of the notion of civil society as a panacea for the evils of European technocratic policy-making. On the one hand, she reinstates the broader Hegelian notion of civil society, which includes economic interactions among individuals and groups; on the other hand, she sees a role for civil society (in more recent understanding, as the sphere of critical discourse and deliberation on public goods and common values) in the formation of a transnational public space in Europe capable of connecting the Europe-wide sphere with the national ones – a better premise, Spini suggests, for the legitimation of the Union.

The theoretical importance of focusing on declared symbolical[3] moments such as how we remember a past of sorrow and how we shaped the 'capital' of the Union has already been underlined. On the substantive level, Therborn's (Chapter 4) and Bottici's (Chapter 3) contributions show how far the EU still is from managing to create a policy on how it wants to define and communicate itself. With his final quote from a Flemish writer 'Brussels is nobody's, and everybody's',[4] Therborn still seems to give the EU a chance to make the *Quartier européen* a space shaped according to its existence as a polity in progress. So far, however, the EC/EU has not shown any intention to shape its space beyond pure bureaucratic functionalism (to meet the functional needs of its own administration), or to give the visitor something to remember as an icon of its existence, for example a building by Santiago Calatrava or Renzo Piano or Sir Richard Rogers. Perhaps it was the resistance of some member states against too visible a representation of (European) power, perhaps it was inability of the Council and Commission to grasp the relevance of symbols around which all images and notions of Europe can coagulate, decades after the time in which the Adonnino Commission invented the European flag. The strategy of establishing themselves by stealth that has been pursued by European bodies according to Therborn's account can work on the institutional level, but remains affected by shortcomings when it comes to communicating the existence and the value of those institutions. In the age of visual communications a polity remains nearly invisible if it cannot be associated with a White House or another landmark building like the UN headquarters on the East River in New York.

Both these explanations may still hit the mark with regard to how the EU is described in schoolbooks (as a purely geo-economic gathering in most French and Italian texts, whereas German books show a different attitude) and how sparingly it is connected with its origins in the Founding Fathers' will to prevent another internecine war on the continent. Fifty years after the Treaty of Rome, it is in a sense as if in the Italy of 1911 or in the Germany of 1921 history textbooks had recounted what happened after 1861 and 1871 from the point of view of the former pre-unification states. This is obviously a heuristic exaggeration, but it helps highlight the astonishing lack of historical awareness about the European process on the part of the Europeans themselves. This can, however, be assumed not to come from a failed or delayed Europeanization of formal education and basic political culture due only to the deep roots of the nation in European souls. The undergraduates whom we as academic teachers find widely if not totally ignorant about the Union and its institutions have little taste for nation and nationalism, as they are rather far away from any involvement in politics and public life. That they as well as the preceding (lamentably also the following, we must assume) generations of European schoolchildren and students are so ignorant about Europe comes mainly from the refusal[5] of the member states and the corresponding national societies (cf. Bottici's

Chapter 3 on academics) to engage in a joint effort to *rethink their own histories* in the light of the European process and project. Even though far from being proactive Eurosceptics, politicians, top bureaucrats and intellectuals have never seriously intended to stimulate such a rethink among schoolteachers and schoolbook authors. Nor have the European institutions (the Council of Europe rather than the EU) done more than promote a couple of conferences and workshops among academics and teachers, regardless of bilateral initiatives like those between France and Germany. Of course, in liberal democracies public authorities are not allowed to author history textbooks themselves or to tell authors how to write them. But between infringing the freedom of speech and doing nothing there is ample room for political leadership to set the problem of how to break the quasi-silence about Europe on the agenda. We do not believe that a Commission president willing to do so would not have enough freedom of manoeuvre and enough authority to launch an initiative in this sense. Provided he or she is convinced that identity formation is crucial to the future of the EU as a political process, and that enough generations of Europeans have grown adult without a chance to learn where, between their national capitals and Brussels, power is located and who should be held accountable for what in all things political regarding their lives. It remains to be understood how politicians, who because of their profession should have known better, could believe that on the back of this aloofness of the EU from the political culture of most Europeans a broad basis of acceptance could be assumed for something as engaging as a Constitution; except if they are obfuscated by old-federalist triumphalism, an episode of which is recounted in Bottici's chapter.

Looking into the future of European politics and research

The *finalité politique* of the Union as it has emerged – more in declarations than in implemented strategies – over the past 20 years, that is an assertive role in the *governance of globalization* in the framework of a rule-based multilateralism, is the dimension in which values and goals constituting the European identity have to redefine themselves, also taking note of the risks of ineffectiveness and rhetorical aftertaste that could prevent the Union from attaining a decent degree of legitimacy among its own citizens. This is said in the awareness that in our and future times the idea of Europe cannot be 'sold' by merely relying on the *finalités politiques* of the origins, peace and prosperity. Nor can the degree of acceptance of the Union be assessed only by looking inwards. In other words, the assessment by Europeans will be influenced to a varying extent by what at least the most far-sighted of them think the role of the EU will be in the world; it is by betting on the growing importance of this feedback effect that we have given so much importance to the external image of the Union.

Let us now come back to the initial reflections on the epistemology of this book and note that the policy considerations we have advanced are no strangers to the scholarly approach. The political identity and legitimacy of the EU cannot be studied in a purely objectivistic manner, as a sequence of mechanical events to observe. The very justification of the importance we have given to that topic depends on the acceptability of our four assumptions. First, that the European process, although post-national and non-federal, has reached a level of politicization that can be reversed or paralysed only with major risks for the stability of the Union. Second, the notion that a political process essentially implies questions of identity formation among citizens and elites as a condition for the institutions to be legitimized (this should be self-evident, but it is not either in EU politics or in many corners of European studies). Third, the belief that even in an *objet politique non identifié*, political identity formation depends on high political acts performed by the leadership as well as on educational and communication policies. Fourth, the assumption that how the EU handles the rest of the world and how they consequently look at us will play an increasing role in shaping our own identity and making the Union legitimate in our own eyes. We hope the volume itself is a credible witness of these connections between epistemological approach, substantive theoretical insights and policy-oriented considerations.

Notes

1 Preposterous not just because of the improper use of 'identity' for conveying something which can be correctly expressed by 'image' or 'stance', but rather because it sounds as if a quality specific to a single entity on its own right were attributed to its relationships with a multiplicity of entities (*inter nationes*). *Unum* cannot be *plures*.
2 This is the case of an element of a shared European culture (there are not all that many of them) that in the age in which science and technology have lost their ethical neutrality becomes relevant to the *political* culture of the EU citizens.
3 In truth, policy-making and policy reception also contains symbolical elements, as nearly everything in the polity does, but not as explicitly as in the dimension we are now talking about.
4 This sentence would acquire a new meaning should Belgium really split.
5 In this refusal there are elements of what Freud dubbed denial, the unconscious act of simply ignoring a new reality that is too disturbing for one's own beliefs and images of the world. This compounds with the (conscious) fear of losing benefits that are embedded in the old order, as in the case of national bureaucracies, academic or professional lobbies.

Index

Aachen 61
acquis communautaire 48, 162, 187–88
Acuti, Elena 36, 212, 213
Adonnino Commission 216
African countries: GM seeds sent by US to 98; and issue of sanctions against Zimbabwe 168, 169, 172; unfair trade practices towards 202
African Union 198
agency 17; in collective remembrance 46
agricultural biotechnology 94–95, 98, 101
agriculture 201–2, 204, 213, *see also* Common Agricultural Policy (CAP)
Al Ahram 199–200
aid/assistance policies 161–62, 162, 164, 167
Alesina, A. 7
Alter Europe 149
Amsterdam 60, 63, 65
Amsterdam Treaty (1997) 81, 133
Antoine, Dominique 50
Apprédéris, Franck 50
Arato, A. 143
architecture: in debate on Brussels 71, 216; European capital cities 60; European institutions 70
Architecture Studio 70
Asia 202, *see also* Southeast Asia
assistance programmes *see* aid/assistance policies; economic assistance (EC)
Athens 60
Attac 148
Australia: images and views of EU 194, *195*, 203; public opinion on EU and US influence 202, *202*
Austria: approach to medical biotechnology 119; approaches to food safety issues 94, 99; Haider's electoral victory 36; public opinion on biotechnology policy 115

Badii, Renata 207, 212
Balfour, Rosa 18, 37, 213
Barroso Commission 148
Beck, Ulrich 144
Beetham, D. 8
Belarus 160, 167–68, 169, 170, 171
Belgium: approach to recombinant DNA technique 94; Brussels as national capital 63, 67, 67–68, 71; contesting of sanctions against Zimbabwe 168; dioxin case 93, 95, 101, 102; ethnic divisions 72; precautionary approach to GMOs 99
Berger, P.L. 5
Berlant, L. 73
Berlin: effect of unification of German small states 66; Second World War fiftieth anniversary celebrations 49; social transformation with modernity 62; urban history 59, 63
Berlin Wall, fall 162
Bern 63, 67
bioethics: debate 119–20; Oviedo Convention 113–15
biosafety policy 17, 99, 212, 213
biotechnology: challenge for democratic societies 108–10; concerns of environmentalists 96; European values and ethics of 112–15; introduction to commerce and industry 94; legitimization of EU policies 98; public opinion on European policy 115–16, 211; public optimism towards 111; strategy promoted by EC (2002) 110–12; US and EU approaches 101, *see also*

220 Index

agricultural biotechnology; food safety policy; medical or red biotechnology
Biotechnology Consultative Forum 109
Bonino, Emma 54
Bonn 63
Bottici, Chiara 12, 18, 32, 37, 212, 216, 216–17
bourgeoisie 61–62
Brazil: images and views of EU 194, 194–98, *195*, 198, 199, 201; public opinion on EU and US influence 202, *202*
Bremen 63
Brewer, M.B..10
Britain: BSE crisis 93, 95, 101; English newspapers' coverage of ESM 135; 'ethical foreign policy' 161, 171; hosting of Hampton Court Informal Summit 133, 135; legislation on recombinant DNA 94; memories of Second World War 50; model of social provision 129; newspapers' linking of BSE food scandal with EU 102; position on raising arms embargo on China 169; press attention to EU external human rights policies 169, 170, *see also* United Kingdom (UK)
Broad Economic Policy Guidelines (BEPG) 130
Brussels: after Belgian secession 63; background and process of becoming European capital 66, 67–68; changes with European role 69, 69–70; debates on architecture for the future 70–71, 216; and delocalization of decisions 150; and European identity 73, 212, 216; grassroots groups and NGOs 149–50; Meunier's Monument to Labour 64; national legacies and problems of identity 16, 71–73; as populists' scapegoat 13
BSE (bovine spongiform encephalitis) 36, 93, 95, 96, 213; newspaper coverage 101, 102
Budapest 60
buildings *see* architecture
Bulgaria 66, 135, 180, 185, 186
Bundesverfassungsgericht ruling (1993) 8
bureaucracy 9, 13; Brussels 16, 73
Bush, George W. 118, 172
business organizations, view of EU market 201–2

Calatrava, Santiago 216
Cameron, J. 97
Canada: images and views of EU 194, *195*, 203; public opinion on EU and US influence 202, *202*
capital cities 12, 18; different roads of development in Europe 65–66; identities and key stages in development 63–65; and national history 59–61; road to modernity 61–63
Cardiff Process (1988) 130
Catholic Church 48, 61
Cavour, Camillo Benso, count of 72
Cedermann, L.-E. 10, 34
Central and Eastern Europe Countries (CEECs): approach to legal norms 188; citizens' trust in judicial systems 185–87; democracy promotion in 177–78, *178*; effect of enlargement on legal elites 181–84; EU differentiation as Other 34; judges and judicial standards 182–83, 214; judicial reforms and reshaping of EU image 176–77; role of human rights in integration into EU 162
Central Europe, architecture of capital cities 60
Cerutti, F. 16, 25, 28, 33, 151, 172, 188, 211, 213
Charlemagne 61
Charter of Fundamental Freedoms 165
Charter of Fundamental Rights (2000) 28, 81, 114, 147
chemical industries 149
China 111, 128, 200; debate on lifting arms embargo on 160, 167, 168–69, 169, 170, 172; images and views of EU 194, 194–98, *196*, 198, 199, 201; multilateralism 200, 201, 207; public opinion on EU and US influence 202, *202*; as world power *199*
Chirac, Jacques 169
churches: conflict with nation-states 62, 65; religious monumentality 61
cities, relationships with states 62–63
citizens: attitudes towards ESM 136–37; importance in constitutional process 146–47; interest in foreign policy 23; level of awareness of climate change policies 77, 83–84; need to promote dialogue with 112; perception of environmental risks 88, 89; perceptions and opinions of food safety policies 94, 98; self-

identification and political identity 3, 4, 5, 32, 151, 218; trust in judicial systems in CEECs 185–87, 188, *see also* public opinion and debate
civil society: external images of EU 201, 206; in food safety policy decisions 103–4; Hegelian model representing system of needs 142, 143, 144, 152, 215; model representing public space and democracy 142, 143–44, 151, 152, 215; in political theory literature 142–43; role in constructing political identity 152; as term 18, 142; two models compared in context of EU 144–48; without constitutional framework 151
civil society organizations (CSOs) 149, 150, 152; external images of EU 194, *195*, 195–7
civilian power 24
class: in development of nations and capital cities 61–62; and identity 14
climate change (CC): citizens' perceptions of EU policies on 83–84; costs and values 81–82, 86–88; EU policies against 17–18, 77–78, 79–80, 85–86; need to consider for future generations 80–81, 84, 90, 214; relevance of EU policies to European identity 88–90, 213; UN conference 203, 204–5, *see also* global warming (GW)
Cohen, J. 143
Cold War, end of 24, 160
collective memory 45, 45–46
collective remembrance 45, 46–47; and history 53–54; institutional 47–49, 50–51, 54; pedagogical 51–53; public 49–51
Cologne 61, 63
Cologne Process (1999) 130
Committee of Experts on the Progress of Biomedical Science (CAHBI) 113
Common Agricultural Policy (CAP) 11, 12
Common Foreign and Security Policy (CFSP) 24, 29, 160, 164, 165, 168
communication structures 15
communist regimes: EU rule of law and dismantling of legacy of 176; judicial policies adopted after break up of 186
Competitiveness Council of European Research Ministers 117, 119
CONECCS 145, 148

Conference on Security and Cooperation in Europe (CSCE) 162
conflict, and differentiation 34
conflict management 24
conflict prevention 202
Conflict Prevention Strategy (2001) 164
conservative governments 94
constitutional process: enlargement and judicial function 180; press coverage of civil society's role 147–48; public interest groups 146, 146–47, *see also* European Constitution
Constitutional Treaty 49, 133, 134; French and Dutch rejection of 12–13, 14; human rights promotion 165; reformulation of foreign policy 161
Consultative Council of European Judges (CCJE) 182, 183
Consultative Council of European Prosecutors (CCPE) 182
consumer protection 98, 101
consumers: early concerns over biotechnology 94; impact on policy-making 148; scepticism about GM soy and corn 95
consumption 87
Convention on the Future of Europe (2002) 160–61
Cook, Robin 171
cooperation: development 29, 207; and integration 11, 201
Copenhagen 64, 65
Copenhagen criteria (1992) 178
Council of Europe: choice of Strasbourg 67, 68; framework for bioethical principles 113, 117; legal norms and principles 178
Council of Ministers, decisions on environmental policy 79, 80, 99
Council of the European Union, principle for autonomous sanctions policy 166–67
Creutzfeldt-Jacob disease 95
crisis management 26
cultural diversity 3
cultural heritage 5–6
cultural identity 7, 27
Cyprus 136, 168
Czech Republic 180–81, 183, 186
Czechoslovakia 60

D'Andrea, Dimitri 32, 37, 104, 207, 212, 214

de Gaulle, Charles 67, 68
De Seixas Correas, Luiz, F. 199
death penalty 28
decision-making: difference between US and EU structures 101; need for civil society to be involved in 103–4; in new polity of EU 13
defence policy 9
Dehaene, Jean Luc 16
Dehousse, R. 142
Delors, Jacques 15, 126, 126–27, 130
Demertzis, Vaïa 18, 215
democracy 8, 11, 13; and civil society 144, 146; EU model and European enlargement 176–77, 177–78; external views of global actors' contributions to 198, 200; as key European value 165–66, 213; use of term 16–17
democracy promotion: public opinion on issues of 170–71, 202; studies 159
Democratic Republic of Congo 168
Denmark 15, 99, 115, 161
Derrida, Jacques 147
d'Estaing *see* Giscard d'Estaing, Valéry
developing countries: and climate change 82; EU's unfair agricultural and trade policies towards 202, 204, 205, 207, 213; inaccessibility of biotechnological products to 110; TEU's promotion of international cooperation 29
development: cooperation 207; external views of EU's contribution to 198, *see also* aid/assistance policies
dialogue: aspects of European governance 145–46; with citizens 112, 149
dioxin case (Belgium) 93, 95, 101, 102
distinctiveness 24–26; and Otherness 33–34
Doha Round negotiations 11, 203, 204
Dublin 66
Duchêne, François 24

Ebeid, H. 202
Eco, Umberto 70
economic assistance (EC) 164
economic policies, Europeanization 130
economics: biotechnology sector 110; costs of fight against climate change 87–88, 89; as criterion for legitimacy of EEC 144; determination of EU policies 15; and legitimacy 3, 11, 12; and populists' scapegoat of 'Brussels' 13; in recurrent external image of EU 199, *see also* market; socioeconomic issues
education *see* history textbooks
Egypt 194, *196*, 198, 199–200, 201
elites: debates on European and US differences 26; external images of EU 194, *195*, *195–7*, 199, 200–201, *201*; and failure of Constitutional Treaty 12; self-identification and political identity 3, 4, 5, 9, 218, *see also* legal elites
emissions *see* European Emissions Trading Scheme (ETS); greenhouse gas emissions
employment 89, 90, 131, 136
employment relations, negotiation between social partners 130
enlargement 24, 159, 201; development of process of 178–80, 187; and judicial reforms 18, 186–87; and media coverage of ESM 135, 138; new member states and human rights 161, 163, 167, 181; role in EU's reformulation of image 176–77, 180, 187
environment: concerns over GMOs 94, 96; US and EU standards 101
environmental policies: early developments 79, 82; external views 203; public perceptions 83–84, 206; sustainable development 81, *see also* climate change (CC); global warming (GW)
ethical policies 17–18, 85, 212
ethics: controversial issues in medical biotechnology 108–9, 113, 118–19; in Denmarks' development policy 161; EU stance in world politics 24; Europeans' position on climate change problem 87, 90; of memory 47, *see also* bioethics
ethnic divisions 72
ethno-nationalist identity 6
Eurobarometer surveys 14, 23, 83–84, 111, 115–16, 136, 147, 168, 185, 186, 212
Eurodis (Rare Diseases Europe – European Association of Patients Affected by Rare Diseases) 116
Euronews 15
Europe: 'born out of the Second World War' narrative 53, 53–54; choosing a capital for 67–69; different roads to national capital cities 65–66; early

western city-belt 63, 67, 72; 'idea of' 5–6; importance of history in group identity 29; non-European perceptions of 194; presentation in history textbooks 51–53, 216; Rumsfeld on New and Old 35, *see also* European identity
Europe Day 48, 49
European Association of Biotechnology Industries (EuropaBio) 116
European Climate Change Programme (ECCP) 80
European Coal and Steel Community (ECSC) 47, 67–68
European Commission: actions on biotechnology 94, 95, 96; approach to social policy 130; creation of arenas for judicial reform 183; creation of ESM 125, 126, 128; and early environmental policies 79; medical biotechnology regulation 112; on precautionary principle 96; process of choosing location for 68, 70; support for promotion of human rights in foreign policy 164, 166; White Paper on governance 146
European Commission for the Efficiency of Justice (CEPEJ) 183
European Constitution: and issues of identity 7, 8; press attention to issues of 49, 138; public opinion on 147; referenda 14, 54, 102, 135, 147, 148; role of civil society 146–47; unifying formula in Preamble 51, *see also* constitutional process
European constitutionalism 178, 185
European construction: in history textbooks 51, 52, 216; narrative of 'Europe out of the Second World War' 54
European Convention on Human Rights (ECHR) 162, 178, 180–81
European Council: adoption of precautionary principle 97; decisions on issues of identity and legitimacy 7, 14; Declaration on Human Rights 160; on human rights and judicial reform for enlargement 178–79; and institutionalization of ESM 125, 132–33
European Court of Human Rights 178, 186, 187, 188

European Court of Justice (ECJ): CEEC citizens' trust in 186, 187, 188; emphasis on rights in enlargement process 185; and EU model of democratic governance 178; as human rights authority in Constitutional Treaty 165, 176–77; legal basis for environmental policies 79; location in Luxembourg 68, 70
European Economic and Social Committee (ESC) 145, 146, 149
European Economic Community (EEC) 68, 144–45
European Emissions Trading Scheme (ETS) 82, 83, 89
European Employment Strategy (EES) 130
European Environment Agency (EEA) 85–86
European federalism 49, 144
European flag 216
European Food Safety Authority (EFSA) 95, 97
European Group on Ethics in Science and New Technologies (EGE) 98, 114
European identity: and application of human rights norms 163; competing with national identities 16; in debate on Brussels as European capital 70–71, 73; and 'distinctiveness' thesis 25–26; diversity of approaches 3–5; importance of civil society 146, 151; importance of legal norms 188; labelling 34; OMC aims in social policy-making 131; relevance of climate change policies 88–90; role of ESM 125, 138; Schroeder's plea 50–51; war and collective remembrance 45–54, 212, *see also* political identity
European Initiative for Democracy and Human Rights 164
European institutions: buildings architecture 70; citizens' concerns regarding food safety 94, 102, 103, 111; conditions set for food safety policy compared to US 93, 96, 97, 101; cooperation with CSOs 150; importance of external human rights policy to 159, 163–64, 171; and issue of legitimacy 8, 14; issues in debate on Brussels 71; need for initiatives in rethinking histories 217; and public interest groups 150; relevance of ESM to legitimacy 125, 137–38; sites

for collective remembrance 47–49, 50–51, 54
European Judges Association 182
European Neighbourhood Policy (NP) 167
European Parliament (EP): adoption of precautionary principle 97; framework for bioethical principles 114, 116, 117; and human rights in EU foreign policy 165; location in Brussels 72; position on raising arms embargo on China 169
European Platform for Patients' Organizations, Science and Industry (EPPOSI) 116
European Security Strategy (2003) 26, 163, 164
European Social Forum, second (Paris, 2003) 147–48
European Social Model (ESM) 18, 125–26, 214–15; citizens' attitudes towards 126, 136–37; national newspaper coverage 126, 134–35; origins and political emergence 125, 126–27; policy content 129–32; politics and legitimacy 132–34, 137, 137–38; socioeconomics 127–29
European Trade Union Confederation (ETUC) 150
European Transparency Initiative 149
European Union (EU): approaches to political identity and legitimacy 3–5, 13–15, 211–12; double nature 3, 11, 15; external images in non-European countries 37, 193, 194–203, 212, 217; external views of as world power *199*, 202, *202*; regulatory role 213, 213–14; universal and particular features 6; as world power 193
European values 32; and climate change policies 77, 81–82, 87–88, 89; and ethics of biotechnology 112–15; in European social models 126–27, 131; and EU's constitutive features 159; in food safety policies 93, 97–98, 103; guiding EU foreign policy 24; human rights 213; in self-identification and political identity 28–30
European Women's Lobby 150
Europeanization: economic policies 130; of judiciary in enlargement countries 18, 188, 214; nomenclature in Brussels 70; in urban foreign policy before 'globalization' 68
Euroscepticism 50, 135, 217

Ferrari, Giuseppe 63
Le Figaro 49, 101, 119, 135, 145, 204–5, 206
Finland 66, 69, 94, 99, 115
Fioramonti, Lorenzo 18, 34, 37, 212–13
First Community Action Programme on the Environment (1973) 79, 82
First World War 64
Flanders 67
Flemings/Flemish people 72, 72–73
food risk: management principles 96; perceptions of 94, 99, 103
food safety policy 93; background history of food biotechnology events 93–96; European public opinion 101–3; GMOs and risk regulation models 100–101; member states' different approaches to GMOs 99–100; need for debate with civil society 103–4; principles and values 96–98
food scandals 94, 101–3, 102, 110–11
foreign policy: background to emergence of human rights element 160–63; and human rights promotion/protection 159–60, 163, 164, 169; influence of European political identity on 30–32; relevance of political identity 27, 28–30; role in European political identity 9, 17, 18, 23, 24–27; and self-identification 35, 36
Fox, G. 28
France 15, 72, 217; approach to recombinant DNA technique 94; benefits of CAP to farmers 12; contesting of sanctions against Zimbabwe 168, 171, 172; debate on food safety issues 103; divisions with UK 168, 213; lack of press attention to EU external human rights policies 169, 170; moratorium on GMOs 99; newspaper coverage of ESM 135; presentation of Europe in history textbooks 52, 216; presidential campaign of 2007 151; press coverage of civil society's role 147; public remembrance of Second World War and Holocaust 49; push for end to arms embargo on China 169; referendum and vote against

Constitutional Treaty 12–13, 14, 49, 102, 135, 215
France 3 50
Francophone people, Belgium 72
Fraser, Nancy 32–33
free trade 29, 198, 201, 204
freedom of choice principle, food safety policy 93, 97, 99
freedom of movement 9
French Revolution 60, 65, 70

Galea, Censu 119
Gaulle, Charles de *see* de Gaulle, Charles
Generalized System of Preferences (GSP) 167, 171
Germany 15, 119, 217; approach to recombinant DNA technique 94; in early western European city-belt 63; historical guilt and national identity 29, 35; model of social provision 129; parliament building 60; position on medical biotechological research funding 119; precautionary approach to GMOs 99; presentation of Europe in history textbooks 51–52, 216; public remembrance of Second World War and Holocaust 49; push for end to arms embargo on China 168–69, 171; significance of 8 May 50–51; split in press over medical biotechnology policy 118–19; unification of small states 17, 66
Giavazzi, F. 7
Giscard d'Estaing, Valéry 133–34
Global Summit of Women in Cairo (2006) 203, 204
global warming (GW): definition and detrimental effects 78; fight against 78–79, 81, 83, 203; Kyoto objectives and EU position 86, 214; perception of threat 77–78; perceptions of EU policy on 77, 203, 207, 211, 212, *see also* climate change (CC)
globalization: changing cultural heritage 5–6; citizens' concerns 89, 136; and concept of civil society 143; EU legitimacy in context of 12, 13, 14, 217; pressures on member states addressed by ESM 130, 132–33, 138
Globescan survey 202
GMOs (genetically modified organisms): Bt10 crisis 95–96, 101, 102; consumer scepticism and public opposition 94, 95, 97, 103, 111; EU directives 94; EU-US dispute and risk regulation models 93, 98, 99–101
governance: and democracy in EU 16–17; enlargement and 'justice' in judicial reform 179, 181, 185; and globalization 12, 217; models 3, 12; multi-level nature of EU 8, 15, 16, 144, 217; participation of civil society in 144, 145–46, 146; technocratic 146
grassroots groups 147–48, 149–50, 151
Greece 66, 99, 168
greenhouse gas emissions: EU achievement of stabilization 85; Kyoto objectives and national trends 85–86; less developed countries 82; monitoring 79, *see also* European Emissions Trading Scheme (ETS)
Greenpeace 149
Greenwood, Justin 145, 148
Groenleer, Martijn 96
group identity 6; and external labelling 34; influence of history on 29; role of EU's foreign policy for Europeans 23; sensitivity to political feedback 35–36; US identity politics 32
Guardian 49, 50, 101, 102, 118, 135, 170, 171, 204, 206
Gulag 53

Habermas, Jürgen 3, 143, 143–44, 147
Haider, Jörg 29–30, 36
Halbwachs, Maurice 45
Hamburg 63
Hampton Court informal EU summit (2005) 133, 135
harmonization 138
Haussmann, Georges Eugène, Baron 60, 65
Hay, C. 129
Hegel, G.W.F.: idea of civil society 142, 143, 146, 152; *Phenomenology of Mind*/study of self-conciousness 5
Helsinki 64
Helsinki Process 161, 162–63
Hermans, Stefan 73
Herrmann, R.K. 8, 10
historians 53, 54
history: capital cities 59; and collective remembrance of war 53–54; in Europe's Other 32; 'idea of Europe'

in 5; influence on evolution of group identity 29; problem for German national identity 29, 35; subjective or active side of 17
history textbooks, images of Europe 51–53, 216
Hix, S. 136
Hoedeman, Olivier 149
Holland *see* Netherlands
Holocaust 18, 49, 53
Holy Roman Empire 69
Honneth, Axel 32–33
Hopf, T. 31–32, 32
housing, post-war social-democracy in capital cities 64
Huddy, Leonie 29, 34
human rights policy 18, 37, 212, 213
human rights promotion/protection: background and emergence in foreign policy 160–63; in biomedical regulation 113–14; in Copenhagen criteria 178; in identity of CEEC citizens 187; importance in EU's political identity 159–60, 163, 171, 185, 213; institutional legitimacy 163–64; public support for EU in 165–66; and use of sanctions 160, 166–71
Hungary 181, 183
Huntington, Samuel 6, 27

identity: CEECs 180, 187; connection with legitimacy 10, 13–15; diversity of approaches 3–5; and foreign policy 27; meanings 3; recognition theory 32–33; role of boundaries in formation of 34–35, *see also* European identity; political identity; self-identification
IDNET research project 26
India 111; images and views of EU 194, *196*, 199, 200, 201, 203; public opinion on EU and US influence 202, *202*
Industry, Transport, Research and Energy Commission (ITRE) 117
information, communication, technology (ICT) 179
institutions: legitimacy and meaning 13–14, 218, *see also* European institutions; national institutions
integration 11, 12–13, 135; enlargement and Copenhagen criteria to protect 178; role of interest/pressure groups 145; socioeconomic 128, 137, *see also* regional integration
intellectual property, biotechnology 109
interest/pressure groups 145, 148, 151, *see also* public interest groups
Intergovernmental Panel on Climate Change (IPCC) 78
International Criminal Court 162
International Labour Organization 167
international relations: China's view of EU's contribution to 200; development cooperation 29
International Relations (IR) 23–24, 31, 32
Iran 11, 200
Iraq: criticisms over sanctions on 167; Japanese view of approaches to conflict 202; press coverage of EU at start of war 203, 205–6; press criticisms over arguments to justify war 170; transatlantic divide regarding war 36; US intervention 8
Ireland 94
Islam 6
Islamic countries, Bonino's proposal regarding 54
Israeli-Palestinian conflict 199–200
Italy 15; debate on choice of capital for new nation-state 63, 72; debate on food safety issues 103; debates about *Partito Democratico* 151; in early western European city-belt 63; lack of press coverage of external human rights policies 169–70, *170*; moratorium on GMOs 99; position on medical biotechological research funding 119; presentation of Europe in history textbooks 51, 216; press coverage of civil society's role 147; relegation of human rights in foreign policy 161; support for sanctions against Belarus 168; unification of small states 17, 66

Jammu-Kashmir 200
Japan 128; images and views of EU 194, *197*, 198, 199, 201, 201–2, 202, 203; public opinion on EU and US influence 202, *202*
Jepperson, R. 27–28
Jepson, M. 131
Joas, H. 7
John Paul II, Pope 48
Jonas, H. 96

Josling, T., European risk regulation model 100–101
judges *see* legal elites
judicial function: CEEC citizens' trust in 185–87, 188; effectivenes of EU rule of law promotion 187–88; in EU model of democracy 176–77; Europeanization in enlargement countries 18, 177–81, 214; views of European judges 182–84, 188, 214
justice: constitutional 180; and EU concept of rule of law 176–77; principles regarding economics of climate change policy 81–82

Kallas, Siim 149
Katiforis, M. 134
knowledge-based economy 130, 131
Koolhaas, Rem 71
Koselleck, Reinhart 45
Kratochwil, Friedrich 30
Kreuzhuber, Gregor 145
Kyoto Protocol: and EU actions on climate change 79, 80, 82, 203, 214; failure to achieve goals 77, 85–86; public awareness and concerns about 83; US refusal to sign 84

labelling policy 97, 99
Laeken declaration (2001) 146
Latin American countries 162, 202
Latvia 136, 168
law *see* judicial function; legislation; rule of law
Lebanon crisis (2006) 11
legal culture 180
legal elites, and CEEC enlargement 181–84, 188
legal norms 178, 181, 187–88; influence on European model of governance 181–82; views of CEEC judges 183–84, *see also acquis communautaire*
legal texts, institutional memory 48
legislation: as executed by national institutions 15; human rights promotion/protection 164–65; national systems in biotechnology sphere 113, 116; social policy 129–30, *see also acquis communitaire*
legitimacy 3, 16; approaches 3–5; aspects highlighted in this volume 211–18; citizens' trust in judicial system 185–87, 187, 188; common usages of concept 10–13; connection with identity 10, 13–15, 17, 85; deficit in formal dimension of human rights policy 164–65; EEC 144–45; effect of EU failures in medical biotechnology sector 116; EU model of rule of law 176–77; and human rights dimension of foreign policy 159, 162, 163–64, 167, 171; importance of climate change policies 77, 89; importance of food safety policy 93, 213; in models of civil society 143–44, 144, 146, 152, 215; role of ESM 125, 132, 137–38
Leopold III, King of Belgium 67
Lezaun, Javier 96
liberalism, in European values interpretation 28–29
Libération 101, 135, 205, 206
Liège 61, 67–68
Lipsius, Justus 70
Lisbon 65
Lisbon strategy 116–17, 130–31, 132–33, 138, 146
Lithuania 69, 119, 168
living standards 137
Livingstone, Ken 64
lobbying: chemical industry 149; function of ESC 145; public interest groups 150, 152
London 48, 60, 64
Lord, C. 8
Low Countries 63, *see also* Belgium; Netherlands
Lucarelli, S. 18, 28, 34, 36–37, 139, 172, 207, 211–13
Luckmann, T. 5
Lukashenko, Alexander 167
Lula da Silva, L.I. 201
Luxembourg (city) 68, 68–69, 69, 70
Luxembourg (country) 72, 94, 99

Maastricht Treaty 11, 13, 24, 126; provisions regarding environment 79; sustainable development and precautionary principle 81, 96; world-changing events at time of 162
Madrid 65
Magnette, Paul 146, 151
Malta 119, 136
man-nature relationship 98, 103
Manners, I. 4, 24, 25
Margalit, Avishai 47
market: EU's protectionism 201–2, 205; liberalization 29; political elites'

external images of EU 199; in popular image of EU 9, 11; side of EU's nature 15; versus individual rights in biotechnology regulation 110, *see also* economics
Marx, Karl 143
media 10, 15, 101, 203; external images of EU 194, *195*, 195–7, 199, *see also* newspaper/press coverage
medical or red biotechnology: differentiation with agricultural biotechnology 94–95, 98; ethical principles 113–15; ethically controversial issues 17, 108–9; EU policy of regulating 108, 113, 213; and promotion of European political identity 115–20, 212; public opinion 111, 116–17, 119
medieval era: nationally important cities 61, 65; religious monuments 61
Mediterranean countries 94, 199–200
member states (MS): in concept of 'Europe' 9; different views of external human rights policy 160, 169, 171; enlargement countries and human rights promotion 161; and EU food safety policy 93, 99–100; human rights policies as accountable to 165; obligations for judicial reform 179; perceptions of social policy 136, 137
memory: as individual 45; of Second World War 18, 37, 45, 212; in self-identification process 32; shared 3, 12, 46, *see also* collective memory; collective remembrance
Meunier, Constantin 64
Middle East 31–32, 199–200
militant organizations 147–48
military intervention 170–71
Mill, John Stuart 143
Minsk 59
Mitterrand, François 48–49
modernity, development of capital cities 60, 61–63
modernization 132–33
monarchies 62, 65
Monnet, Jean 68, 144
monumentality 60–61; in debate on future identity of Brussels 71
monuments: plans for Schuman Roundabout 70; style in European capital cities 60
moral issues *see* ethics
Morgan, G. 4

Morocco 34
Movement for Rights and Freedoms (Bulgaria) 180
Mugabe, Robert 168, 169
multilateralism 205, 206, 207, 217; and multipolarism 200–201
Mummendey, A. 7
El Mundo 101, 117
museums, European capital cities 60, 70
Muslim Brotherhood 200
Myanmar 169

NAFTA *see* North American Free Trade Agreement
Napoleon 65
Napolitano, Giorgio 49, 54
nation-states: citizens' identity 9; conflict with prince and church 62, 65–66; legitimacy model 11; relationships with cities 62–63
National Allocation Plans (NAPs) 83, 89
national history, capital cities 59–61
national identities 3, 14; conflict with European identity 16, 17; and development of capitals 65–66; key moments in development of capitals/identities 63–65
national institutions: 'EU-bashing' 15; in European capital cities 62
national welfare states: and ESM social policy 125–26, 127, 129–32, 132–33, 137, 138; role of liberalism 29
NATO (North Atlantic Treaty Organization) 11
neo-liberalism 204–5, 207
Nepal 200
Netherlands: human rights promotion in foreign policy 161; official and unofficial capitals 63; position on raising arms embargo on China 169; precautionary approach to GMOs 99; referendum and vote against Constitutional Treaty 12–13, 14, 49, 135; seats of government in history 67
Neumann, I.B. 32, 33
New York 216
newspaper/press coverage: civil society's role in constitutional process 147–48; ESM 134–35, 138; EU external human rights policies 169–70; EU's global image regarding specific events 203–6; external images of EU 193,

194, 200, 201, 201–2, 202, 207; food scandals and debates 101–3, 103; global warming 83–84; relevance of EU climate change policies 88–89; Second World War memories 49–50; two events about biomedical technology 117–19
NGOs (non-governmental organizations): chemical industries' battle with 149; in constitutional process 148, 151; criticisms of EU trade and agricultural policies 202, 206; early concerns over biotechnology 94; influence on policies on GMOs 99; professionalization 149–50
Nikonoff, Jacques 148
Nora, Pierre 47
North American Free Trade Agreement (NAFTA) 198
North Korea 200
Norway 94

OECD (Organization for Economic Cooperation and Development) 113
Onuf, Nicholas 30
Open Method of Coordination (OMC) 131–32
OPTEM study on European citizens 136
Oslo 66
Otherness 37
Others: non-European countries' views of EU 193–94; role in shaping European political identity 26–27, 32, 33–34, 193
Oviedo Convention (on Human Rights and Biomedicine) 113, 113–14, 117

El País 101, 117, 135, 170, 172, 205
Palestine *see* Israeli-Palestinian conflict
Paris: fiftieth anniversary celebrations of Second World War 48; Haussmann's architecture and layout 60, 65; urban naming system 60
parliament buildings, in European capital cities 60, 62
Partnership and Cooperation Agreement 167
Patterson, L.A., European risk regulation model 100–101
peace/peacemaking: external views of EU's contribution to 198, 199–200, 200; as key European value 165, 193
peacekeeping 24
Pei, I.M. 70

philosophical ideas: 'idea of Europe' 5; subjective side of history 17
Piana, Daniela 18, 214
Piano, Renzo 216
Pizzorno, Alessandro 32–33, 33
Plato 4
Poland 119, 168, 186
policies 10; feedback to political identity 32–35; as framework of values interpretation 28, 29, 32; precautionary principle 81; science related to 111–12
policy-making: cross-national OMC model 131–32; ESM as mobilization term for 137; legitimacy and meaning 13–14; and political identity 17–18, 29, 150, 213–17
political elites *see* elites
political identity 3, 16; aspects explored in this volume 17–18, 211–18; common usages of concept 5–10; diversity of approaches 3–5; EU policies against climate change 77, 77–78, 80, 87–88; Europeanization of judicial function 188; feedback from policy to 32–35, 213–17; and group identity 35–36; human rights promotion in foreign policy 159–60, 163, 171; importance of food safety policies 93, 103; importance of legitimacy of policies 85; importance of values 80, 83; influence on foreign policy 30–32; issue of medical or red biotechnology 115–20; relationship with EU human rights policy 37, 165; relevance of external images of EU 203–6, 207, 217; relevance of foreign policy to 24–27, 28–30; role of acts of remembrance 47, 53–54; role of civil society 152; values interpretation 28–30, *see also* European identity
political parties 151
polity: civil society's relationship with 146, 152; difference with society 6; importance of human rights protection 213; nature of EU 15; post-national 9, 16
Portugal 66, 99
Portzamparc, Christian de 70
Prague, monument to ending of plague 61
precautionary principle 81, 96; in EU food safety policy/food risk management 93, 97–98

press *see* newspaper/press coverage
princes: battle between nation-states and 62, 65, 65–66; and capital cities 61
Prodi, Romano 70, 71
protectionism, EU market 201–2, 204, 205, 206
public interest groups 143, 146–47, 148–49, 151
public opinion and debate: biotechnology issues 115–16, 119–20; BSE scandal 95; democracy promotion 170–71; development aid 168; ESM 135, 138; EU external human rights policy 160, 171; and EU foreign policy 26; external images of EU 194, 194–98, *195–7*; failed Europeanization of 15; food safety policies 94, 94–95, 101; impact of external image of EU on 206–7, 212; issue of Brussels as capital 71; in liberal/EU model of civil society 142, 143–44, 146–48, 152; medical biotechnology issues 109, 111, 116–20; political identities and values 29–30; science and man-nature relationship 98; sources used 203, 212; support for EU human rights promotion 165–66, *see also* citizens; newspaper/press coverage

Rappagliosi, Andrea 116
Rare Diseases Europe *see* Eurodis
Rawls, John 4
REACH 149
recognition theory 32–33
recombinant DNA technique 94
red biotechnology *see* medical or red biotechnology
referenda: citizens' choices 9; Constitutional Treaty 14, 54, 147, 148, 215; results as a tool 9
Regensburg 61
regional integration 201, 207
remembrance 53, *see also* collective memory; collective remembrance; memory
Resolution on Human Rights in Development Policy 160
Reykjavik 66
Rhineland 61, 63
Ricoeur, Paul 46
Rifkin, J. 4, 206
rights: enforcement as key point of EU membership 176–77, *see also* human rights policy; human rights promotion/protection
Rio Conference (Earth Summit, 1992) 79
risk, moral and social elements in notion of 94
Riss, Jorgo 149
Risse, Thomas 8
Rogers, Richard 64, 70, 216
Rokkan, Stein 63
Roman Empire 61, 72
Romania 135, 182, 183, 185, 186
Rome 66
Rudolph, E. 4, 27
rule of law: in Copenhagen criteria 178; promotion of EU model in CEECs 176–77, 180, 181–82, 183–84, 187–88
Rumelili, Bahar 34
Rumsfeld, Donald 35
Russia: identity politics 31, 32, 33; nature of conflict leading to union of nations 66; new member states' critical positions towards 161

Saarbrücken 68
sanctions 160, 166–71, 171
Saran, Shyam 200
Scharpf, F. 10, 130
Schavan, Annette 118–19
Schlegel, Friedrich 53
Schmidt, V. 4, 10, 16
Schröder, Gerhard 50–51, 54, 169
Schuman, Robert 48, 68, 70
Schuman Declaration (9 May 1950) 48
Schütz, Alfred 5
science: European values 97–98, 103; evidence on climate change 81; policy-related 111–12; and precautionary principle 96–97
science–society relationship 109–10, 110–11
Scottish Enlightenment 143
Second World War: institutional acts of remembrance 47–49; memories 18, 37, 45, 212; narrative of 'Europe out of' 53, 53–54; pedagogical remembrance 51–53; public acts of remembrance 49–51
security: external views on EU's contribution to 199–200; and human rights 164; political identity and legitimacy 9, 11
self-identification 3, 7, 9, 211–12; and re-elaboration of memory 32; relevance of external images of EU

193, 203–6, 206–7, 212; relevance of foreign policy 23, 25, 35; sensitivity to group identity 35–36; social identities 31; in substantial legitimacy 13; values interpretation for 28–29
Serrano Pascual, A. 131
settler states 67
Sewerynski, Michal 119
Shoah 49
Simmel, George 34
Singh, Manmohan 199
Single European Act (SEA) 79, 82, 146
Single Market 127
Sivan, Emmanuel 46
Sixth Environment Action Programme 86
Slovakia 119
Smith, Antony 27
social cohesion 90, 131
social democracy: influence on ESM 126–27; post-war popular housing 64
social dumping 135
social identity theory (SIT) 23–24, 35
social life, issues in fight against climate change 87, 89–90
social norms, identity 27, 31
social policy: citizens' values and expectations 136–37; ESM 125–26, 129–32, 137, 138; 'Social Europe' working group 133–34, 134–35
society: and polity 6, see also civil society; science–society relationship
socioeconomic issues: ESM 127–29, 135, 136–37, 138; Lisbon strategy 130–31, 132–33; national and European 126–27, 127–28
Solana, Javier 169
Il Sole 24 Ore 101, 205, 206
solidarity 114, 127, 207
South Africa: capital cities 67; images and views of EU 194, 194–98, *197*, 198, 199, 201; public opinion on EU and US influence 202, *202*
Southeast Asia 129
Soviet Union, dissolution 162
Spain: lack of press attention to EU external human rights policies 170; precautionary approach to GMOs 99; warring princes in nineteenth century 66
Spinelli, Altiero 49
Spini, Debora 18, 215
Sri Lanka 200

Stability Pact 15
stakeholders 146, 148
La Stampa 49, 101, 205, 206
the state, and civil society 143, 144
state identity 30–31
state sovereignty: China's protection of 201; and EU human rights policy 162, 165
stem cell research 108, 117
Stockholm 60, 64, 65
Strasbourg 67, 68, 70
Süddeutsche Zeitung 49, 101, 117
sustainable development 81
Sweden: agencies located outside capital 69; approaches to food safety issues 94, 99; in line with emissions objectives 85–86; model of social provision 129; parliament building 60; public opinion on biotechnology policy 115; support for sanctions against Belarus 168; tradition of human rights promotion 161
Switzerland 63, 65, 67, 94
symbols 3, 7, 12, 71, 214–15

Taiwan 169
Taylor, Charles 32–33, 33
Taylor, Peter 72
television 15, 203, 212
Telò, M. 4, 24
terrorism 28, 164, 167, 170, 200
Thatcher, Margaret 50
The Hague 63, 65, 67
theatres, European capital cities 60, 62
Therborn, Göran 12, 18, 211–212, 216
The Times 101, 117, 135, 204, 206
toponymy, European capital cities 60
Torgerson, H. 95
totalitarian regimes/post-totalitarian regimes 176
trade: in external images of EU 199, 201, 202; human rights factors 164, 169; impact of sanctions on Belarus 168, 169, 170; tariffs and non-tariff barriers 201, 213
trades unions 130, 201, 202
Transatlantic Trends 166
Treaty constituting the European Coal and Steel Community (ECSC) 47
Treaty of Rome (1957) 68, 79, 145
Treaty on European Union (TEU) 29, 160, 162
TRIPS (Trade-Related Intellectual Property Rights) agreement 29

Troebst, Stefan 53
Turkey 34, 135

UNESCO (United Nations Educational, Scientific and Cultural Organization) 113
United Kingdom (UK) 15; debate on food safety issues 103; divisions with France 168, 213; line with emissions objectives 85–86; support for sanctions against Belarus 168; support of sanctions against Zimbabwe 168, 170, see also Britain
United Nations (UN) 166, 198, 201; Climate Change Conference, Nairobi (2006) 203, 204–5; headquarters in new York 216; Universal Declaration of Human Rights 162, see also UNESCO
United Nations Charter 167
United States (US): accused of double standards regarding human rights 172; aspects of identity 25, 27, 28, 29; Biotechnology Consultative Forum 109; biotechnology market 111; cultural influence on India 198; dichotomy with EU socioeconomic model 128, 128–29, 135, 138; difference with EU in justice principles 28; external views of role as world power 198, 199, *199*, 200, 202, *202*; GMO dispute and differences with EU risk regulation 95, 95–96, 98, 99–101; identity politics underlying relations with Middle East 31–32; institutional differences with EU regarding food safety policy 93; intervention in Iraq 8; position on raising arms embargo on China 169; public opinion on international role of 26; public opinion on man-nature relationship 98; recombinant DNA technique 94; refusal to sign Kyoto Protocol 84, 214; science-based regulation model for biotechnology 112; view of Belarus 167; views of EU as counterbalance to 6, 34, 202, 204, 205, 206, 207, see also Washington
Universal Declaration of Human Rights (UN) 162
universal norms 25

University of Siena, Elite Survey 166

values: and choice of historical perspective 54; conflict with interests and effect on policy 85; in EU biotechnology regulation 111; in meaning of identity 3, 28; and political identity 32, 80, 83, 217; reallocation produced by social policy 136, see also European values
Ventotene, island of 49, 54
Verhofstadt, Guy 70
Versailles 65, 70
Vienna 60, 61, 64, 72

Wæver, Ole 32
Waldzus, S. 7
Wallonia 67
Walloon people 72–73
Walzer, Michael 29
war: acts of collective remembrance 46; divisive effects 50, see also Second World War
Warsaw 59, 69
Washington 67, 73, 145
Weber, Max 12
Weldes, Jutta 27
welfare state see national welfare states
Welsh, Ian 98
Wen Jiabao 200
Wendt, Alexander 30–31
Wesselius, Erik 149
Wiegandt, K. 7
Winter, Jay 46
World Bank 161–62, 198
World Health Organization (WHO) 113
World Powers Survey 198, *199*
World Social Forums (WSF), Porto Alegre (2001, 2002) 203, 204
World Summit on Sustainable Development (WSSD), Johannesburg (2002) 203, 204, 205
World Trade Organization (WTO) 15, 29, 99, 198, 203
World Value Surveys 185–86
Worms 61

Yugoslavia, break up 162

Zaventem (Brussels airport) 72
Zielonka, Jan 16
Zimbabwe 160, 167, 168, 169, 170